Speech
DIS

K.H.S.

3-92

Speech
DIS
K.H.S.
3-95

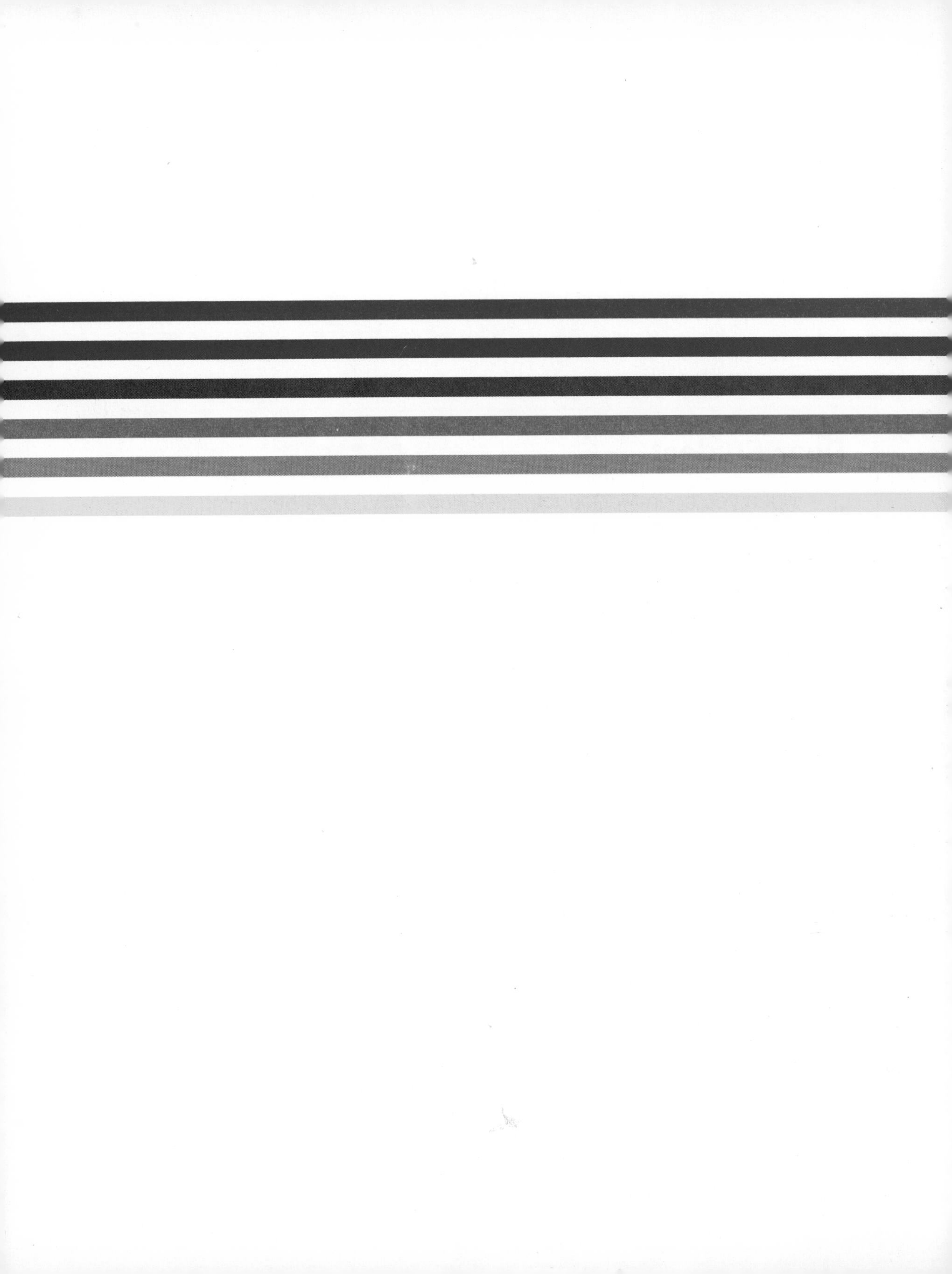

Dear Student,

When you open *McDougal, Littell English,* you are beginning a journey. You will be traveling through the world of words. You will discover your own talent for shaping ideas into words.

McDougal, Littell English uses literature as your guide. Below is a list of some of the titles and authors of the literature you will read as models of good writing. Let those models lead you to the books themselves so that you can discover and enjoy the power of words in the world of literature.

The Editors

Literary Selections in *McDougal, Littell English, Silver Level*

Abercrombie, Barbara, "Poems Like Dreams," *The Other Side of a Poem.* ▸*Cat-Man's Daughter*

Aiken, Joan, "The Third Wish," *Not What You Expected.* ▸*A Necklace of Raindrops*

Alexander, Scott, "Pictures on the Flying Air," *Instructor.*

Ciardi, John, "A Man in the Woods Said," *I Met a Man.* ▸*The Man Who Sang the Sillies*

Crane, Stephen, from *The Red Badge of Courage.* ▸*The Complete Short Stories and Poems of Stephen Crane*

Doyle, Arthur Conan, from *The Complete Sherlock Holmes.* ▸*The Hound of the Baskervilles*

Dunbar, Paul L., "Roses and Pearls," *The Complete Poems of Paul Laurence Dunbar.* ▸*Little Brown Baby: Poems for Young Children*

Frank, Anne, from *The Diary of a Young Girl.* ▸*The Works of Anne Frank*

▸*An additional work by the author*

Continued on page 490.

McDougal, Littell ENGLISH

Green Level
Red Level
Gold Level
SILVER LEVEL
Aqua Level
Brown Level
Plum Level
Pink Level
Cherry Level (K)

ML
McDougal, Littell & Company
Evanston, Illinois
New York Dallas Sacramento Raleigh

Authors

Kathleen L. Bell, Assistant Director of Composition, Department of English, University of Miami, Coral Gables, Florida

Frances Freeman Paden, Ph.D., Lecturer, Department of English and Communicative Arts, Roosevelt University, Chicago, Illinois

Susan Duffy Schaffrath, Consultant in Educational Materials for the Elementary and Middle Grades, Chicago, Illinois.

The Editorial Staff of McDougal, Littell & Company

Consultants

Deborah Kay Bossmeyer, Middle School Team Leader and Language Arts Teacher, DuValle Middle School, Louisville, Kentucky

Patricia Brackenrich, Principal, White Sulphur Elementary School, White Sulphur Springs, West Virginia

Ann E. Davis, Assistant Superintendent, Washington County Education Service District, Portland, Oregon

Karla J. Dellner, Coordinator of Staff Development, San Juan Unified School District, Carmichael, California

Joy C. Fowles, Ph.D., Coordinator for Secondary Education, Clear Creek Independent School District, League City, Texas

Susan Vignes Hahn, Assistant Superintendent for Instruction, Archdiocese of San Francisco, San Francisco, California

Nana E. Hilsenbeck, Language Arts Supervisor, Volusia County School District, Daytona Beach, Florida

Bobbi Mulholland-Mahler, Coordinator of Curriculum, Irvine Unified School District, Irvine, California

James W. Reith, Program Coordinator for Language Arts, Foreign Languages, and Libraries, Scottsdale School District, Phoenix, Arizona

Cover Art: *Sailing* **by an elementary school student, courtesy of The International Collection of Children's Art, University Museums, Illinois State University.**

Acknowledgments: See page 489.

ISBN: 0-8123-5090-1

91 92 93 94 / 15 14 13 12 11 10

Contents

Grammar

Chapter 3 Using Nouns 41
with Applied Writing Activities

Grammar

Chapter 4 Verbs for Sentence Power 57
with Applied Writing Activities

Composition

Chapter 10 The Process of Narrative Writing 175

Speaking and Listening

Chapter 11 Improving Speaking and Listening Skills 197

McDougal, Littell
ENGLISH
Silver Level

UNIT 1

Steppingstones to Writing

In Unit 1, you will learn about the tools of good communication. You will see how to use these tools to build steppingstones to clear writing and speaking.

You will learn how to unlock the meaning of new words. Then you will turn words into sentences and paragraphs. Finally, you will explore the choices writers make as they put ideas on paper.

These skills will be useful to you both in and out of school. Your vocabulary skills will be helpful as you learn new terms in science or do a crossword puzzle. Use your writing skills for a school assignment, an entry in your diary, or a letter to a friend.

Unit 1 can serve as a stepping stone to expressing yourself clearly. It will provide you with the tools you need to put your ideas into words.

A BAG OF TOOLS

Isn't it strange
That princes and kings,
And clowns that caper
In sawdust rings,
And common people
Like you and me
Are builders for eternity?

Each is given a bag of tools,
A shapeless mass,
A book of rules;
And each must make—
Ere life is flown—
A stumbling block
Or a steppingstone.

—R. L. SHARPE

Chapter 1

Building Word Power

Thomas Edison might find it difficult to read some of the words in today's books, magazines, and newspapers. Even to an inventor like him, words such as *laser, Styrofoam, Telstar,* and *Dacron* would seem quite puzzling. Perhaps you, too, do not understand some of the words you hear and read. The world is changing rapidly. You must keep learning new words so that you can read and talk about these changes. The job you choose also may have special words you must learn. It is helpful to know different ways to discover what a new or unfamiliar word means.

In this chapter, you will learn how to tell the meaning of a word from context. *Context* means the words or sentences around a specific word. You will learn how the meanings of words change when prefixes and suffixes are added to base words. With these skills you will more easily understand what you read. You will also be building a strong vocabulary so that you can speak and write more effectively.

1 Using Context Clues: Definition, Restatement, and Example

Focus

Context clues can help you learn the meaning of an unfamiliar word in a sentence. A context clue may define, restate, or give an example of an unfamiliar word.

When a writer knows that a certain word will be new to many readers, he or she may use a **context clue**. *Context* means the words or sentences around a particular word.

Definition or Restatement

The writer may give a **definition** of the word or **restate** the unfamiliar word in a different way. Read these sentences.

She saw a colony of *gannets*—large, white sea birds—perched on the rocks. (definition)

The balloonists *ascended,* or went up, more slowly than they came down. (restatement)

Example

Sometimes the writer helps the reader understand a new word by giving an example. When you read, check to see if an unfamiliar word is explained by one or more examples somewhere else in the sentence. Read this sentence.

Implements, such as screwdrivers and pliers, are handy to have around the house. (example)

The context tells you that screwdrivers and pliers are examples of *implements*. This helps you understand the meaning of *implements*.

Certain key words and punctuation marks signal that a writer is giving a context clue.

Key Words Signaling Definition or Restatement

which is	or	also known as
that is	in other words	also called

Punctuation Marks Signaling Definition or Restatement

dashes, commas, and parentheses

Key Words Signaling an Example

and other	for example	for instance
like	especially	such as

Exercises **Mastering Context Clues**

A. Use the context clues in these sentences to write definitions for the words in italics. Check your definitions in a dictionary.

1. I enjoy Japanese food—*sukiyaki*, for example.
2. Samantha is a *philatelist*. In other words, she is a person who collects stamps.
3. Old pottery, like *majolica*, is hard to find.
4. Stay away from *toxic* plants such as poison ivy.
5. Diana can do a *half gainer* and other difficult dives.

B. Write what each word in italics means. Then write what key words or punctuation marks helped you tell the word's meaning.

1. Dexter worked with a *farrier*, a blacksmith, to shoe the horses.
2. A *vista*—a distant view—of pine forests and lakes opened before us.
3. Julio asked the grocer for *plátanos* (bananas).
4. Stock up on *gherkins* and other kinds of pickles.
5. I used an *adz*, which is a flat-bladed ax.

2 Using Word Parts: Base Words

Focus

A **base word** is a word to which a beginning or an ending can be added to form a new word.

Context clues are not always available to help define an unfamiliar word. Sometimes, careful study of the word itself offers clues to its meaning.

Many words are made from other words and word parts. That is, a beginning or an ending is added to a **base word** you already know. For example, the beginning *un-* is added to the base word *tie* to make *untie*. Adding the ending *-ment* to the base word *move* makes the word *movement*.

Beginning	Base Word	Ending	New Word
un-	+ tie		= untie
	move	+ -ment	= movement

What base word is in these three words?

reader misread readable

The base word is *read*. The ending *-er* was added to make *reader*. The beginning *mis-* was added to make *misread*. The ending *-able* was added to make *readable*. These three new words were built on the same base word.

What Is the Base Word?

preview
viewer
review

senseless
nonsense
sensible

Exercises Building on Base Words

A. Copy each of the following words on a sheet of paper. Find the base word in each. Write the base word after each word.

1. rebuild
2. unthinkable
3. nonspeaker
4. laborer
5. precooked
6. joyous
7. misspell
8. hopeless
9. thoughtful
10. unfit

B. Add a beginning or ending to each of the following base words. Write the new words you have made on your paper.

1. care
2. require
3. cook
4. call
5. act
6. hazard
7. thunder
8. state
9. make
10. harm

3 Using Word Parts: Prefixes

Focus

A **prefix** is a word part added at the beginning of a word.

You can add a word part to the beginning of a base word to change the meaning of that word. These beginning word parts are called **prefixes**.

Prefix	Base Word	New Word
mis-	+ use	= misuse

In this example, the prefix *mis-* changed the word *use* into *misuse*. *Mis-* means "wrong" or "wrongly." Therefore, the base word *use* was changed to mean "wrong use" or "wrongly used" by adding the prefix *mis-*.

Here are four other prefixes often used in English.

non-	This prefix always means "not." *Nonliving* means "not alive." *Nonstop* means "having no stops, continuous."
pre-	This prefix always means "before." *Preschool* is the school before elementary school. *Presoak* means "to soak clothes before they are washed."
re-	This prefix has two meanings. It may mean "back." *Repay* means "to pay back." The prefix may also mean "again." *Reappear* means "to appear again."
un-	This prefix may mean "not." *Unnamed* means "not named." The prefix may also mean "the reverse of." *Unzip* means the reverse of *zip*. Therefore, it means "to open or unfasten."

Not all beginning letters that look like prefixes are prefixes. For example, the letters *un* are not a prefix in *unit*. The letters *re* are not a prefix in *real*.

Exercises Adding Prefixes to Base Words

A. Here are lists of prefixes and base words. Build as many new words as you can. Use any of the prefixes with any of the base words. For example, from the base word *pay* you could make *repay* and *prepay*. Not all of the base words and prefixes will go together. Use your dictionary to check your new words.

Prefixes	Base Words
mis-	name
non-	call
pre-	stop
un-	made
re-	heat

B. Answer these questions.

1. If a *conception* is an idea, what is a *misconception*?
2. If *compliance* is giving in to the wishes of others, what is *noncompliance*?
3. If *dawn* is the beginning of daylight, what does *predawn* mean?
4. If a *grateful* person is thankful, what is an *ungrateful* person?
5. What do these mean?
   a. to *redo* a project
   b. to *replay* a tape

4 Using Word Parts: Suffixes

Focus

A **suffix** is a word part added at the end of a base word.

You have learned that you can change the meaning of a base word by adding a prefix at the beginning of the word. Another way to change the meaning of a base word is to add an ending. These endings are called **suffixes**. See how the base words *breath* and *help* are changed by adding the suffix *-less*.

Base Word		Suffix		New Word
breath	+	-less	=	breathless
help	+	-less	=	helpless

The suffix *-less* means "without." *Breathless* means "without breath." *Helpless* means "without help."

Here are four other common suffixes and their meanings.

-able or **-ible**	These suffixes have two meanings. They can mean "can be." For example, a *divisible* number can be divided. A *crushable* box can be crushed. The suffixes can also mean "having this feature." For example, a *comfortable* chair has the feature of comfort. A *sensible* question has the feature of good sense.
-er or **-or**	These suffixes mean "a person or thing that does something." For example, a *traveler* travels, and a *collector* collects. The suffix *-er* may also mean "more." *Colder* means "more cold."

-ful	This suffix has two meanings. It can mean "full of." A *handful* of dirt means "a hand that is full of dirt." The suffix can also mean "having." A *beautiful* person has beauty.
-ous	This suffix also means "full of" or "having." A *vigorous* person is full of vigor or energy.

Be careful! Sometimes the spelling of the base word changes when a suffix is added. Notice how these words change.

beauty	sense	flip
beaut**iful**	sens**ible**	flip**per**

Exercises Adding Suffixes to Base Words

A. Copy these words on a piece of paper. After each word write the base word. Then write the suffix that was added.

Examples: dipper = dip + -er   ridiculous = ridicule + -ous

1. carrier
2. eventful
3. thoughtless
4. continuous
5. pitiful
6. famous
7. valuable
8. actor
9. lovable
10. fearless

B. Answer these questions.

1. If *pacify* means "to bring peace," what is a *pacifier*?
2. If *decipher* means "to change a code into plain language," what does *decipherable* mean?
3. If *worth* means "value," what does *worthless* mean?
4. If *glee* means "joy," what does *gleeful* mean?
5. If *advantage* means "benefit or favor," what does *advantageous* mean?

Exercises for Mastery

Chapter 1

Building Word Power

A. Using Context Clues Number a sheet of paper from 1 to 10. Use the context clue to write a definition for the word in italics in each sentence.

1. Nora enjoys reading books about *marsupials*, especially kangaroos.
2. Mario took a course in *linguistics*, which is the study of languages.
3. The wall needs some outside support—perhaps a *buttress*—to keep it solid.
4. Kim always uses *enoki*, or some other Oriental mushrooms, in that dish.
5. Today some old musical instruments, like the *serpent*, are almost forgotten.
6. For breakfast, I ate a *scone* (a round, flat biscuit) with butter.
7. We saw a picture of a *unicorn* (a mythical animal that looks like a horse with one long horn growing out of its forehead).
8. Some kinds of sugar—*glucose*, for example—are found naturally in fruit.
9. Pearl especially likes Greek dishes, such as *souvlaki*, prepared with lamb.
10. The campers put their food in a *cache*—a hiding place—to keep it away from the bears.

B. Finding Base Words Copy each of the following words on a sheet of paper. Write the base word after each word.

1. unfold
2. noiseless
3. preschool
4. replace
5. wonderful
6. misjudge
7. printer
8. unsinkable

C. Finding Meaning from Word Parts Answer these questions on your paper.

1. If an *informed* person is one who has information, what is a *misinformed* person?
2. If something *flammable* is something that will burn, what is something *nonflammable*?
3. If *natal* refers to birth, what does the word *prenatal* mean?
4. Something *remarkable* is something unusual enough to be noticed. What is something *unremarkable*?
5. If the word *construct* means "build," what does *reconstruct* mean?

D. Using Word Parts for Meaning Number your paper from 1 to 5. Answer these questions.

1. If *melody* means "a pleasant sound," what is a *melodious* tune?
2. If *excuse* means "to forgive," what is an *excusable* act?
3. If a *defense* is a way of protecting something, what is a *defenseless* animal?
4. If *fret* means "to worry," what is a *fretful* person?
5. If *thunder* is a loud sound, what is *thunderous* applause?

Using English in Computer Studies

Many work and leisure activities have their own special vocabularies. These special vocabularies are called **jargon**. Football players use jargon when they call a *blitz*. So does a newspaper reporter when she *wires* her story to the paper. Farmers use jargon when they talk of a *bumper crop* of grain.

Exercise Understanding Jargon

The words in italics in the following paragraph are part of computer jargon. Write these words on your paper. Use context clues to learn what each word means. Write the computer meaning next to each word on your paper.

Today is Laurie's first day in computer class. Two students will work at each *terminal*. Sometimes the keyboard, screen, and computer are talked about together as a terminal. Laurie puts a *disk* (a piece of special plastic covered with paper) into the computer. Laurie's disk contains a *program*, that is, a set of instructions for the computer to follow. Laurie can also *store*—save—information on her disk. First the students learn to get the computer running or *boot the system*. Then a *menu* (a list at the beginning of the program) lets Laurie choose what she will do. Laurie's program allows her to draw pictures, designs, and other *graphics*. After she has drawn a design, Laurie can get a *printout*. A printout is a printed version of Laurie's design put on paper. If Laurie likes working with computers, perhaps she will become a computer *programmer*, one who puts instructions into a computer.

Chapter 1 Review

A. Using Context Clues Use context clues to discover the meanings of the word in italics in each sentence. Number your paper from 1 to 10. Write each word and its meaning.

1. Mom poured the spaghetti and hot water into a *colander,* which is a strainer.
2. Do the wheels *shimmy,* or wobble, on your bike?
3. *Kale* and other forms of cabbage provide vitamin C.
4. One sign of *gentility,* or politeness, is having good table manners.
5. The king and queen hired several *yeomen* and other servants to work in the royal household.
6. The speech teacher told us that you can tell much about a person from his or her *stance* (the way one stands).
7. The new hospital has a *solarium,* a room where people can enjoy the sun.
8. The logs were shipped on a *flatcar,* which is a railroad car without sides or a roof.
9. I read that every successful person has a *mentor,* a wise and loyal teacher.
10. *Tempestuous* storms, like hurricanes and tornadoes, often do great damage.

B. Identifying Word Parts Copy the following words. Write the base word. Then write any prefix or suffix used with it.

1. miscast
2. returnable
3. glorious
4. unspeakable
5. nonsmoker
6. mislead
7. heartless
8. runner
9. presoak
10. carrier

Chapter 2

Writing and Studying Sentences

Language is like a jigsaw puzzle. It is made up of many pieces. In Chapter 1, you learned about one piece of the puzzle—words. You saw that a great deal of meaning can be expressed by one small group of letters. Words, in turn, can be fitted together to make sentences. These sentences give a more definite shape to our ideas. Through sentences, we explain our thoughts, ask questions, even create new people and places. In every great story, in every exciting paragraph, there are good sentences.

In this chapter, you will learn about sentences. You will learn to identify the parts of a sentence. You will also learn about the four types of sentences. You will discover how sentences can be used to express almost every kind of thought or feeling you experience.

1 What Is a Sentence?

Focus

A **sentence** is a group of words that expresses a complete thought.

Read these three groups of words. Each group is a complete thought or idea. Each group of words is a **sentence**.

Richard plays the drums.
Laura studies violin with Mr. Kim.
The Colorado River winds through the Grand Canyon.

Notice that a sentence always begins with a capital letter. Every sentence ends with a punctuation mark.

Not all groups of words are sentences. Read the group of words below.

Dominic and his brother

This group of words does not express a complete thought. The words do not tell you what the boys did or what is happening to them. A group of words that does not express a complete thought is a **fragment**.

Now look at this group of words.

won the three-legged race

This group of words tells *what happened,* but not *who* won. It is also a fragment.

A sentence must always tell *whom* or *what* the sentence is about. It must also tell *what happened*. This group of words is a sentence.

who or what	what happened
Dominic and his brother	won the three-legged race.

Exercises Identifying Sentences

A. Number your paper from 1 to 10. Label each group of words below *Sentence* or *Fragment*.

1. We built a snowman.
2. The lifeguard.
3. An anthill in the yard.
4. Carved the turkey.
5. Our class took a field trip to the museum.
6. Rides a bike to school.
7. Our hamster got loose last night.
8. Alice swam across the lake in two hours.
9. The cattle rancher.
10. Makes jewelry of wire and rhinestones.

B. Number your paper from 1 to 10. Identify what is missing in each group of words by writing either *Who or What* or *What Happened*. Then complete each sentence by adding the missing information.

1. the boy with the sled
2. the large, hungry dog
3. made a sand castle
4. my two older sisters
5. played football
6. the portable TV set
7. told a secret
8. found a fossil
9. almost all the birds
10. talked on the phone

C. Writing The fragments below are all related to the same idea. Number your paper from 1 to 5. Read all the groups of words. Then turn each fragment into a complete sentence.

1. the snake in the science corner
2. kept it in a glass aquarium
3. one day during class
4. found it one week later
5. had crawled into a desk

2 Parts of the Sentence

Focus

The **subject** of a sentence tells *whom* or *what* the sentence is about. The **predicate** of a sentence tells what the subject *does* or *is*.

Every sentence has two parts. One part of the sentence is the **subject**. The subject tells *whom* or *what* the sentence is about.

The other part of the sentence is the **predicate**. The predicate tells something about the subject. The predicate tells what the subject *does* or *did*. It can also tell what the subject *is* or *was*.

See if you can find the subjects and predicates in the sentences below. Then look at the chart to see if you were right.

1. The small kitten scratched my arm.
2. My brother read *Where the Sidewalk Ends*.
3. Hector's aunt is a pianist with the St. Louis Symphony.

Subject	Predicate
1. The small kitten (what)	scratched my arm. (what happened)
2. My brother (who)	read *Where the Sidewalk Ends*. (what the subject did)
3. Hector's aunt (who)	is a pianist with the St. Louis Symphony. (what the subject is)

Exercises Working with Subjects and Predicates

A. Copy these sentences. Draw one line under the subject of each sentence. Draw two lines under the predicate.

1. Tammy went to the beach with Audrey.
2. The fierce tiger growled in his cage.
3. Two boys raced on roller skates.
4. The soybean fields need water.
5. Aunt Beth is a chemical engineer.
6. The baby reached for her toy telephone.
7. The first show was at six o'clock.
8. Casey and Timmy built a tree house.
9. The new-born colt hobbled on weak legs.
10. Susan is an excellent storyteller.

B. Each sentence below is missing either a subject or a predicate. Supply the missing part for each sentence.

1. The single-engine plane ________.
2. A team of oxen ________.
3. ________ swirled overhead.
4. ________ lined up.
5. ________ set off the fireworks.
6. The champion gymnast ________.
7. ________ was on the pier.
8. ________ buried the treasure.
9. Four astronauts ________.
10. The famous magician ________.

C. Writing Create a new story by changing only the words in italics.

Our class *decided to write a mystery play*. *Our teacher* made a list of things we needed to think about. *Everyone* wanted to tell the whole school about it. Several of the kids *wanted to make posters*. No one *wanted to miss the chance to perform*. *The class play* was a great success.

3 The Simple Predicate, or Verb

Focus

A **verb** is a word that tells about an action, or that tells what someone or something *is*.

In part 2 of this chapter, you learned about the two parts of a sentence. When we divide a sentence into these two parts, we call the subject part the **complete subject**. We call the predicate part the **complete predicate**.

The complete subject may be short or long. It includes all the words that tell *who* or *what*.

The complete predicate may be short or long. It includes all the words that tell what the subject *does* or *is*.

Read these examples.

Complete Subject	Complete Predicate
The weary zebras	walked.
The weary zebras	walked slowly.
The weary zebras	walked slowly toward the water hole.
The tall girl	played.
The tall girl	played basketball.
The tall girl	played basketball for our team.

In each complete predicate, there is one part that is more important than the rest. This part is the verb. The first three sentences above have the same verb: *walked*. The last three sentences also have the same verb: *played*.

The verb is sometimes called the **simple predicate**. In the rest of this book, we will speak of the simple predicate as the *verb*.

Two Types of Verbs

There are two types of verbs. They are called action verbs and state-of-being verbs.

Some **action verbs** tell of an action you can see.

> The trained lion *jumped* through a hoop.
> Cary *dived* from the highest platform.

Other action verbs tell of action you cannot see.

> I *remember* all the words of that poem.
> We *heard* the blast of the trumpet.

A **state-of-being verb** tells that something or someone *is*.

> That book of riddles and jokes *is* in the library.
> Our birthdays *are* on the same day.

Here are some common state-of-being verbs.

State-of-Being Verbs

is	was	has been	seem
are	were	have been	appear
am	will be	had been	look

Exercises Finding the Verb

A. Number your paper from 1 to 10. Write the verb in each sentence.

1. Miss Morgan writes with a quill pen.
2. My uncle is an Air Force test pilot.
3. The space shuttle *Discovery* blasted into orbit.
4. Margie rested before the high-hurdle competition.
5. Three penguins waddled to the water.
6. The sky looked pink and orange at sunset.
7. At noon, the zookeeper feeds the sea lions.
8. Hand pumps are on many old fire engines.
9. Our class made cornhusk dolls and table decorations for the Harvest Festival.
10. Adam hoped for better luck in his third vault.

B. Number your paper from 1 to 10. Write the verb in each of the following sentences. After the verb, write *Action* or *State-of-Being* to show what kind of verb it is.

1. The colors of the Italian flag are green, white, and red.
2. Valerie's dog performed a new trick.
3. Sean and Rhoda paddled their canoe for three miles down the Manistee River.
4. The spotted lizard darted up the cottonwood tree.
5. Our class visited Children's Hospital.
6. Father seemed anxious about his speech.
7. Eli used the microphone at the student assembly.
8. The Girl Scouts are at the Chippewa National Forest.
9. Navajos made these brightly beaded necklaces.
10. The home team fans were excited about their victory in the championship game.

C. Writing Pretend that you are an animal. What kind are you? Are you a hungry lion, an ornery bear, a timid fawn, or a fearless eagle? Write a paragraph that tells what you do from morning to night. Use as many action verbs as possible in your paragraph.

4 Subject of the Verb

Focus

The **subject of the verb** is the most important part of the complete subject.

In each complete subject, one word is more important than the others. This key word is sometimes called the **simple subject**. In this book, we will call it the **subject of the verb**.

In the examples below, the subject of the verb is in italics.

Complete Subject	Verb
The *clock*	stopped.
The old *clock*	stopped.
The old *clock* on the shelf	stopped.

Finding the Subject of the Verb

To find the subject of the verb, first find the verb. Then ask *who*? or *what*? before the verb. Look at these examples.

1. Monkeys escaped from the zoo.

Verb: *escaped*
Who or what *escaped*? *Monkeys*
Monkeys is the subject of *escaped*.

2. Three young monkeys from South America escaped from the zoo.

Verb: *escaped*
Who or what *escaped*? *Monkeys*
Monkeys is still the subject of the verb.

See if you can find the verb, and then the subject of the verb, in this example.

3. The lifeguard shouted a warning to the swimmers.

Did you find the action verb *shouted*? The subject tells you *who* shouted. What is the subject? *Lifeguard* is the subject of the verb.

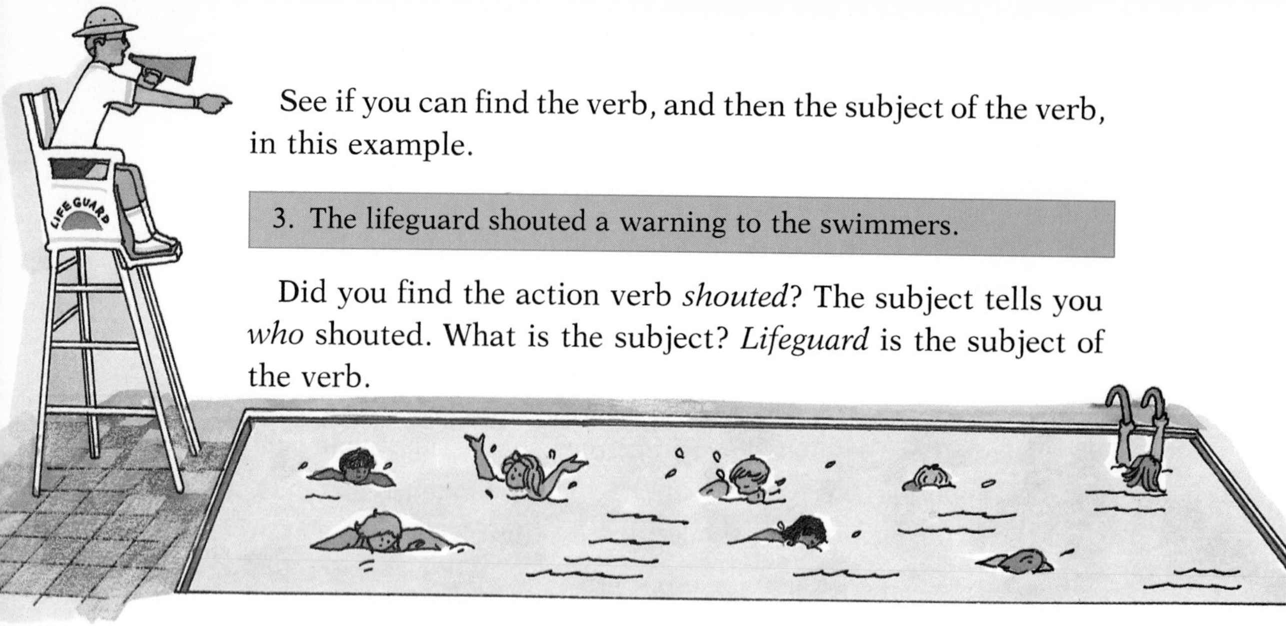

In the next example, look for a state-of-being verb. Then find the subject of the verb.

4. Our new computer is in Mom's study.

Did you find the state-of-being verb *is*? The subject tells you *who* or *what* is. What is the subject?

Exercises **Finding the Verb and Its Subject**

A. Copy each sentence. Draw two lines under the verb. Then draw one line under the subject of the verb.

1. Waves splashed over the cold, black rocks.
2. Juanita added to her butterfly collection.
3. Claudia hung her watercolor paintings.
4. The tents are waterproof.
5. Tom Sawyer found a secret hideout.
6. Jocelyn was her sister's bridesmaid.
7. Street musicians played for holiday shoppers.
8. Skiers sped down steep, icy slopes.
9. The shimmering desert seems endless.
10. The attic was dark and dusty.

B. Copy the following sentences. Draw two lines under the verb. Draw one line under the subject of the verb.

1. Large hailstones fell for several minutes.
2. Melinda leaped over the parking-lot fence.
3. That green parrot speaks Spanish.
4. The golden coach turned into a pumpkin at midnight.
5. The heavyweight boxer was ready for the match.
6. Dr. Méndez taped my sore wrist after the accident.
7. Three jugglers in the main ring tossed balls and pins.
8. Our school had a surprise fire drill today.
9. A stray dog slept on our steps all afternoon.
10. The knight on the black charger won the joust.

C. Writing Create a short paragraph about a circus. Write at least one sentence with *clown* as the subject, one sentence with *acrobat* as the subject, and one with *elephant* as the subject. Add other sentences to complete your paragraph. Draw one line under the subject of each sentence.

5 The Subject in Unusual Positions

Focus

The subject does not always come at the beginning of a sentence.

Writers often change the word order in sentences to add variety and interest to a paragraph. Read the following.

1. The rocket soared toward the planet Venus.

Rocket is the subject of the verb *soared*. It is placed before the verb near the beginning of the sentence.

2. Toward the planet Venus, the rocket soared.

Rocket is near the end of the sentence, still before the verb.

3. Toward the planet Venus soared the rocket.

Rocket has been moved again. Now it follows the verb.

When you look for the subject in sentences like examples 2 and 3, find the verb and ask *who* or *what*.

Example: Faster and faster ran the greyhounds.
Verb: *ran*
Who or what *ran*?
Greyhounds is the subject of *ran*.

Notice how the subject and verb change positions in the following examples without changing the meaning.

The lobster crawled over the rocks.
Over the rocks, the lobster crawled.
Over the rocks crawled the lobster.

Exercises Finding the Subject

A. Copy each sentence. Draw two lines under the verb. Then draw one line under the subject of the verb.

1. Down the steep hill raced José.
2. In the early evening, fireflies appeared.
3. On the top branch of the evergreen tree sat a brilliant red cardinal.
4. From the sugar maple fell the multi-colored leaves.
5. Down poured the rain.
6. Into the stadium the brass band marched.
7. Up into the clouds sailed the balloons.
8. Into the lake fell our tackle.
9. Out of the dark cave came a strange howl.
10. Across the range the cowboys rode.

B. Copy each sentence. Draw two lines under the verb. Draw one line under the subject. Rewrite each sentence, moving the subject to a new position in the sentence. You may have to move other words.

1. Around the barnyard waddled a gray goose.
2. Through the door sauntered the cat.
3. After the storm, a misty rainbow appeared.
4. A great green frog hopped into the pond.
5. Over the trees, my kite sailed.
6. In front of the grocery store, Mom waited patiently.
7. A large lumber wagon rumbled through the gate.
8. Across the snow whooshed a shiny sled.
9. The plane soared above the clouds.
10. In the parade were two prancing horses.

C. Writing Write a paragraph. Begin with this sentence. *I woke up one morning and found that I had wings.* Tell what happened on this day. What did you do? How did people treat you? When you finish, trade papers with a partner. Rewrite your partner's sentences, changing the positions of the subjects in some of the sentences.

6 Four Kinds of Sentences

Focus

There are four kinds of sentences: **declarative**, **interrogative**, **imperative**, and **exclamatory**.

When you speak, you have one of several purposes in mind. You may wish to make a statement or ask a question. At other times you give an order or show surprise. There is a special type of sentence to use in each of these situations.

The Declarative Sentence

A declarative sentence tells or states something. The word *declarative* comes from the Latin word *declarare* which means "to make clear." Use a declarative sentence when you want to make a statement. Always use a period after a declarative sentence.

Machu Picchu is the name of an ancient Inca city in Peru.

The Interrogative Sentence

An interrogative sentence asks a question. The word *interrogative* comes from the Latin word *interrogare,* which means "to ask." Use an interrogative sentence when you are looking for information or when you want an answer. Always use a question mark after an interrogative sentence.

Is Thai food very spicy?

The Imperative Sentence

An imperative sentence makes a request, gives a direction, or gives an order. The word *imperative* comes from the Latin word *imperare* which means "to order." Use an imperative sentence to make a polite request. Use a period at the end of most imperative sentences.

Please feed the dog before you leave for hockey practice.

If an imperative sentence shows strong feeling, use an exclamation point.

Stop yelling!

Study these examples of imperative sentences. Look for the subjects.

Switch off the light.
Turn left at the gas station.

In each of these sentences, the subject is not expressed. The subject is understood to be *you.*

(You) switch off the light.
(You) turn left at the gas station.

The Exclamatory Sentence

An exclamatory sentence shows strong emotion. The word *exclamatory* comes from the Latin word *exclamare,* which means "to cry out or say suddenly." Use an exclamatory sentence to show surprise, shock, or amazement. Use an exclamation point at the end of every exclamatory sentence.

We won!

Exercises Finding Four Kinds of Sentences

A. Number your paper from 1 to 10. Tell what kind of sentence each of the following is. Then tell what punctuation mark should be used at the end of each sentence.

Example: Are you going shopping Saturday
interrogative, question mark

1. What luck you have
2. Bring the yardstick
3. I heard a rumor
4. Tom takes a bus
5. Aim for the target
6. Tomorrow is my birthday
7. Are you telling the truth
8. Do you have a skateboard
9. When will the train leave
10. That's fantastic

B. Number your paper from 1 to 10. Rewrite each sentence below, changing it to the type shown in parentheses. Punctuate each sentence correctly.

1. Did we score a touchdown? (exclamatory)
2. Did Katie see the circus? (declarative)
3. Please stay with me. (interrogative)
4. Does the trail end in the mountains? (declarative)
5. Ken erased the chalkboards. (imperative)
6. Something in the shadows moved! (interrogative)
7. Did I lose my keys? (exclamatory)
8. Have we made a mess? (declarative)
9. Have another plate of spaghetti. (interrogative)
10. Those fireworks are noisy! (interrogative)

C. Writing Imagine that you have built a robot. In a paragraph, tell your robot how you feel about it. Explain how you built it. Give it commands. Ask it questions. Use all four sentence types in your paragraph.

Exercises for Mastery

Chapter 2

Writing and Studying Sentences

A. Making Sure That Sentences Are Complete Number your paper from 1 to 10. Write *Sentence* after each number that comes before a sentence. Write *Fragment* after each number that comes before a fragment. Then turn all fragments into sentences by adding the missing parts.

1. Use your skateboard on the sidewalk.
2. A frisky young mare.
3. Took the train across Europe.
4. We fed the panda bear.
5. A United States atlas.
6. My brother plays the flute.
7. Kermit and Miss Piggy.
8. Watched an exciting magic show.
9. The campers on the bus sang.
10. The giant yellow helium balloon popped.

B. Finding Subjects and Predicates Copy these sentences. Draw one line under the complete subject of each sentence. Draw two lines under the complete predicate.

1. Our family vacationed in the Catskills.
2. Baby garter snakes look like rubber bands.
3. Walter's calico cat has four kittens.
4. The clanging fire truck sped through traffic.
5. The sheriff's deputy made the arrest.
6. Tracey picked a bushel of Cortland apples.
7. Two girls joined our baseball team.
8. The librarian helped us find an answer to our question about Poland.
9. Each planet revolved around the sun.
10. The drum and bugle corps marched up the street.

Exercises for Mastery Continued

C. Finding the Verb Number your paper from 1 to 10. Write the verb in each sentence.

1. Our art class drew self-portraits.
2. The marathoners raced for more than twenty-six miles.
3. Ronnie drives a three-wheeler.
4. The Sioux scouts followed the trail.
5. All computers store information in a memory bank.
6. Tyrone met his friends at the mall.
7. The forward scored the final goal.
8. Your backpack seems heavier than those of the other campers.
9. Jenny has a strong volleyball serve.
10. The President held a press conference yesterday afternoon on the White House lawn.

D. Finding the Verb and Its Subject Copy each sentence. Draw two lines under the verb. Then draw one line under the subject of the verb.

1. A hydroplane landed on the glassy lake.
2. Alice chased the March hare.
3. My pen leaked purple ink all over my desk.
4. Spencer reads many books about whales, sailing ships, and the sea.
5. The cactus in that flowerpot is very prickly.
6. A blue iceberg floated on the choppy sea.
7. Lobsters thrive in the cold waters along the coast of Maine.
8. Slowly, Nina crawled through the tunnel.
9. My older sister camped for a week at Yellowstone National Park.
10. Vendors at the stadium sell peanuts.

E. Finding the Subject Copy each sentence. Draw two lines under the verb. Then draw one line under the subject of the verb.

1. During the fourth inning, the rain started.
2. Close overhead, a Navy helicopter hovered.
3. Around the corner roared a motorcycle.
4. Over the fence bounded the hounds.
5. Out of the water splashed a playful seal.
6. Under our porch, some red squirrels nested.
7. Toward the straw-filled target flew the arrow.
8. On the tape, my voice sounded strange.
9. High in the air fluttered the flag.
10. On Ann's T-shirt was a picture of Mickey Mouse, Pluto, and Goofy.

F. Four Kinds of Sentences Number your paper from 1 to 10. Tell what kind of sentence each is. Tell what punctuation mark should be used at the end of the sentence.

1. Listen to this new song
2. Hooray for our team of champions
3. Where is the subway exit
4. The *Concorde* taxied down the runway to begin its nonstop flight to New York
5. Olga has adopted a pet rabbit and has named it Hoppity
6. Can you fill in this crossword puzzle
7. Turn to page 80 before starting the homework assignment
8. Look out for the speeding car
9. Would you like some hot popcorn during the movie
10. I read the *Peanuts* comic strip every day

Using Grammar in Writing

A. The sound on the TV set is acting up. Because it keeps going off and on, you hear only part of the news, sports, and weather. You hear a few complete sentences but other groups of words are only fragments. Write three sentences that you hear clearly when the sound is working. Then turn three fragments you hear into sentences. You hear: *broke her own record in the high jump*, *two-day old hurricane Elena*, and *collapsed as the final beams were raised*.

B. Today is Monday, but it is *not* like every other Monday. You just had the most exciting weekend of your life! You cannot wait to tell your best friend about it. Write this conversation between you and your friend. Use all four sentence types. Here are two lines to get you started.

ME: You won't believe what happened!
FRIEND: Tell me.

C. Using Sentences To Write About History Imagine that you and your family travel back to the year 1903. You are on a beach at Kitty Hawk, North Carolina. You see Orville and Wilbur Wright prepare their first airplane for a test flight. You watch as Orville takes off on the first successful flight.

Write sentences that you or other members of your family might say as you watch this historic event. Use at least one sentence of each kind.

Chapter 2 Review

A. Identifying Sentences and Fragments Study the following groups of words. Write whether each group of words is a *Sentence* or a *Fragment*. Then tell whether each complete sentence is *Declarative*, *Interrogative*, *Imperative*, or *Exclamatory*. Finally, write the punctuation mark you would use at the end of each sentence.

1. The taxi circled the block for almost an hour
2. Where are you going after school
3. The pigs at the county fair
4. It's going to be a great day
5. Whistling down the street
6. The carpenter fixed the warped window
7. Don't start singing "Happy Birthday" yet
8. A blue-and-white van at the curb
9. Look out for that hairy green monster
10. Have you mailed the thank-you letter

B. Finding the Verb and Simple Subject Copy each of the following sentences. Draw two lines under the verb. Draw one line under the simple subject.

1. Into the library marched the principal.
2. Michael often hides under the table.
3. Please check the mailbox for a small package.
4. Behind the lunch counter, the waitress worked quickly and neatly.
5. On the raspberry bushes are many sharp thorns.
6. The players shot baskets in the gym before the game started.
7. Grate the cabbage for cole slaw.
8. Every day for an hour the symphony violinist practiced.
9. The lost picture was in the album all that time.
10. Get the air mattress out of the trailer.

Chapter 3

Using Nouns

Imagine that you are at the circus. Jugglers, acrobats, and clowns crowd the ring. You see trained elephants and hear roaring tigers. You eat hot buttered popcorn, roasted peanuts, and sticky cotton candy.

Without nouns you would not be able to tell your friends about the circus. Nouns name people, places, things, and ideas. You can use nouns to name all that you see, hear, and taste at the circus.

In this chapter, you will learn about nouns. You will practice using nouns when you speak and write. You will learn to use nouns to name the persons, places, things, and ideas that are a part of your world.

1 What Are Nouns?

Focus

A **noun** is a word that names a person, place, thing, or idea.

Look around your classroom. What do you see? What do you hear? Think of the games you play and the food you eat. The words that you use to name these things are **nouns.**

Some nouns name things that can be seen. *Firefighter, ranch,* and *pencil* are nouns.

Some nouns name things that cannot be seen. They are ideas. *Honesty, courage,* and *peace* are also nouns.

Here are some other examples of nouns.

Persons	Places	Things	Ideas
Bill Cosby	frontier	caterpillar	friendship
aunt	Milwaukee	robot	hunger
Sally Ride	universe	Congress	happiness

Key to Writing and Speaking When you write and speak, give a clear picture by using specific nouns. Choose *collie* rather than *dog*. Choose *cabin* instead of *building*.

Exercises Finding Nouns

A. Number your paper from 1 to 10. Write the nouns in each sentence below.

1. Stacy saw the fireworks last July.
2. A surfer rode a huge wave.
3. Clowns and puppets performed at the fair.
4. My brother has excellent eyesight.
5. My cousin lives in the mountains of Montana.
6. Jason plays the piano and the trombone.
7. The Dodgers will play in the World Series.
8. Keith has a picture of the space shuttle on his new green notebook.
9. Ms. Mason told the story of the first Thanksgiving.
10. Many students do chores to earn an allowance.

B. On your paper, make a chart like the one on page 42. Find the nouns in each of the following sentences. Write each noun in the correct column of the chart.

1. The wind scattered leaves all over the lawn.
2. Tabby, the cat, is sitting in the window.
3. Honesty and loyalty keep friendships strong.
4. From the airplane, Adele saw distant mountains.
5. Carolyn made a good suggestion at the meeting.
6. Do more people live in Los Angeles or in Boston?
7. My puppy chewed on the cover of the book.
8. Do you live in the city, the country, or a suburb?
9. Jack and his father planted the rosebush near the porch steps.
10. Mr. Bielski talked to the class about freedom.

C. Writing Pretend that you are traveling in a time machine. Where are you going? What year are you traveling to? Whom will you meet? What will you see? What will you do? Make a list of these things. Then, write a paragraph that tells about your adventure.

2 Common Nouns and Proper Nouns

Focus

A **common noun** is a general name for a person, place, thing, or idea.

A **proper noun** names a particular person, place, thing, or idea.

When you call Thomas Edison an inventor, you are giving him a name shared by all those who create new gadgets. The name *inventor* is common to a whole group of people. Many other names are also shared by a group. Examples are *cat, country,* and *baby*. These are **common nouns.**

Other nouns name particular persons, places, or things. *Grand Canyon, Switzerland,* and *Christopher* are a few examples. They are called **proper nouns**. A proper noun always begins with a capital letter.

The map below shows both proper and common nouns.

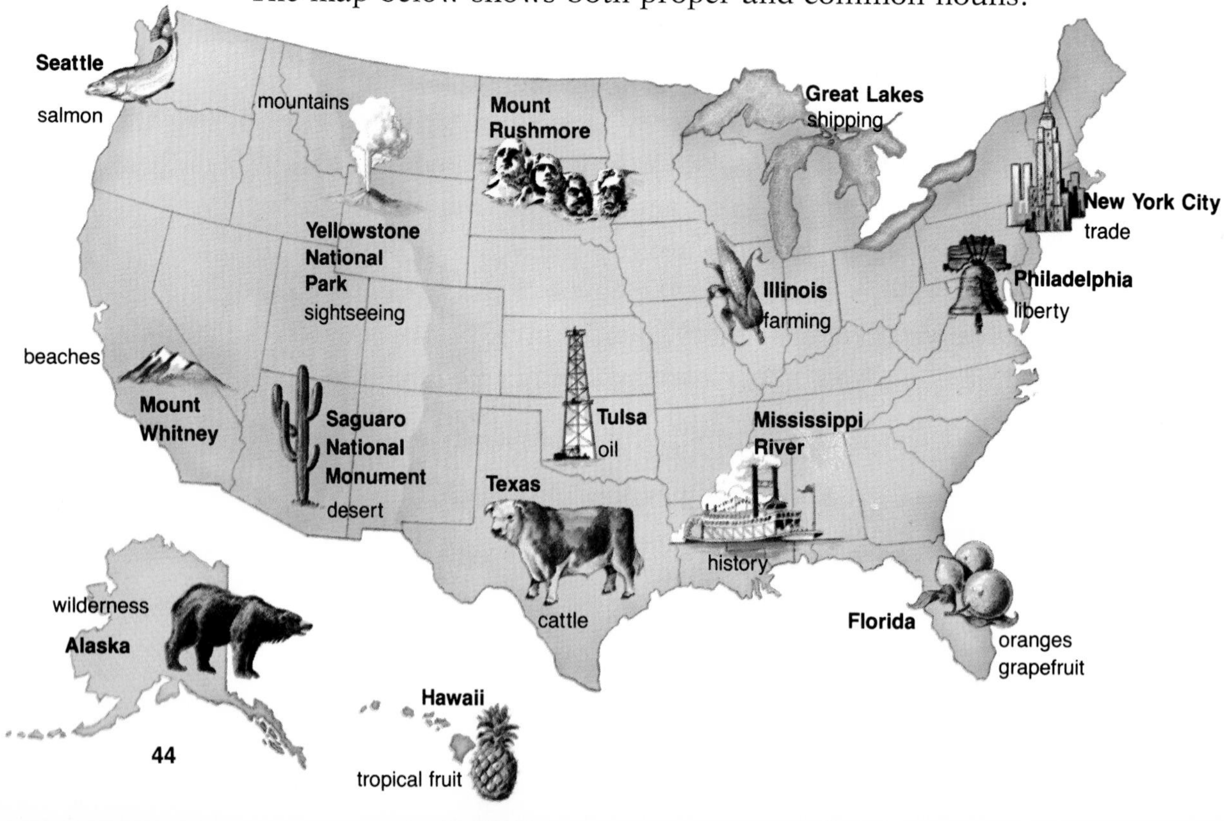

Key to Writing and Speaking Make your writing and speaking more interesting to your readers and listeners. Use proper nouns for particular people, places, and things.

Common noun: I sailed on a lake last summer.

Proper noun: I sailed on Lake of the Isles last summer.

Exercises Finding Common and Proper Nouns

A. Divide your paper into two columns. Label one column *Common Nouns* and the other column *Proper Nouns*. Number from 1 to 12 down the left-hand margin. After each number, write the noun from the list below in the correct column. Begin every proper noun with a capital letter.

1. person
2. barn
3. houston
4. ms. steele
5. paper
6. albert
7. maria
8. supermarket
9. africa
10. building
11. mr. ruiz
12. state street

B. Write the following common nouns on your paper. After each common noun, write a proper noun that matches it.

Example: ocean—Indian Ocean

1. river
2. boy
3. planet
4. restaurant
5. company
6. store
7. city
8. street
9. soap
10. building
11. singer
12. actress

C. Writing Pretend that you have been granted a wish by the travel genie. You may visit any country in the world. Think about where you would go. Think about whom and what you would see. List these people, places, and things. Then use these common nouns and proper nouns in a paragraph about your travels.

3 Singular and Plural Nouns

Focus

A **singular noun** names one person, place, thing, or idea.

A **plural noun** names more than one person, place, thing, or idea.

What is the difference between the words in these columns?

cake	cakes
person	persons
planet	planets

The nouns in the first column name one person, place, or thing. They are called **singular nouns**. The nouns in the second column name more than one. They are called **plural nouns**. Changing a word from singular to plural is called forming the plural of the noun. Here are seven rules for forming plurals.

1. To form the plural of most nouns, just add an -s.

sticks	cows	bikes	drinks
stones	dogs	skates	snacks

2. When the singular noun ends in s, *sh*, *ch*, x, or z, add -es.

buses	ashes	foxes
classes	lunches	quizzes

3. When the singular noun ends in o, add -s.

studios radios stereos banjos

Exceptions: For the following nouns ending in *o*, add *es*:

echoes heroes tomatoes potatoes

4. When the singular noun ends in *y* with a consonant before it, change the *y* to *i* and add -es.

fly—flies	penny—pennies
pony—ponies	candy—candies

5. For most nouns ending in *f* or *fe*, add *-s*. For some nouns ending in *f* or *fe*, however, change the *f* to *v* and add *-es* or *-s*.

belief—beliefs	elf—elves	loaf—loaves
chief—chiefs	self—selves	calf—calves
roof—roofs	wife—wives	knife—knives
dwarf—dwarfs	life—lives	wolf—wolves
cuff—cuffs	leaf—leaves	shelf—shelves
hoof—hoofs	half—halves	thief—thieves

6. Some nouns are the same for both singular and plural.

deer trout sheep moose salmon

7. Some nouns form their plurals in special ways.

mouse—mice	man—men	tooth—teeth
goose—geese	woman—women	foot—feet
child—children		

Key to Writing If you are unsure how to form the plural of any noun, check your dictionary. If your dictionary does not give the plural form, simply add an *-s* to the word.

Exercises **Forming Plurals**

A. Number your paper from 1 to 15. Write the plural form of each noun below. Then write the number of the rule that tells how the plural was formed.

1. bench	6. tomato	11. shelf
2. party	7. man	12. box
3. tax	8. thief	13. cameo
4. pencil	9. turkey	14. sheep
5. lady	10. tooth	15. roof

B. Number your paper from 1 to 10. Write the correct plural form of each word in italics.

1. The *woman* in Shawn's family all have blond hair.
2. Kathy sold the two *sheep* that she had raised.
3. There are eight *child* in Ned's family.
4. We set our *watch* to the correct time.
5. Make enough *copy* of the poster for everyone.
6. Mario and Faith came to the costume party dressed as *mouse*.
7. The brisk wind swept the *leaf* from the trees.
8. The *hero* pulled the child from the icy river.
9. Will there be any *sandwich* left?
10. Crackling *noise* came from the old radio.

C. Writing Pretend that your family has just moved into a very old house. In the attic, you discover many strange old collections. Think about the kinds of collections you might find. Make a list of the collections and some of the things each collection might contain. Then write a paragraph about your discoveries.

4 Making Nouns Show Possession

Focus

A **possessive noun** shows who or what owns something.

In this chapter, you have learned that nouns may be proper or common. You know that nouns are singular or plural. Now you will learn that nouns can also show ownership.

Here is *Zachary's* magnet.
Who owns the magnet? *Zachary*

This is the *girl's* book.
Who owns the book? the *girl*

Zachary's and *girl's* are possessive nouns. Possessive nouns show ownership.

Making Singular Nouns Show Possession

To make a singular noun show possession, add an apostrophe and *s*.

Singular Noun	Possessive Noun
mechanic	mechanic's
James	James's
Ms. Roberts	Ms. Roberts's

Making Plural Nouns Show Possession

There are two rules for making a plural noun possessive.

1. **If the plural noun ends in s, simply add an apostrophe after the s.**

Plural Noun	Possessive Noun
workers	workers'
nurses	nurses'

2. If the plural noun does not end in *s*, add an apostrophe and an *s*.

Plural Noun	**Possessive Noun**
men	men's
women	women's
children	children's

If you are not sure where to add the apostrophe, write the word by itself first. Then follow the rules.

When writing *'s* in cursive handwriting, you should not connect the *s* following the apostrophe to the last letter before the apostrophe. The apostrophe should separate the two letters.

Key to Writing Be sure to use punctuation carefully when forming possessives. Notice how changing the position of the apostrophe changes the meaning of these phrases.

Pirate's treasure means the treasure belongs to one pirate.

Pirates' treasure means the treasure belongs to more than one pirate.

Exercises Making Nouns Show Possession

A. In each sentence one word is in italics. Write this word so that it shows possession. Write the word first. Then add the apostrophe or apostrophe and *s*.

1. Michael gave me one of his *Labrador* puppies.
2. *Juan* laughter was catching.
3. The *twins* sixth birthday party was held at the roller-skating rink.
4. *Ladybugs* shells are black and orange.
5. Jamie Gilson, the author of our favorite book, answered our *class* letters.
6. Ray was amazed when the *robot* voice called him by his nickname.
7. *Stephanie* report was almost finished.

8. Six *detectives* hard work finally solved the case.
9. The *girls* chorus rode in a parade.
10. The principal complimented the student council on the clean-up *crew* good work.

B. Number your paper from 1 to 10. In each sentence, find the possessive noun that is not written correctly. Write it correctly.

1. Jacks paragraphs were about his mother's work.
2. The dog carried Laura's shoe to Billys yard.
3. Juans' parakeet is the same color as Bob's shirt.
4. Judys sisters shouted to get their father's attention.
5. The mail carrier's truck delivered a large package to Jakes house.
6. My hockey teams' annual party was held in Richard's basement.
7. Max's hobby is collecting ballplayers autographs.
8. Steves ticket is from Mr. Doonan's puppet show.
9. Jean's homework was left at her best friends house.
10. Yoko's ride on Charleses skateboard was scary.

C. Writing Pretend that Count Dracula had a Monster Bash. Each guest left behind one item. Using possessive nouns, make a list of what was forgotten and who left it. For example, Dracula's cape or the witch's broomstick may have been left behind. Then write a paragraph that tells about these forgotten belongings.

Exercises for Mastery

Chapter 3

Using Nouns

A. Finding Nouns Number your paper from 1 to 10. Write the nouns in each sentence below.

1. The girls tried their new skateboards.
2. A driver asked for directions.
3. Children played on the slide and swings.
4. Thomas Jefferson drew the plans for his new home.
5. Emeralds, rubies, aquamarines, and diamonds are precious gems.
6. My birthday is in August.
7. Practice will begin on Friday.
8. Colorado has beautiful mountains.
9. Vanessa put the change in her pocket.
10. The twins wore identical sweaters.

B. Finding Common Nouns and Proper Nouns Divide your paper into two columns. Label one column *Common Nouns* and the other column *Proper Nouns*. Number from 1 to 20 down the left-hand margin. After each number, write the noun in the proper column. Begin each proper noun with a capital letter.

1. utah
2. bird
3. doctor neff
4. gum
5. michael j. fox
6. glasses
7. pacific ocean
8. pretzel
9. bijou theater
10. garbage
11. mrs. thorpe
12. taxi
13. people
14. statue of liberty
15. basketball
16. oven
17. denver
18. camera
19. movie
20. disneyland

C. Forming Plurals Write the plural form of each of these nouns.

1. shoe	11. boss
2. ax	12. foot
3. lion	13. lunch
4. loaf	14. calf
5. crutch	15. salmon
6. navy	16. goose
7. wolf	17. brush
8. story	18. bath
9. hero	19. factory
10. chief	20. tomato

D. Writing the Possessive Form In each sentence one word is in italics. Write this word so that it shows possession. Write the word first. Then add the apostrophe or apostrophe and *s*.

1. All *raccoons* eyes are masked in black.
2. *Alonzo* victory made him feel like running a marathon again.
3. The nurse took the *man* pulse.
4. Leslie borrowed *Carla* ruler.
5. I clean my two *birds* cages every day.
6. *Archie* car is second-hand.
7. *Pamela* winning streak at checkers is over.
8. Our club is selling *children* T-shirts.
9. The *boys* locker room is filled with steam.
10. An *ant* strength is amazing.

Using Grammar in Writing

A. Write your own myth. Use it to explain some part of nature. Use at least five common nouns and five proper nouns in your myth. You may want to write about one of these topics.

how geese got webbed feet
how the kangaroo got its pouch
how the unicorn got its horn
how the raccoon got its mask

B. You are a movie director. You are getting ready to shoot the opening scene of your new fantasy movie. The camera focuses on the set. The action begins. In a paragraph, tell what happens next. Include the plural forms of some of the following words in your paragraph.

echo	chief
banjo	penny
elf	glass
bridge	foot
canyon	

C. Using Nouns in Science Australia is known for its wide variety of unusual animals. Use an encyclopedia to find information about Australian animals. Then choose one to write about. In your paragraph, describe the animal. What does it eat? In what part of the country does it live? Do you think that the animal would be a good pet?

Chapter 3 Review

A. Finding Nouns Write the nouns in each of the following sentences. Tell whether each noun is common or proper.

1. Jim swam in the ocean last summer.
2. The forgotten loaf of bread was covered with mold.
3. Maxine pins up her hair on hot, humid days.
4. Is it true that the Philippines is made up of more than seven thousand islands?
5. The shops in the mall are open two nights a week.
6. The little lamp fell apart when Helen picked it up.
7. Joy waits until the light changes before crossing the street.
8. Bright paint made the old bike look like new.
9. Please open the window so we can get a breeze.
10. Mr. Winn stenciled tiny white and yellow flowers on the cabinet.

B. Using Correct Plural and Possessive Forms Rewrite the sentences. Write the correct plural form for the first noun in italics in each sentence. Write the correct possessive form for the second noun in italics in each sentence.

1. The *box* contain my *family* old clothes.
2. In two *minute* I'll find *Charles* address.
3. Boxes of *tomato* filled the *farmer* truck.
4. The *pony* ate the *farmers* lunch.
5. *Stereo* for every class is *Mr. Wolf* dream.
6. My *tooth* were cleaned by a *dentist* assistant.
7. We took two *bus* to get to my Aunt *Fay* house.
8. Turn up the *cuff* on *Norris* trousers.
9. Trading in the *coupon* for new team uniforms was the *coach* idea.
10. There are *flower* in a vase on the windowsill of *Christine* room.

Chapter 4

Verbs for Sentence Power

Do oysters sneeze beneath the seas,
or wiggle to and fro,
or sulk, or smile, or dance awhile
. . . how can we ever know?

Which words made you smile when you read this poem? You probably never thought about oysters sneezing before. The words *sneeze, wiggle, sulk, smile,* and *dance* probably put funny images in your head. These words are called verbs. Verbs are words that express action or state-of-being.

In this chapter, you will learn about the different kinds of verbs and how to use them correctly. You will learn how to use helping verbs, and how to use verbs to show time. You will master the use of confusing pairs of verbs. This chapter will teach you all about verbs.

1 What Are Verbs?

Focus

Verbs are words that express action or state that something *is*.

There are two different kinds of verbs, **action verbs** and **state-of-being verbs**.

Action Verbs

Some verbs express action you can see.

Brian *hit* the ball.
The track team *ran* the race.
Melinda *rode* the unicycle.

Other verbs express action you cannot see.

Sarah *worried* about her performance.
Tony *wanted* a new baseball jacket.
Linus *believes* in the Great Pumpkin.

State-of-Being Verbs

Some verbs do not show any kind of action. Instead, they show that something *is*. Look at the following sentences. The verbs in italics are used to say that something *is*. They are called state-of-being verbs.

We *are* late.
School *is* over.
The boys *were* funny.
I *am* the last one.
The snow *was* heavy.
She-ra *is* He-Man's twin.

Here are the most common state-of-being verbs.

State-of-Being Verbs

am	be	was
are	being	were
is	been	

Several other verbs can also be used as state-of-being verbs. Look at the sentences below and study the verbs in the box.

The team *seemed* excited.
The apricot *tasted* sweet.
Evan *sounds* worried.
We *remained* calm.
The pillow *felt* soft.
The attic *smelled* musty.

Other State-of-Being Verbs

look	appear	smell	seem	sound
feel	taste	become	remain	grow

Key to Writing and Speaking Use action verbs whenever possible. Action verbs make your writing and speaking livelier.

The red fire engine *roared* down the street.
Pete Rose *powered* the ball over the left-field fence.
The wild stallion *bolted* across the prairie during the storm.

Exercises Recognizing Verbs

A. Number your paper from 1 to 10. Write the verb in each sentence.

1. The squirrel raced up the tree.
2. Jason called his brother in Utah.
3. The deep-dish pizza looked delicious.
4. I hoped for a good fishing trip.
5. The acrobats leaped onto the platform.
6. I like the smell of fresh sawdust.
7. The artist works on his masterpiece every day.
8. Susan began dance classes at Ms. Page's studio.
9. My science class visited the airport.
10. Dad lost the keys for his car.

B. Number your paper from 1 to 10. Write the verb in each of the following sentences. After the verb, write *Action* or *State-of-Being* to tell what kind of verb it is.

1. Wes plays the drums in a marching band.
2. Gino's parents own a toy store.
3. These library books are overdue.
4. Gloria is the club president.
5. The sparrow injured its wing.
6. The soup tastes spicy.
7. Gail hid in the hay loft.
8. The tulips were in bloom.
9. The mime entertained us.
10. Pecos Bill became a hero of tall tales.

C. Writing Imagine that you are walking through a jungle. Maybe you are searching for Tarzan. As you trek along a narrow path, you hear many animal noises. Describe your adventure. Use a variety of verbs to tell about what you see and hear.

Example: The pride of lions *rested* peacefully in an open area. One lion *roared* loudly as I passed.

2 Main Verbs and Helping Verbs

Focus

A verb may be a single word or a group of words.

Some verbs are single words. Look at these sentences.

Betsy *walks* home. Steve *called* you.

Other verbs are made up of two or more words. Look at the verbs in italics in the following sentences.

Betsy *is walking* home.
Betsy *has been walking* home.

Steve *was calling* you.
Steve *might have called* you.

When there are two or more words in the verb, the last verb part is the **main verb**. All of the other words in the verb are called **helping verbs**.

Helping Verbs	Main Verb	Verb
is	walking	is walking
has been	walking	has been walking
was	calling	was calling
might have	called	might have called

The most common helping verbs are the forms of *be, have,* and *do*.

be—am, are, is, was, were
have—have, has, had
do—do, does, did

These words can also be used by themselves as main verbs.

Used as Helping Verb	Used as Main Verb
Janet *was visiting*.	Janet *was* in Indiana.
Ralph *does enjoy* math.	Ralph *does* his work.

There are several other helping verbs that can be used with main verbs.

can	shall	will	may	must
could	should	would	might	

Separated Parts of the Verb

Sometimes another part of the sentence comes between the helping verb and the main verb.

Ezra *may* not *pitch* today.
Joanne *will* probably *stay* for the weekend.
The gate *should*n't *have been locked* last night.

Notice that *not* and the ending *n't* are not parts of the verb.

In questions, there are often one or more words between the helping verb and the main verb.

Does the Tin Man *need* oil?
Were you *looking* for me?
Have you ever *seen* a meteor shower?

Exercises Main Verbs and Helping Verbs

A. Number your paper from 1 to 10. Make two columns. Label the first column *Helping Verb*. Label the second column *Main Verb*. Write the verbs for each of these sentences in the proper column.

Example: Joseph didn't see the curb.

Helping Verb	Main Verb
did	see

1. Our goalie has blocked many shots.
2. Vicky had never missed a Yankees game.
3. Would you repeat your answer?
4. The students were awarded a prize for their float.
5. The champ was waiting to enter the ring.

6. Devonna will probably break the school record in the 100-yard dash.
7. We couldn't cross the railroad tracks.
8. The queen has ordered this entertainment.
9. They had often visited Disneyland.
10. Didn't immigrants come to Ellis Island?

B. Write the following sentences. Add a helping verb to each one. Choose helping verbs from the lists on pages 61 and 62.

1. I ______ only joking when I said the game was cancelled.
2. ______ there be fireworks after the parade?
3. Grandma ______ never missed my birthday party.
4. Winona ______ barely reach the rings.
5. Barry ______ almost finished the crossword puzzle.
6. My little brother ______ impatiently waiting for Halloween.
7. When ______ your family move to Seattle?
8. The freshly baked bread ______ quickly eaten.
9. I ______ learn this computer language.
10. Eula ______ drawn a cartoon strip in art class.

C. Writing Write and illustrate a story booklet for younger children. Tell about a trip to a beach or an amusement park. You might write about the games, rides, or food. You could also describe the other people you might see. Be sure to use main verbs and helping verbs in your story.

3 Using the Right Form of *Be*

Focus

Some forms of the verb *be* may be used alone or as helping verbs. Other forms of the verb *be* may be used only with helping verbs.

The verb *be* has many forms.

am	are	were	being
is	was	be	been

Here are five rules to remember when using forms of the verb *be*.

1. If the subject names one person, place, thing, or idea, use the form *is* or *was*.

Christine *is* gone. She *was sitting* near me.

2. If the subject names more than one person, place, thing, or idea, use the forms *are* or *were*.

The children *are* late. They *were riding* their horses.

3. When the subject is *you*, use the forms *are* or *were*.

You *are* my best friend. *Were* you going along?

4. When the subject is *I*, use the forms *am* or *was*.

I *am* here. I *was studying* English.

5. Use a helping verb before *be*, *being*, and *been*. These words may not be used alone or without another helping verb.

Karen *will be* here. Alex *was being taken* to surgery.

Jeff *has been looking* for you. The tests *have been* hard!

Exercises Using the Right Form of *Be*

A. Number your paper from 1 to 10. Choose the right form of the verb *be* from the parentheses. Write each sentence correctly.

1. Batman and Robin (is, are) superheroes.
2. I (am, are) a loyal friend.
3. You (is, are) the team captain.
4. The comet (been, has been) spotted.
5. You (was, were) blocking my view.
6. Craig and Cecile (was, were) tossing the beach ball.
7. The St. Bernard (being, was being) watchful.
8. Your bucket (is, are) loaded with seashells.
9. Nancy (be, is) a talented figure skater.
10. The boys (was, were) jumping over puddles.

B. Number your paper from 1 to 10. If a sentence uses an incorrect form of the verb *be*, rewrite the sentence correctly. If the sentence is correct, write *Correct* on your paper.

1. Tammy and I are building a sand castle.
2. I be guessing the number of marbles in the fish bowl.
3. You is a good sport to play guard.
4. The trainer be feeding the porpoises.
5. Because Mom is running for mayor, I am helping her deliver campaign leaflets.
6. Eric and Sam been early every day this week.
7. The haunted house being scary.
8. They were throwing snowballs.
9. I were snorkeling when the storm began.
10. The pilots is boarding the Navy transport plane.

C. Writing Imagine that you and your friends are living in either the year 1787 or the year 2187. In a paragraph, describe your life. You may want to tell about the transportation, food, education, or clothes of the time. Be sure to use helping verbs in your paragraph.

4 Using the Right Verb After *There*, *Here*, and *Where*

Focus

In a sentence beginning with *There*, *Here*, or *Where*, first find the subject to decide whether the verb should be singular or plural.

Many sentences begin with *There, Here,* or *Where*. These words are usually followed by a form of the verb *be,* such as *is, are, was,* or *were*. How do you know which verb is the correct verb to use?

First, find the subject. *There, Here,* and *Where* are never subjects. To find the subject, reverse the order of the sentence.

Read these sentences.

There (is, are) the parrot.
The *parrot* (is, are) there. (*Parrot* is the subject.)

Where (was, were) the caterpillars?
The *caterpillars* (was, were) where? (*Caterpillars* is the subject.)

After you have found the subject, follow these rules.

1. When the subject names one person, place, or thing, use one of these forms.

There is	Here is	Where is
There was	Here was	Where was

There *is* a sailboat on the lake.

2. When the subject names more than one person, place, or thing, or is the word *you*, use one of these forms.

There are	Here are	Where are
There were	Here were	Where were

Where *were* the buses?
You *were* the first to arrive.

Exercises Using the Right Verb After *There*, *Here*, and *Where*

A. Number your paper from 1 to 10. Write the subject of each of the following sentences. Then choose the correct form of the verb *be* from the parentheses. Write the correct form of the verb.

1. Where (is, are) your brother's paints?
2. There (is, are) five kites in the sky.
3. Where (is, are) the batteries?
4. There (is, are) a strong wind from the west.
5. Here (is, are) the oldest tree in the park.
6. There (was, were) a carnival in town.
7. Here (is, are) several children that you met at the pool.
8. Where (is, are) the Big Dipper?
9. Where (is, are) the sour apples that you picked?
10. Here (is, are) the Canadian geese.

B. Rewrite the following sentences. Change singular subjects to plural subjects. Change plural subjects to singular subjects. Be sure to change the verb to fit the subject.

1. Where are the basketballs?
2. There is the boy with the skateboard.
3. Here is the astronaut who walked on the moon.
4. Where are the campsites?
5. Here is your missing gym shoe.
6. There is a good reason for my mistake.
7. Here is your birthday present.
8. Where are the best fishing spots?
9. Here is the yellow rose.
10. There are our new computer games on that shelf.

C. Writing Imagine that you are showing a new student around your school. Make a list of the interesting places. Write a paragraph describing your tour. Use such phrases as "Here is . . . ." or "Over there are . . . ." Begin the tour from your classroom.

5 Regular Verbs

Focus

Regular verbs express action that happened in the past by adding the ending *-ed* to the basic form.

Verbs do more than show action or tell that something *is*. Verbs also tell about time. **Present tense** verbs tell about action that is taking place at the present time.

The sentences below all show verbs in the present tense.

1. I *play*.
2. You *work*.
3. He *paints*.
4. They *dance*.

Notice that when the subject is plural, as in sentence 4, the basic form of the verb is used. When the subject is singular, as in sentence 3, *-s* is added to the basic form of the verb. Use the basic form of the verb with the pronouns *I* and *you*.

Other verbs tell about action that happened in the past. These verbs are said to be in the **past tense**. Study the following examples to see one way in which the basic form of the verb is changed to make the past form.

Basic Form	Past Form
talk	talked
stop	stopped
study	studied

Most verbs add *-ed* to the basic form of the verb in order to show past tense. Verbs that follow this rule are called **regular verbs**. Notice that the spelling of some verbs is changed when the *-ed* ending is added.

stop becomes **stopped** (the final consonant is doubled)
study becomes **studied** (*y* changes to *i*)
dance becomes **danced** (the silent *e* is dropped)

Exercises **Using Regular Verbs**

A. Number your paper from 1 to 10. Change each of the following verbs to the past form by adding *-ed*. Remember that the spelling of some verbs will change when you add *-ed*.

1. march
2. number
3. order
4. hop
5. color
6. slam
7. hammer
8. hope
9. finish
10. hurry

B. Number your paper from 1 to 10. If the verb in italics is in the present tense form, write the past tense form. If the verb is in the past tense form, write the present tense form.

1. We *traveled* in a camper through the Black Hills.
2. The search team *discovered* clues to solve the mystery.
3. Natalie *belongs* to the Girl Scouts.
4. The blind woman *crosses* the street with the help of her seeing eye dog.
5. My mother *bakes* chicken for Sunday dinner.
6. I *watched* my favorite TV program on Thursday.
7. Dad *planted* tulip bulbs in November.
8. Vince *practiced* every day after school.
9. Adam *fishes* in the pond every Saturday morning.
10. In the spring, my family *picks* thirty pounds of strawberries to make jam.

C. Writing Imagine that you had a great adventure yesterday. You woke, not as yourself, but as a great hero or heroine from the past. Who were you? Were you Robin Hood, Cleopatra, a Viking king or queen, a samurai warrior, or Annie Oakley? Write down everything that happened in your adventure. Then write a paragraph that tells about it. You may want to use some of the action verbs listed below.

charged	dropped	splashed	evaded	grabbed
clutched	arrived	guessed	searched	decided

6 Using Helping Verbs To Show Past Tense

Focus

The helping verbs *has*, *have*, and *had* can be used with the verb to show action in the past.

You have seen one way that verbs can express action in the past. There is also a second way. Sometimes, the helping verb *has, have,* or *had* can be used with the verb to show past tense. The form of the verb that is used with *has, have,* or *had* is called the **past participle**. With regular verbs, the past form and the past participle are the same.

Past	Past Participle
I *talked.*	I had *talked.*
He *painted.*	He has *painted.*
You *called.*	You have *called.*
We *played.*	We had *played.*

Now you have learned about three forms that a regular verb can have. A regular verb can have the present form, the past form, or the past participle form. These three forms of the verb are called the **principal parts of the verb**. Below are the principal parts for several regular verbs.

Principal Parts of Verbs

Present	Past	Past Participle
watch	watched	(have) watched
save	saved	(have) saved
trade	traded	(have) traded
grab	grabbed	(have) grabbed
carry	carried	(have) carried

Exercises Using the Principal Parts of Verbs

A. Divide your paper into three columns. Label the columns *Present*, *Past*, and *Past Participle*. Write each of the following words in the *Present* column. Then write the past and past participle forms of each verb in the proper columns. Remember to use a helping verb with the past participle.

1. like
2. crash
3. marry
4. trot
5. notice
6. add
7. skip
8. erase
9. nudge
10. tally
11. flap
12. cry

B. Number your paper from 1 to 10. Write the form of each verb asked for in parentheses. Then use each verb in a sentence.

1. explode (past participle)
2. cover (present)
3. fix (past participle)
4. subtract (past)
5. move (past participle)
6. squeal (present)
7. change (past)
8. remember (present)
9. show (past)
10. measure (past)

C. Writing You may have heard the saying, "A cat has nine lives." Imagine that you also have nine lives, and that you have already lived three. In one life, you were an object, and in another you were an insect. In your third life, you were an animal.

Write a paragraph telling just what you were in each of those three lives. Then, in another paragraph, tell about something funny or unusual that happened in one of your lives. Use the past tense and one or two past participles (with *had*) in your story.

7 Irregular Verbs

Focus

Some verbs form the past tense in special ways. These verbs are called **irregular verbs.**

You have learned that some verbs are called **regular verbs.** The past form of a regular verb is made by adding *-ed* to the present form.

listen—listened   scurry—scurried

Some verbs, however, do not make the past tense by adding *-ed.* These verbs are called **irregular verbs.** Irregular verbs have special past forms.

sleep—*slept*   teach—*taught*   sit—*sat*

Sometimes, the past form and the past participle of an irregular verb are the same.

He *slept.*	We *taught.*	They *sat.*
He has *slept.*	We have *taught.*	They had *sat.*

Other irregular verbs, however, have special past participles. The chart on page 73 shows the principal parts of many of these verbs.

When you use irregular verbs, remember these rules.

1. The past form of a verb is used without a helping verb.

Rick *saw* a shuttle launch at Cape Canaveral.
Karen *did* a graceful somersault from the diving board.
Chris *took* first place at the 4-H fair.

2. The past participle *must* be used with a helping verb.

Incorrect: They *seen* a rodeo.
Correct: They *have seen* a rodeo.

Principal Parts of Common Irregular Verbs

Present	Past	Past Participle
begin	began	(have) begun
break	broke	(have) broken
bring	brought	(have) brought
choose	chose	(have) chosen
come	came	(have) come
do	did	(have) done
drink	drank	(have) drunk
eat	ate	(have) eaten
fall	fell	(have) fallen
fly	flew	(have) flown
freeze	froze	(have) frozen
give	gave	(have) given
go	went	(have) gone
grow	grew	(have) grown
have	had	(have) had
know	knew	(have) known
lay	laid	(have) laid
lie	lay	(have) lain
ride	rode	(have) ridden
ring	rang	(have) rung
rise	rose	(have) risen
run	ran	(have) run
say	said	(have) said
see	saw	(have) seen
sing	sang	(have) sung
sit	sat	(have) sat
speak	spoke	(have) spoken
steal	stole	(have) stolen
swim	swam	(have) swum
take	took	(have) taken
teach	taught	(have) taught
throw	threw	(have) thrown
wear	wore	(have) worn
write	wrote	(have) written

Exercises Using Irregular Verbs

A. Rewrite each of the following sentences. Change the present form in parentheses to the past form.

1. I (wear) my father's old top hat to school on Hat Day.
2. Maria (know) all the answers on the game show.
3. The explorers all (see) a strange creature.
4. The pond (freeze) before Thanksgiving.
5. We (choose) our favorite spot in the park to eat lunch.
6. Mr. Okamoto (teach) us all of the state capitals.
7. My mother (run) in a marathon this summer.
8. Alex (ride) his horse in the rodeo last week.
9. The phone (ring) four times before I could answer it.
10. The home team (steal) three bases in the ninth inning.

B. Number your paper from 1 to 10. Write each sentence twice. First, use the verb in italics in the past tense. Then use the past participle.

1. The animal trainer *speaks* calmly to the tigers.
2. The Vienna Boys' Choir *sings* at the Vatican.
3. Many tourists *come* to Australia.
4. Branches *fall* from the trees during storms.
5. The fans *sit* in the east bleachers for home games.
6. We *bring* towels and a picnic lunch to the beach.
7. We *eat* tortillas for breakfast.
8. Some clowns actually *go* to clown school.
9. The kittens *grow* rapidly until the age of six months.
10. My dog Inky *swims* in the muddy waters of the Mississippi River.

C. Writing Imagine that your school had a Track and Field Fun Day. The most popular event was the Crazy Obstacle Course. Write a paragraph that gives a play-by-play account of this race. Include the past form of some of these irregular verbs: *begin, break, bring, come, do, fall, go, have, lie, run, see, sit, take, throw*.

8 Direct Objects of Verbs

Focus

The **direct object** is the noun or pronoun that completes the action of the verb.

In many sentences, a subject and a verb are enough to express a complete thought.

Subject	**Verb**
The child	fell.
The telephone	rang.

In other sentences, the thought is not complete until other words have been added.

Kirk spilled the *glue*.
Jeannie dialed the *number*.

The noun that completes the action of the verb is the **direct object** of the verb. *Glue* tells what Kirk spilled. *Number* tells what Jeannie dialed. *Glue* and *number* are direct objects.

To find the direct object in a sentence, first find the verb. Then ask *whom*? or *what*? after the verb. The word that answers *whom*? or *what*? after the verb is the direct object.

The sailors anchored their ship.
The sailors anchored *what*? their *ship*
The direct object is *ship*.

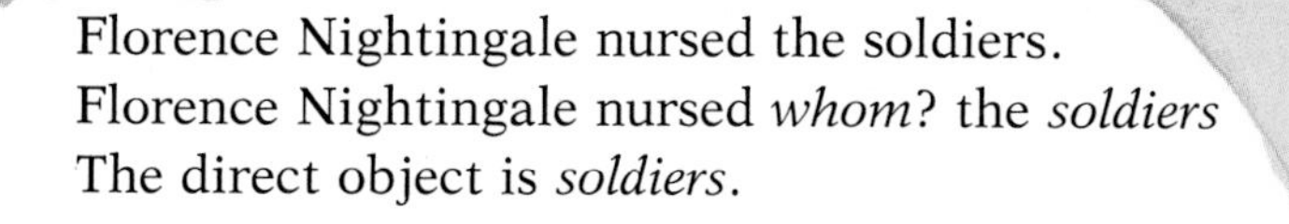

Florence Nightingale nursed the soldiers.
Florence Nightingale nursed *whom*? the *soldiers*
The direct object is *soldiers*.

Exercises Using Direct Objects

A. Copy the following sentences. Draw one line under the verb. Draw two lines under the direct object.

Example: Della was riding her bicycle.

1. Teresa broke her leg on the ski slope.
2. Tim borrowed my newest album.
3. The fielder should have caught that ball.
4. The conductor will collect tickets.
5. John Smith guided the colonists.
6. Sally rolled the ball down the bowling alley.
7. The strong tide tugged the weary swimmer.
8. Phyllis and Marni were working a puzzle.
9. Long ago, Native Americans hunted buffalo.
10. Lyndon cut the watermelon into small pieces.

B. Number your paper from 1 to 10. Write the direct object in each of the following sentences. Then rewrite each sentence using a different direct object.

1. Mosquitoes attacked us shortly after dark.
2. The children liked the puppets at the fair.
3. The scientist prepared an experiment.
4. We were building a fort of snow and ice.
5. The bears ate blueberries all morning long.
6. Heidi will read *Charlotte's Web* during Book Week.
7. My father plants a garden after the last frost in May.
8. Jane washed her puppy in an old metal tub.
9. Over eight thousand fans cheered the musicians.
10. My friends and I wrote a skit for our block party.

C. Writing On a sheet of paper, write sentences using the following verbs. Put a direct object in each sentence.

1. lost
2. dropped
3. will fill
4. likes
5. was writing
6. should have read

9 Some Confusing Verbs

Focus

There are some pairs of verbs that are confusing. These include *set* and *sit*, *let* and *leave*, *may* and *can*, and *teach* and *learn*.

Look at the correct way to use these confusing verb pairs.

Set* and *Sit

Set means "to put something somewhere."
Sit means "to rest in one place."

Say these sentences over until they sound natural.

Set your skates on the bench.
Set the lamp here.
Sit in the first row.
Don't *sit* on that tree limb.

Let* and *Leave

Let means "to allow or permit."
Leave means "to go away or depart."

The following sentences show you the correct way to use *let* and *leave*.

Let me borrow your watercolors.
Will you *let* me see that movie?
When did you *leave* Arkansas?
Do not *leave* your poncho at the campsite.

May and _Can_

May means "to allow" or "to permit."

Can means "to be able to."

Read the following sentences. Notice how they show the difference between *may* and *can*.

You *may* have more salad.
May we use your skateboard?
Nina *can* walk on stilts.
You *can* swim very well.

Teach and _Learn_

Teach means "to show how" or "to explain."

Learn means "to understand" or "to gain knowledge."

Study the following sentences to see how to use these verbs.

Will you *teach* me how to make that square knot?
I *taught* my dog to do the trick last week.
Thomas will *learn* to say the alphabet backward.
My dog Gilly *learned* how to shake hands.

Exercises Choosing the Right Verb

A. Number your paper from 1 to 10. Choose the right verb from the parentheses. Write it on your paper.

1. (Set, Sit) that water cooler under the willow tree.
2. The diver (let, leave) the shark come near.
3. Dad (lets, leaves) me win at Scrabble.
4. (Set, Sit) the vase on the piano.
5. William Perry (let, leave) the reporter ask him several questions.
6. My dog Rex (sets, sits) by my side.
7. The President will (set, sit) at the head of the table.
8. Will Mom (let, leave) the baby with a sitter?
9. Birds (let, leave) their nests whenever something disturbs them.
10. Did the player (set, sit) his helmet on the bench?

B. Number your paper from 1 to 10. Choose the right verb from the parentheses. Write it on your paper.

1. Mr. Dior (teaches, learns) ballet classes.
2. My sister (taught, learned) me to ride a horse.
3. A magician (may, can) make things disappear.
4. I (taught, learned) to fish for trout.
5. Yes, you (may, can) snack on some raisins.
6. Cats (may, can) see in the dark.
7. Magnets (may, can) attract metals.
8. (Teach, Learn) me that yo-yo trick, Raoul.
9. People (teach, learn) from their mistakes.
10. (May, Can) we please feed the geese?

C. Writing Use each of these pairs of words in a tongue twister: *sit-set*, *let-leave*. As many words as possible should begin with the first letter of the exercise word.

Example: Larry and Leon *leave* limes on the lawn, but they won't *let* little Lucy lift the limes.

10 Using Contractions

Focus

Some verbs may be combined with another word to make a new word. The new word is called a **contraction**.

Look at these frequently used contractions.

Commonly Used Contractions

I'll = I will	here's = here is
I'd = I would, I had	there's = there is, there has
I'm = I am	they're = they are
I've = I have	they've = they have
she'd = she would, she had	isn't = is not
he's = he is, he has	aren't = are not
we'll = we will	weren't = were not
we're = we are	hasn't = has not
you're = you are	wasn't = was not
it's = it is, it has	can't = cannot
that's = that is, that has	don't = do not
what's = what is, what has	won't = will not
where's = where is, where has	shouldn't = should not

Always use an **apostrophe** (') when you write a contraction. The apostrophe shows where letters are left out when the words are combined.

You + *are* = *you're* (The apostrophe replaces the *a* in *are*.)

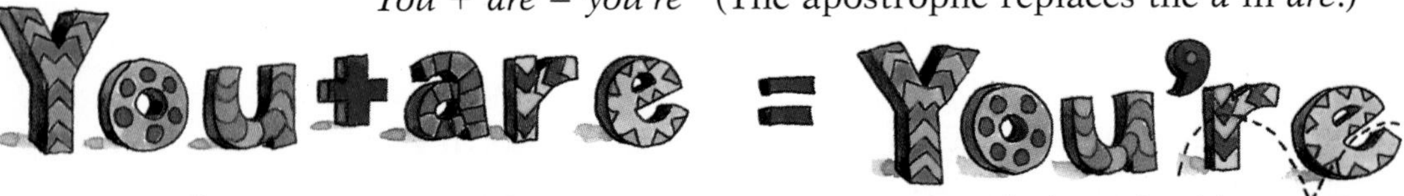

Key to Writing Do not use contractions in formal writing, such as school work. Use contractions only in informal writing. For example, in a letter to a friend, you may use *don't* rather than *do not*.

Exercises Forming Contractions Correctly

A. Copy each of the following contractions. Place apostrophes where they belong.

1. well
2. theres
3. youre
4. thats
5. Im
6. werent
7. theyve
8. wont
9. whats
10. wheres

B. Copy the following sentences. Make contractions from the words in italics in each sentence.

1. *It is* my birthday next Wednesday.
2. This mule *has not* been fed yet.
3. The plane *will not* land in the fog.
4. *They are* always on time.
5. Jeremy *was not* outside when the grass fire started.
6. "*What has* happened here?" asked Mrs. Kaplan.
7. I think *she would* like to go.
8. Most animals *will not* go near snakes.
9. *There is* the start of the movie.
10. *You are* the team captain for this round.

C. Writing Imagine that you and a friend decided to earn some money. Think about the project you chose. List the steps you took to organize your money-making project. Write a letter to another friend about this project. Use the items in your list. Tell your friend how successful your project was. Use contractions in this friendly letter.

11 Using Negatives Correctly

Focus

Never use **double negatives** when you speak or write.

Contractions that contain the word *not* are called **negatives**. They are made by joining certain verbs with the word *not*. *Are* + *not* = *aren't* (The apostrophe takes the place of *o* in *not*.)

Here are some other examples of negatives.

is + not = isn't	should + not = shouldn't
was + not = wasn't	can + not = can't
do + not = don't	could + not = couldn't

The following words are also negatives, even though they are not contractions.

no	no one	nothing	never
none	nobody	nowhere	

Two negatives should never be used together in the same sentence. Two negatives used together make what is called a **double negative**. Avoid double negatives.

Wrong: She *can't* do *nothing* right.
Right: She *can't* do anything right. *or* She can do *nothing* right.

Look at the following sentences. They show how to use negatives correctly.

Never touch the hot stove.
Don't ever touch the hot stove.

The doctor *hasn't* seen anyone.
The doctor has seen *no one*.

There are *none* left.
There *aren't* any left.

Exercises Using Negatives Correctly

A. Number your paper from 1 to 10. Write the correct word from the two given in the parentheses.

1. Doesn't (anybody, nobody) know the time?
2. Don't you have (anything, nothing) to eat?
3. Haven't you (ever, never) seen the Grand Canyon?
4. There isn't (any, no) reason to be afraid.
5. Ellie doesn't take her dogs (anywhere, nowhere).
6. There really weren't (any, no) easy problems.
7. No one (is, isn't) wearing a sweatshirt.
8. (Does, Doesn't) nobody want to roller skate?
9. Isn't (anyone, no one) using the computer?
10. (Were, Weren't) none of the girls working on their science experiment?

B. Find the sentences that contain double negatives. Rewrite the sentences correctly. If a sentence is correct, write *Correct*.

1. There wasn't anything wrong with your paper.
2. The strike didn't solve nothing.
3. Does anything happen when you push that button?
4. She doesn't know nobody in her music class.
5. Nothing was ever too spicy for Ken.
6. We don't want no trouble.
7. I couldn't see anything on the stage.
8. These scissors won't cut nothing.
9. The bus had no empty seats when I boarded.
10. Manuel's glasses weren't nowhere to be found.

C. Writing Imagine that there is a cartoon character called Dismal. Dismal has a difficult time. Nothing ever seems to go right for Dismal. Think about what might happen to this character on his walk home from school one day. List the problems that he might run into. Then write a paragraph about Dismal's walk home. Use negatives correctly in your paragraph.

Exercises for Mastery

Chapter 4

Verbs for Sentence Power

A. Identifying Main Verbs and Helping Verbs Number your paper from 1 to 10. Write the complete verb in each of the following sentences. If there is a helping verb, label the *Helping Verb* and the *Main Verb*.

1. Spiderman climbed the building.
2. Pete and Michele are watching the Independence Day fireworks.
3. Roberta is a frisbee champion.
4. Where does the eagle build its nest?
5. Fozzie Bear wore a top hat.
6. Dennis hasn't ever played in left field.
7. The runners were thirsty.
8. Claire will always be my friend.
9. The tadpole changed into a frog.
10. The air suddenly has become muggy.

B. Choosing the Right Form of *Be* Number your paper from 1 to 10. Choose the right form of the verb *be* from the parentheses. Write the sentence.

1. Paul (is, are) going to an auction this Saturday.
2. I (is, am, are) in charge of clean-up.
3. Carlos and Heather (was, were) soccer teammates.
4. We (will be, be) playing kickball when the weather warms up.
5. You (was, were) making me laugh with those silly jokes you always tell.
6. I (been, have been) thinking of a better plan.
7. (Was, Were) I talking too fast?
8. Hurry up! You (is, are) taking too long.
9. Snoopy (be, is) Charlie Brown's dog.
10. The wind (is, are) whistling through the branches.

C. Using the Right Verb After *There*, *Here*, and *Where* Number your paper from 1 to 10. Find the subject of each of the sentences below. Write it. Then choose the correct form of the verb *be* from the parentheses and write it after the subject.

1. There (is, are) the caboose.
2. Here (is, are) your racket.
3. Where (was, were) the first settlements in Virginia?
4. There (was, were) enough apples for everyone.
5. Where (was, were) the accident that you saw?
6. There (was, were) many stars on that show.
7. Where (is, are) Sanibel Island?
8. There (is, are) no rivers flowing out of Nevada's Great Basin.
9. Where (was, were) your collection of beetles?
10. There (is, are) the stadium.

D. Using the Past Form Number your paper from 1 to 10. Change the verbs in italics from the present tense to the past tense. Write the past tense on your paper.

1. The tail of the comet *points* away from the sun.
2. My new leather shoes *squeak* on the tile floor.
3. Karen's brother *pumps* gas at the service station every day after school.
4. Mums *bloom* in the fall until the first hard frost of the season.
5. Mud slides *wash* away big chunks of highway.
6. Our dentist *rents* an office near our home.
7. Brett's family *farms* in Idaho.
8. A sudden loss of power *causes* a plane to tailspin.
9. A family of field mice *lives* in the hayloft.
10. The rocket *soars* in space.

Exercises for Mastery Continued

E. Using the Past Form and Past Participle Change the verbs in italics from the past form to the past participle by adding *has* or *have* to the verb. Write the past participle on your paper.

1. My cousin Elaine *studied* Chinese.
2. Many students *learned* computer languages.
3. I always *wanted* to be a police officer.
4. Rita *visited* her grandparents in Ohio.
5. Spiders *nested* in the giant hollow log.
6. Native Americans *designed* turquoise jewelry.
7. I *shared* riddles with the Cub Scout pack.
8. The defensive line *sacked* the quarterback.
9. Few *traveled* to the Australian Outback.
10. Water *filled* the canal.

F. Mastering Irregular Verbs Write the correct verb.

1. Have you (drank, drunk) all of the apple juice.
2. We (flew, flown) over the huge limestone quarry.
3. I (saw, seen) the seeds we planted begin to sprout.
4. It has (took, taken) us six hours to reach Phoenix.
5. Sammy (chose, chosen) me to play on his team.
6. The children have (rode, ridden) the train.
7. Tim (brang, brought) pumpkins for everyone.
8. Ms. Bakken (teached, taught) us first aid.
9. All the leaves had (fell, fallen) by early November.
10. I have (gone, went) to the Catskill Mountains.

G. Finding Direct Objects Copy these sentences. Draw one line under the verb. Draw two lines under the direct object.

1. The movers packed furniture in the truck.
2. Bert will frame the sketch he drew.
3. At the movie, we bought popcorn.
4. The police officer was directing traffic.

5. Scientists have measured distances between stars.
6. Fire destroyed the hotel in two hours.
7. I can climb any tree in the woods.
8. Sherman might have seen this show before.
9. Winnie the Pooh ate Rabbit's honey.
10. Robots assemble cars in factories.

H. Choosing the Right Verb Choose the right verb from the parentheses. Write it on your paper.

1. Does your dog (set, sit) on command?
2. The guards won't (let, leave) us past the iron gate.
3. (May, Can) I please read that magazine?
4. Mom (taught, learned) a class in yoga.
5. Did you (let, leave) some dessert for Dad?
6. Marka (may, can) punt farther than Sherry.
7. My class will (teach, learn) Spanish.
8. The jury (sets, sits) in a special room.
9. Little Miss Muffet (set, sat) on a tuffet.
10. Kerry (lets, leaves) a treat for Santa every year.

I. Using Negatives Correctly The following sentences have double negatives. Number your paper from 1 to 10. Write each sentence correctly.

1. Milton hasn't never had a cavity.
2. The police can't find no clues.
3. Isabella didn't like nothing on the menu.
4. This maze doesn't lead nowhere.
5. Aren't none of the actors ready to audition?
6. Can't no one on this team pitch a curve?
7. That tire doesn't have no air.
8. Nobody wasn't watching the robot in the store.
9. He wouldn't never want to run a steam shovel.
10. The broken door won't never budge.

Using Grammar in Writing

A. The year: 2158

Latest scientific discovery: A formula that prevents aging.

Vincent and Camille are ten years old. Vincent thinks that it would be great to stay ten years old forever. Camille decides against the formula because she imagines that life as an adult will be even better. Each tries to convince the other that his or her way is best.

Write in dialogue form the conversation between Vincent and Camille. Correctly use contractions and negatives in your dialogue. Identify your characters in this way.

VINCENT:

CAMILLE:

B. You have suddenly found yourself on another planet. It is called Velco. The Velconians want to know how you got to their planet. Since you cannot remember, you must make up a story. In a paragraph, tell how you came to Velco. Use several of these irregular verbs: *begin, bring, choose, come, do, eat, fall, fly, go, have, ride, ring, rise, say, see.*

C. Using Verbs in Science The word *volcano* came from an early Roman tale. The Romans believed that a god named Vulcan kept fires burning deep in the earth. He was thought to be bad-tempered. When he was angry, the Romans thought he split the earth. Today scientists know much more about what happens when a volcano erupts. Gather information about volcanoes from science books, encyclopedias, or other sources. List in order the stages of a volcanic eruption. Then write a paragraph, using the details from your list. Use action verbs to tell about this powerful flow of molten rock.

Chapter 4 Review

A. Finding Verbs and Direct Objects Number your paper from 1 to 10. Write the complete verb in each sentence. Tell whether it is an *Action Verb* or *State-of-Being Verb.* Then write the direct object of each action verb.

1. Melissa plays the flute well.
2. It is too cold for a picnic.
3. Would you put the mask near the snorkel and fins in my locker?
4. Cora has never learned French.
5. The "Top Secret" documents must be extremely important.
6. Anita was a professional dancer.
7. Charlie will never change his mind.
8. *Peter Pan* was the first English play for children.
9. The matador couldn't spear the bull.
10. Sun quickly melted the icicles.

B. Using Verbs Correctly Number your paper from 1 to 10. Each sentence contains one or two errors in the use of verbs. Find the errors. Then write each sentence correctly.

1. Ed been the best trail blazer in our troop.
2. The homemade raisin bread are fresh.
3. Here is the envelopes for your pen pal's letters.
4. I never seen two frogs jump at the same time.
5. Haven't you never ate an avocado?
6. I learned Casey how to play marbles.
7. Where should I set for the slide show?
8. Brad hasn't never said his speech out loud.
9. The kitten were hungrily lapping its milk.
10. The old trunk have been stored in the basement for many years.

Chapter 5

Learning About Paragraphs

Suppose someone asked you to describe your favorite relative. Could you do that in a single sentence? What if you had to write about your most frightening experience? Could you fit all of the details into one sentence? The answer to each of these questions is "no." Many of the ideas you want to communicate are too detailed for single sentences.

Whenever you want to write about an idea that is too complicated for a single sentence, write a paragraph. A paragraph is a group of sentences that tells about one main idea. Learning about paragraphs is important. Paragraphs allow you to tell stories, explain opinions and processes, and describe people, places, and things.

In this chapter, you will learn about what makes a good paragraph. You will discover how sentences work together to explain one main idea. You will find out what a good topic sentence is and how to write one. Once you know how paragraphs are formed, good writing will be easier.

1 What Is a Paragraph?

Focus

A **paragraph** is a group of sentences that tells about one main idea.

A **paragraph** is a group of sentences. The sentences work together to tell about one main idea. The **main idea** is what the paragraph is about. In many paragraphs, the main idea is expressed in the first sentence. Read this paragraph.

> Lizards move around in many different ways. One type of giant lizard swims between islands. Another type of lizard, called a *flying dragon*, actually flies from tree to tree. Some lizards are able to climb straight up on rough or smooth surfaces. That is because they have sharp claws and brush-like hooks on their legs. There are some lizards that raise the front parts of their bodies and walk on their hind legs. Others slither along without any legs at all.

Notice that the first line of the paragraph begins a little to the right. The first line of a paragraph is always indented.

In this paragraph, the main idea is how lizards move around. This main idea is expressed in the first sentence. All of the rest of the sentences work together to tell about the main idea. These sentences give you the following information.

Some lizards swim.
Some lizards fly.
Some lizards climb.
Some lizards walk on their hind legs.
Some lizards slither along without legs.

All of these sentences work together to tell how lizards move in different ways.

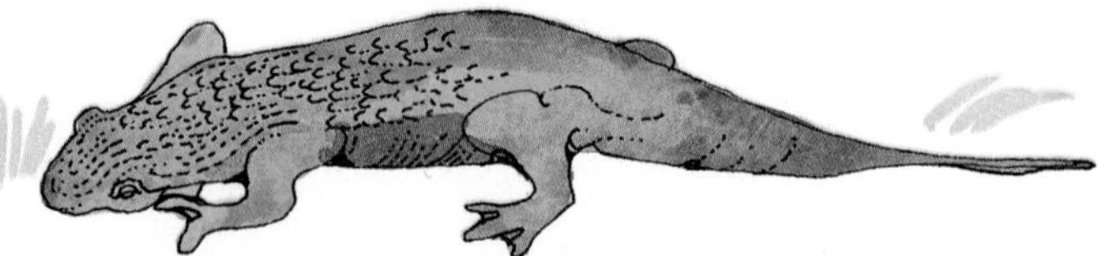

Whenever you write a paragraph of your own, check to see that it is a good paragraph. Ask yourself these questions.

1. Does the paragraph have one main idea?
2. Do all of the sentences work together to tell about the main idea?
3. Is every sentence a complete sentence?

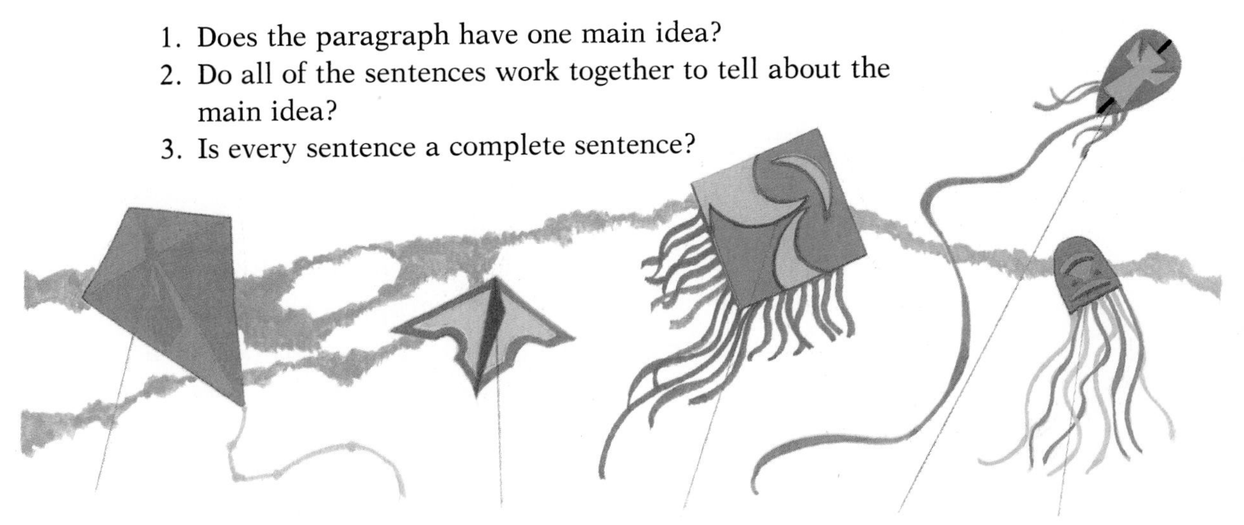

Exercise **Studying Paragraphs**

Recognizing Good Paragraphs Read these paragraphs. Think about what you have learned in this lesson. Then decide if each is a good paragraph or not. Explain the reasons for your choice.

1. One of the largest kites ever flown was a Japanese kite made in 1906. Hot-air balloons were also popular then. The kite measured sixty feet across. Its tail was four hundred and eighty feet long. Some giant airships were bigger, like the *Hindenburg*. The kite weighed over five thousand pounds.

2. One day a change came over the woods and the pond. Warm breezes blew through the trees. The ice, which had softened during the night, began to melt. Patches of open water dotted the pond. The forest animals, sensing that spring had finally arrived, left their nests and burrows and scampered in the sunlight. Winter, at long last, was over.

3. Redwoods are the biggest trees in the world. Redwoods grow to about 90 meters, or over 300 feet, high. The trunk of a full-grown redwood is about three meters, or ten feet, across. Its bark can be 30 centimeters, or nearly a foot, thick. Some redwoods have enough wood to build four houses.

2 Good Topic Sentences

Focus

The main idea of a paragraph is presented in the **topic sentence**.

In part 1 of this chapter, you learned that all of the sentences in a paragraph work together to tell about one main idea. You also learned that the main idea of a paragraph is expressed in a sentence. The sentence that expresses the main idea of a paragraph is called a **topic sentence**. The topic sentence is often the first sentence in a paragraph.

Look again at the paragraph on page 92. What is the topic sentence of this paragraph? What main idea does it express?

A good topic sentence does two important jobs. First, it must tell the reader what the paragraph is about. Second, the topic sentence must be interesting enough to make the reader continue reading. Read these two topic sentences.

> My paragraph is about golden lion marmosets.
>
> I am going to write about how Jim Gary creates a sculpture.

Each of these topic sentences presents the main idea of a paragraph. The first paragraph is about marmosets and the second paragraph is about Jim Gary's sculpture. Neither sentence, however, is a good topic sentence. Why? Because neither sentence is interesting. An interesting topic sentence never begins with words like "My paragraph will be about. . . ." or "I am going to write about. . . ." An interesting topic sentence presents the main idea in a way that makes the reader want to read more. Read these revised topic sentences.

> Golden lion marmosets are little monkeys with big problems.
>
> When Jim Gary has an idea for a new sculpture, he heads for the junkyard.

These topic sentences not only present main ideas, but they also capture the reader's attention. The reader wonders, "What problems do marmosets have?" or "What does Jim Gary look for in a junkyard?" The reader wants to read the paragraph to find the answers to these questions.

Exercise Good Topic Sentences

Writing Topic Sentences Here are three paragraphs. Each paragraph needs a good topic sentence. First decide what each group of sentences is about. Then write a topic sentence that presents the main idea of that group of sentences. Be sure each topic sentence will capture a reader's attention.

1. ______________________________ He was the son of an English Lord. As a boy he was lost in an African jungle. Apes taught him to survive in the jungle. They showed him how to get from place to place by swinging through the trees on vines. As he grew up, he learned to communicate with all the animals. He called to them with his special jungle cry.

2. ______________________________ Dark clouds were moving in from the west. The air was heavy and still. The sky had taken on a queer green color, and thunder rumbled in the distance. Animals scurried for shelter. Parents gathered their children and headed for home.

3. ______________________________ The city has famous buildings like the White House and the Capitol. There is also the Smithsonian Institution, where visitors can see everything from dinosaur bones to rocks from the moon. The city has a beautiful zoo with some rare giant pandas. Washington also has the National Archives Building where people can see the Declaration of Independence and the Constitution.

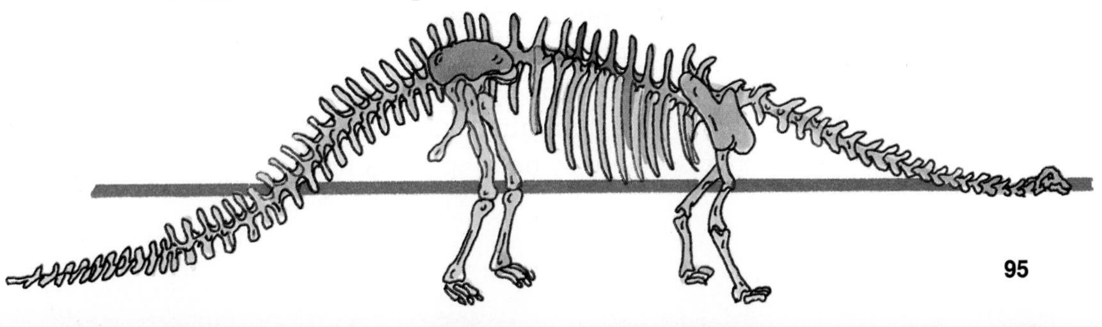

Using English in Reading

Knowing about paragraphs is also important when you read. You have learned that every paragraph has a main idea. Picking out the main idea of a paragraph helps you understand the paragraph when you read. For example, reviewing the main ideas in the paragraphs of a social studies chapter will help you remember what the whole chapter is about.

Exercise Finding the Main Idea

Read the following paragraphs taken from a social studies textbook, a health book, and a book about hobbies. On your paper, write the main idea for each paragraph.

1. For many years Europeans made guesses about the Atlantic Ocean. These guesses led to frightful rumors. People feared that nobody could survive a trip across the dangerous ocean. Some thought ships were swallowed by huge monsters or pools of swirling water. Generally, people felt that the Atlantic was a dark and dangerous ocean. They thought no clear-thinking person should sail on it far from the sight of land.

2. Less than 100 years ago, storing foods without having them spoil was a serious problem. People had only one main way to prevent passing along disease germs in a package of food. This was to cook the food at a very high temperature and to store it in an airtight jar or can. However, this strong heating destroyed some important nutrients in foods, especially the vitamins.

3. It's easy to play a comb kazoo. A comb kazoo is an ordinary comb around which a piece of tissue paper is wrapped. Hold the paper over the teeth of the comb and put the comb against your lips. Then, keeping your lips open a little, sing or hum a tune into the comb. The humming or singing tone is changed by the tissue paper to sound something like a brass band.

Chapter 5 Review

A. Organizing Sentences To Form a Paragraph Some of the following sentences can form a paragraph. Read the sentences. Decide which sentence is the topic sentence. Rewrite the sentences in paragraph form. Write the topic sentence as the first sentence in the paragraph. Leave out any sentence that does not stick to the main idea.

1. The giraffes live in a very tall building.
2. The snakes live behind glass in the reptile house.
3. I really enjoy the art museum, too.
4. All the animals in the zoo have different homes.
5. The bears live in caves and have wading pools.
6. The camels have their own piece of land.

B. Supplying a Topic Sentence Read each of the following paragraphs. Decide what the main idea is in each paragraph. On your paper, write a topic sentence that gives the main idea.

1. ______________________________ Some nights we'd play "Red Light." Other nights we'd play "Kick the Can." The game we played most often, though, was "Hide-and-Seek." We'd use the entire block for hiding. No one wanted to be "it" because it was almost impossible to find people before they reached home.

2. ______________________________ Paul and Maria, the stars of the show, paced nervously behind the drawn curtain. The narrator read and reread the script. The nervous director gave last-minute instructions. The lighting engineer made her final adjustments. So did the people in charge of make-up and costumes.

Chapter 6

Choosing a Process for Writing

No two people write exactly the same way. Still, most people follow a general pattern when they write. First, they plan their writing. Next, they write. Then, they try to improve what they have written. Finally, they share their writing.

In this chapter, you are going to learn about these four stages that writers follow. **Prewriting** is the planning stage. **Drafting** is the writing stage. **Revising** is the improving stage. The last stage is **Sharing**. During each stage, you will make many decisions about your writing. Your decisions might be different from those of your classmates. However, all of you will learn to choose a process for writing that best helps you achieve your goal—to become a better writer.

1 Prewriting: Ways To Find Ideas

Focus

Good writing begins with discovering good ideas.

Have you ever stared at a blank sheet of paper and said, "I just can't think of anything to write about"? If you have, you are not alone. Try some of the following methods. They will help you to discover interesting ideas for writing.

Journal Writing Get a spiral notebook. Write down your ideas, thoughts, feelings, and experiences in it. Try to write in your journal regularly. It will provide good writing ideas.

Brainstorming Begin with one general idea. Then think of as many related ideas or topics as you can. You could talk about your ideas with others, or you could brainstorm alone. In either case, write down everything that pops into your mind. You might make a **clustering chart** like the one below.

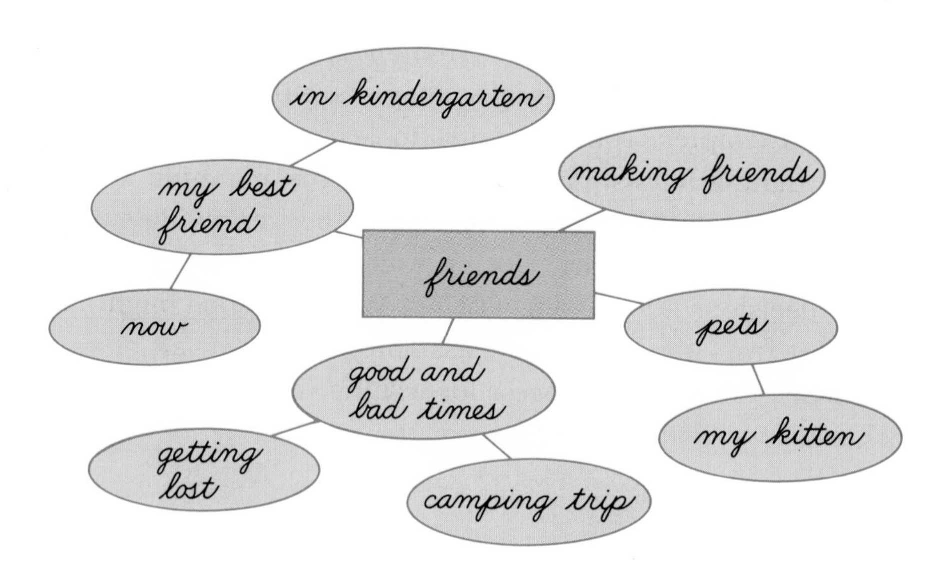

Talking with Others Ask people questions and listen carefully to their answers. Other people's thoughts and experiences often make interesting reading.

Reading and Researching Look through books, magazines, and newspapers. Clip out stories or write down topics that catch your interest. Save these ideas in a writing folder or in your journal. Encyclopedias or other resource books also can help you find out more about subjects you are interested in.

Observing Look at what goes on around you. Make notes in your journal about interesting people and events that you see and conversations that you hear.

Questioning Ask yourself questions such as the following.

What are my hobbies?
What would I like to know more about?
Who are my heroes and heroines?
What do I think is important?
What places do I enjoy?

Exercises **Finding Topics**

A. Talking with Others Choose a person who is older than you are. Ask that person to tell you about an interesting memory from when he or she was eleven years old. In your journal, write the person's story. Ask others and record their stories.

B. Reading Look through books, magazines, or newspapers for writing topics. Clip out any interesting articles or write down any topics you find. Bring your writing ideas to class and collect them in a resource box that can be used by anyone in the class.

C. Researching Write "I wonder how" five times on a sheet of paper. Finish each line with a different response. Then do the same with "I wonder why." Next, look up these subjects in a reference book. Write down any interesting information you discover.

2 Prewriting: Choosing and Limiting a Topic

Focus

Select a topic that interests you and that you would like to share with others. Limit your topic by making it specific.

Sometimes your teacher will assign a writing topic to you. At other times, you will need to find your own. When the topic is your choice, use the methods described in part 1 to discover some interesting writing ideas.

Once you have a general subject, you will have to limit it. Limiting a subject means making it specific. First decide how long your writing will be. If you will be writing just a single paragraph, your topic will have to be very specific. If you write a **composition** of several paragraphs, your topic can be broader.

How do you make a topic specific? You can use some of the same methods you used to find a topic. You might use **brainstorming** and **questioning** to limit a general subject.

Sample Prewriting Notes

Tim began limiting the subject *families* by brainstorming. He wrote down everything that came into his mind about families. Here is his list.

parents	vacations
our family reunion	Sunday dinner
family pets	my sister Anne
fights with my brother	learning to get along
aunts and uncles	sharing

As Tim looked over his list, he thought he would write something about his older sister, Anne. To limit his topic further, he began asking himself questions about his sister. What do I like about Anne? When does Anne make me angry? What activities does Anne enjoy? What things do Anne and I do together?

Tim decided he would write about how he had helped his sister during a triathlon race.

Purpose and Audience

Once you have a limited topic, you must answer two important questions. First, you must decide on your purpose, or reason for writing. Are you going to give instructions, explain an opinion, or tell a story? Do you want to explain how something happens or describe a favorite place? Then ask yourself who your audience, or readers, will be. Will they be your classmates, friends, or the judges in a student poetry contest? Knowing your purpose for writing and who your audience is will help you to choose the best information and the right language for your writing.

Exercises Limiting a Topic

A. Limiting a General Subject Imagine that you have to write a paragraph. The general subject is "food." Limit this general subject to a specific topic you could cover well in a paragraph. Use brainstorming and questioning to limit your subject. Share your specific topic with your classmates. Do they think it is specific enough for a paragraph?

B. Choosing and Limiting Your Topic Look over the list of topics you developed in part 1. Select one, or think of a new idea. Pages 412–414 in the **Power Handbook** may help you. Limit your topic so that it can be covered well in a paragraph. Decide on your purpose for writing. Identify your audience. Save your notes in your writing folder. You will use them later in this chapter.

3 Prewriting: Developing a Topic

Focus

Develop a topic by gathering information about it.

Once you have chosen a topic, you have to develop it. This means that you have to gather information that explains or supports your topic.

How can you gather information about your topic? You can use many of the methods you learned in part 1 for developing ideas. You can brainstorm, look through your journal, and talk with other people. You can also observe or do some reading or research in the library.

What kind of information should you look for? The answer to that question depends on the kind of writing you are doing. The following list will help you decide.

Types of Details

Sensory details appeal to sight, hearing, touch, smell, and taste. They help you to give your readers a clear picture of a person, place, or thing. Sensory details, for example, would help you to describe the monkey house at the zoo. You can gather sensory details by observing something, by remembering what something was like, or by using your imagination.

Stories tell about something that happened to you or to someone else. A brief story can help your readers understand an idea or opinion you are trying to explain. For instance, you might write a letter telling why you think your neighbor should receive a citizen heroism award. To support your opinion, your letter would include the story that tells how your neighbor saved a child from a burning building.

Examples help to explain your main idea. Suppose you were writing about how the space program has benefited all Americans. Two or three examples would help you explain that idea.

Facts and figures can help you to prove a point you are trying to make. Facts and figures can be proven true. You can gather facts and figures by doing research about your topic.

Reasons are explanations that tell why you think your main idea is true. Reasons are necessary when you are explaining an opinion or telling why something happened. Look for reasons in your own experiences or when you are doing research.

Exercises **Developing a Topic**

A. Selecting Details Look over these topics. Decide which type or types of development would be best for each. Then give several details you might use.

Good things that can happen on Saturdays
A friend who disappointed me
Holiday decorations
Why I read books
Bicycle accidents are increasing

B. Developing Details Gather the information you need for the topic you chose in part 2. Use the methods presented in parts 1 and 3. Select details that suit the type of writing you are doing. Keep your notes in your writing folder.

4 Prewriting: Organizing Ideas

Focus

Arrange your details in a logical order. Then make a writing plan.

Now that you have gathered information about your topic, you must decide which details are useful and which are not. Look over your list of details. Cross out any details that do not develop your topic. Add new details if you wish.

Organize Your List of Details

It is important to arrange your details into some logical order. Otherwise, they will not make sense to your readers. There are several ways to organize details.

Ways To Organize Details

Time Order Details are presented in the order in which they happened. Use time order when you are planning a story. Time order is also the right choice when you are explaining a process, such as how to build a model plane.

Natural Order Details are presented as you would see them. This might be from side to side, from top to bottom, from bottom to top, from near to far, or from far to near. Use natural order when you are planning a description of a person, place, or thing.

Order of Importance Details are arranged from the least important to the most important, or the reverse. Use the order of importance when you are arranging reasons that tell *why* something is so.

You will learn more about these and other types of orders in later chapters.

Making a Writing Plan

Once you have your details organized, you will want to make a writing plan. It should include your topic and your reason for writing. It should tell who your reader will be. Also, it should show your organized list of details.

Tim's writing plan is below. Notice that he used numbers to organize his details. Notice his thoughts as he wrote his plan.

topic: my sister's first triathlon
purpose: to tell about Anne's and my experiences
audience: my classmates
details:
(7) time—1 hour, 22 minutes
(6) Anne didn't win
(2) I was Anne's assistant
(3) swimming—quarter mile
(5) running—four miles
(4) biking—ten miles
~~Anne had a very expensive new bike~~
(1) Anne likes all sports

I'd better mention these in the order in which they happened.

This really isn't important to the story.

Organizing a Composition

As you organize your details, you may find that your topic includes two or three main ideas. In that case, you will need to write more than one paragraph. First, decide what the main idea of each paragraph will be. Then, group together the details that tell about each main idea. Finally, organize the details within each paragraph.

Exercise Organizing Details

Make your own writing plan. Use the topic and details you developed in part 3. Cross out details that do not develop your topic. Add details, if necessary. Choose an order for your details. Keep your writing plan in your folder.

5 Drafting

Focus

Follow your writing plan as you turn your ideas into sentences and paragraphs.

You have finished planning what you are going to write. The next stage in the process of writing is drafting.

Writing a Draft

Now you are ready to write your notes as sentences and paragraphs. This is called **drafting**. Use your writing plan as a guide. Do not be afraid, however, to add new ideas. Just be sure that they help you to develop your topic. If you decide some details from your notes are unnecessary, leave them out.

Remember, your draft does not have to be perfect. You can change your ideas and decisions at any time. You might write several drafts before you are satisfied with your work.

Choose a drafting style that is right for you. Some people start writing and do not stop until they reach the end. Then they check over what they have written. Other people write a sentence or two. Then they check what they have written, fix it if necessary, and write another sentence or two. Still others combine these two methods.

Using the Right Language

As you write, choose language that is right for your readers and that suits your reasons for writing. Always use standard English. **Standard English** follows all the rules of good grammar and usage. Standard English is understood everywhere English is spoken.

Standard English can be informal or formal. **Informal English** is the language of everyday speech. It is relaxed and casual. **Formal English** often uses longer sentences and an advanced vocabulary. If you were writing a letter to a friend, you could use informal English. If you were writing a composition for an essay contest, you would want to use formal English.

A Sample Draft

Here is a draft of Tim's story. He made several changes as he worked. Notice his thoughts as he wrote.

This was my sister's first triathlon and I was her

assistant. It seemed natural for my sister to com-

pete in this event. She likes all sports and is on the

track and swim teams at school. The triathlon

began with a quarter mile swim. Anne got into the

water with the other racers. I went to the other side

and met her with a towel, shoes, and her bicycle.

of the lake. After drying off, my sister got on her

Later, Anne told me that she felt dizzy and cramped during

bike for the ten-mile cycling leg of the race. I met *this part of the race.*

Anne once more to catch her bike as she ran off on

her four-mile race. My sister didn't win. Her time

was one hour and twenty-two minutes.

I'd better explain what I did.

I'll add some details so my readers know how Anne was feeling.

Exercise Writing a Draft

Write a draft of the paragraph you have been planning. Follow your writing plan as you work. Add or take out details as your draft develops. Keep your purpose and audience in mind. You may need to write more than one draft. Save your work in your writing folder.

6 Revising and Proofreading

Focus

Careful revision and proofreading will make your writing the best it can be.

Revising is the third stage in the process of writing. When you revise, you make corrections and try to improve what you have written.

When you have finished writing, put your draft away for a day or two. Then take it out and read through it carefully. It is often a good idea to read your draft aloud. You might hear mistakes that you wouldn't notice if you were reading silently. As you read your draft, look for the answers to the following questions.

Guidelines for Revising

1. Have I chosen the right kinds of details for my topic?
2. Are my details organized in a logical order? Does the order suit the kind of writing I am doing?
3. Have I included enough details to explain my topic well? Should I add some information? Have I included any unnecessary details that do not develop my main idea?
4. Does each paragraph have a strong topic sentence that states one main idea? Do all the sentences in a paragraph tell about the main idea?
5. Have I used standard English? Have I made the right choice between formal and informal English for the type of reader I am writing for?

As you revise, you may want to add, take out, or replace entire sentences. You may even decide to rewrite a complete paragraph. You can change your draft as much as you want. Remember, your goal is to improve what you have written.

Working with a Revising Partner You may find it helpful to work with a revising partner. A revising partner is a friend, classmate, brother or sister, or even a parent. Ask your partner to read your writing and to suggest ways that it can be improved. You may also want to have your partner use the "Questions for Revising." Use your partner's suggestions to help you revise your draft.

If you are asked to be a revising partner, try to make your suggestions as helpful as possible. For example, do not say "I don't like your beginning," or "Use better words." Instead, give specific suggestions. You might say "Your first sentence doesn't catch my interest. Try to make it livelier," or "You need to add some adjectives to make your description clearer."

Proofreading

When you think you have revised your draft well, read through it again. Look for mistakes in grammar, capitalization, punctuation, and spelling. This is called **proofreading**.

Proofreading is an important part of revising. Sometimes you are so concerned with the ideas in your writing that you forget to check the little things. The guidelines at the top of the next page will help you proofread your draft.

Guidelines for Proofreading

1. Look for errors in grammar and usage. Use the grammar chapters in this text to help you correct any mistakes you find. For example, if you think you have used the wrong pronoun in a compound subject, see Chapter 9, pages 161–162, for help. If you are not sure about the past form of an irregular verb, see Chapter 4, pages 72–74.
2. Be sure you have capitalized correctly, including titles used with names and the titles of books, songs, movies, and so on. See the "Guide to Capitalization," pages 416–431, in the **Power Handbook.**
3. It is important to punctuate your writing correctly. If you are not sure when to use a comma or how to use apostrophes or quotation marks properly, see the "Guide to Punctuation," pages 432–453, in the **Power Handbook.**
4. Check your work for spelling errors. Be sure to check the spelling of proper nouns, especially the names of any people you have mentioned. Use the "Guide to Spelling," pages 454–462, in the **Power Handbook,** or look up the word in a dictionary or encyclopedia.
5. Check the correctness of dates, figures, and facts.

Using Symbols for Revising and Proofreading

The following symbols for revising and proofreading will help you to change and correct your drafts neatly.

Symbols for Revising and Proofreading

∧ Add leters or words.	— Take out letters or woords.
⊙ Add a period	¶ Begin a new paragraph.
≡ capitalize a letter.	∧ Then add a comma.
/ Make a capital Letter lower-case.	∿ Trade the position of letters or wrods.

Here is how Tim revised and proofread his paragraph. Notice his thoughts as he worked.

I'll make my opening livelier.

I was tired at the end of ~~This was~~ my sister's first triathlon, and I was *just* her assistant! ~~It seemed natural for my sister to compete in this event. She likes all sports and is on the track and swim teams at school.~~ The triathlon began with a quarter-mile swim. *At the gun,* Anne ~~got~~ *dove* into the water with the other racers. I ~~went~~ *hurried* to the other side of the lake and met her with a towel, shoes, and her bicycle. After drying off, my sister ~~got~~ *hopped* on her bike for the ten-mile cycling leg of the race. Later, Anne told me that she felt dizzy and cramped during this part of the race. I met Anne once more to catch her bike *and yell encouragement* as she ~~ran~~ *dashed* off on her four-mile race *to the finish line.* ~~My sister didn't win.~~ *I was there to see Anne finish. She was exhausted but happy.* Her time was one hour and twenty-two minutes. *She wasn't first, but she was a champion in my eyes.*

These two sentences are not really about my main idea.

I need a hyphen here.

I'd better use some strong action verbs.

My ending should be more exciting.

Exercise Revising and Proofreading Your Draft

Revise the draft you have been working on. Ask yourself the questions on page 110. Do not hesitate to make changes. You may even want to change your writing plan as well as other early decisions you made.

After you have revised your work, proofread it. Use the proofreading guidelines on page 112. As you revise and proofread your work, use the revising and proofreading symbols on page 112.

7 Making and Sharing the Final Copy

Focus

Make a neat final copy of your writing. Decide on a way to share it with your readers.

Make a Final Copy

At some point, you will decide that your writing is the best you can make it. Then you will make your final copy. First, write a good title for your work. Then as you write, make all the changes and corrections you marked on your revised and proofread draft. Write as neatly and as clearly as possible. Leave wide margins.

As a final check, proofread your work one last time. If you discover a mistake, correct it neatly.

Share Your Writing

Decide on a way to share your writing with your readers. There are many possibilities. You and your classmates might make a booklet. Your booklet could be a collection of different types of writing. Or, it could be writings on a single theme like "Our Pets" or "Our Favorite Adventures."

Oral presentations are another form of sharing. You and your classmates could take turns reading your work aloud either to the whole class or to small groups. You might invite students from the primary grades to hear your stories.

Display your writings on a bulletin board in your room, in the hall, or in the library. This will allow other students in the school to see and read what you have written.

You might make a poster. Glue a neat copy of your writing on a piece of posterboard or a large sheet of paper. Make drawings on your poster that highlight your writing.

You can also submit your writing to contests and to magazines or newspapers. Your teacher can give you additional information about where and how to submit your writing.

Sample Final Copy

Here is Tim's final copy. Compare it with his first draft. See how much Tim has improved his story.

Three Races in One

I was tired at the end of my sister's first triathlon, and I was just her assistant! The triathlon began with a quarter-mile swim. At the gun, Anne dove into the water with the other racers. I hurried to the other side of the lake and met her with a towel, shoes, and her bicycle. After drying off, my sister hopped on her bike for the ten-mile cycling leg of the race. Later, Anne told me that she felt dizzy and cramped during this part of the race. I met Anne once more to catch her bike and yell encouragement as she dashed off on her four-mile race to the finish line. I was there to see Anne finish. She was exhausted but happy. Her time was one hour and twenty-two minutes. She wasn't first, but she was a champion in my eyes.

RACE

Exercise **Making and Sharing a Final Copy**

Make a final copy of your work. Write a good title. Then, proofread your final draft one last time. Finally, choose a method for sharing your writing.

Speaking and Listening

Group Discussion

You know that ideas for writing topics can come from many sources. Journals, research, and brainstorming are a few. The ideas of other people can also provide a great supply of topics. To really use this source, you must first learn to ask questions and to listen carefully to the answers.

Talking to others also helps you sort out your own ideas. What someone else says may make you see a problem in a new way. Once you have sorted through your ideas by sharing them with others, you can organize details. You can then continue with the writing process.

Exercise Having a Class Discussion

Think about the situation described below. Discuss this situation with your class. After the discussion, write down what you would do if you found yourself in this situation. Include the reasons for your actions. Organize your ideas. Then, write a paragraph explaining these ideas.

> One day you come home from school and find your art supplies strewn all over your room. Pencils are broken and paints are spilled. As you stare in disbelief, your five-year-old sister walks into the room carrying the "art" she made for you. What would you do?

Creative Writing

A. Imagine that your pen or pencil can talk. What would it say about your process of writing from its point of view? Write a paragraph in which your pen or pencil explains how you write!

B. Imagine that the oldest bank building in town has just been purchased by the town council. The council has decided to turn the building over to the town's youth. The council will provide the money, construction workers, and supervision for the project. The boys and girls must decide what will be done with the building. Write a paragraph that describes exactly what this new youth center will look like. Tell what it will be used for and what special features it will have.

C. Have you ever heard the expression "There ought to be a law"? People usually say this when they are angry, annoyed, or worried. A number of real laws sound as if they became law because someone said "There ought to be a law." Look at some examples.

> In Galveston, Texas, it is illegal for camels to roam the streets. In Columbus, Georgia, cats are forbidden to howl after 9:00 P.M. In Brawley, California, it is illegal for snow to fall in the city limits.

What humorous law would you like to see passed? Briefly describe a law that you think should exist. Explain what it would restrict or enforce. Also, explain why you think the law is needed.

Using English in Other Subjects

In part 1 of this chapter, you learned that good writing begins with good ideas. You also learned some ways to find ideas for writing, such as brainstorming, doing research, and writing in your journal. Another way to use your journal is to keep a learning log. A **learning log** is a written record of ideas, thoughts, and experiences you get in all of your classes.

For example, in science class you might make some notes about how you did an interesting experiment. You might write down the results of the experiment and what you learned from doing it. In history class, you might wonder how the Plains Indians survived the harsh winters. Jot down your questions in your learning log for history. How about that day in math class when fractions suddenly started to make sense to you? In your learning log, write down what happened that day and how you felt.

As you can see, a learning log can be a good way to learn and to build on what you have learned. It can also be a great place to store ideas for future writing assignments. You'll be surprised at how quickly your collection of ideas will grow!

Exercise Keeping a Learning Log

Begin keeping a learning log for all of your classes. Try to write something in it every day. Let your learning log be a part of your journal. Read through your learning log whenever you need writing ideas.

Chapter 6 Review

A. Limiting a Topic Look at the six general topics listed below. Choose two topics. Then, use the methods you learned in this chapter to limit each topic. Limit each topic so that it can be covered in one paragraph. Finally, share your ideas with your classmates.

movies	science	music
sports	biking	books

B. Organizing Details Imagine that you were going to write a short composition about the galago, a relative of the monkey. Read the following list of details about this animal. Divide your paper into two columns, *Appearance* and *Actions*. Then list each of the following details in the proper column.

move very fast, making long hops like kangaroos
some as large as cats
jump long distances from one tree branch to another
have eyes that do not move, whole head must turn
hunt at night
some as small as squirrels, called "bush babies"
eat mostly fruits and insects
are nimble and have strong feet for climbing
have soft fur and bushy tails
make good pets, but tend to chew objects like a puppy

C. Proofreading Proofread the following paragraph about the Portuguese man-of-war. You should find two errors in punctuation, two spelling errors, and two errors in capitalization. Copy this paragraph on your paper. Use the proofreading marks on page 112 to make your corrections.

The dedliest jellyfish is the portuguese man-of-war. This beautiful creature floats gracefully in the water As fish or other sea animals float by, the jellyfish paralyzes the victim with pioson darts on its feelers. Then, the Man of war uses its long streamers to put the food in its mouth.

Cumulative Review

Unit 1

Composition

A. Process of Writing Write the following sentences. Fill in the blanks with the word or words that complete the statement.

1. Prewriting includes four major activities: ______ , ______ , developing ideas, and ______ .
2. A ______ is several paragraphs written about the same subject.
3. Types of information you may add to develop a topic include ______ , ______ , ______ , ______ , and ______ .
4. If you describe a building from top to bottom, you are using ______ order.
5. Checking for errors in spelling, punctuation, and grammar is called ______ .

B. The Paragraph Supply a topic sentence for each of the paragraphs below.

______________________________ . My breath came out in huge bursts of steamy fog. My face felt as if it would never thaw. Even under my heavy jacket, my skin had goosebumps. My toes were numb.

______________________________ . Salmon sometimes swim two thousand miles to lay their eggs. They must battle swift currents and swirling rapids. They even leap over waterfalls that are more than ten feet high.

______________________________ . On December 26, 1620, the *Mayflower* landed at Plymouth. It had sailed from Southampton, England, bringing the first colonists. Before leaving the ship, the Pilgrims drew up the Mayflower Compact, which provided for the temporary government of the colony.

Grammar

Sentences, Nouns, and Verbs Each item below has two errors. Write each item as a complete, correct sentence.

1. Sit the camping supplys in the canoe.
2. I had never seen nothing like the childrens' zoo.
3. Six wolfs in a den at the zoo.
4. There is many beautiful buildings in china.
5. Free roller-coaster ride's at the carnival.
6. Is watermelons and potatos in the grocery cart?
7. Can I please have the map of oklahoma?
8. Here are the invitation to Jims barbecue.
9. Where was the books about the wild gooses?
10. Chipmunks was nibbling in Beckys bird feeder.

Related Skills

Vocabulary Read the following paragraphs. Use context clues to tell what each underlined word means. List the underlined words and the meaning for each on your paper.

Fossils offer clues to what the world was like millions of years ago. Many fossils are found in stone. These are imprints, or outlines, of prehistoric plants or animals. Paleontologists—scientists who study fossils—sometimes find bones, teeth, and other remains in tar or ice. Some insects and small animals are fossilized in amber, which is the sticky fluid that oozes out of evergreen trees.

My first visit to an Italian restaurant is a special memory. The maitre d', the head of the restaurant staff, led us to our table. Everyone ordered an Italian vegetable soup called minestrone. The main course was linguini (thin, flat noodles).

UNIT 2

Sharing Experiences

In Unit 2 you will learn more about sharing ideas with others. You will discover more skills that can help you in all of your speaking and writing.

First, you will learn about different study methods. Then your word power will increase as you explore the dictionary and thesaurus. Your improved word skills will be helpful as you create and write a story. Finally, you will sharpen your speaking and listening skills.

Your new skills can help you give a talk in social studies. They will help you listen to instructions for a science project. The world around you is filled with marvelous things to notice and respond to. Your language skills will make it possible for you to capture in words the sighing of the wind or the wonder of a rainbow.

"CALLED AWAY"

I meant to do my work today—
But a brown bird sang in the apple tree,
And a butterfly flitted across the field,
And all the leaves were calling me.

And the wind went sighing over the land
Tossing the grasses to and fro,
And a rainbow held out its shining hand—
So what could I do but laugh and go?

—RICHARD LE GALLIENNE

Chapter 7

Study and Test-Taking Skills

Good study and test-taking skills are important in school. Do you realize how important they are in other parts of your life, too? You study directions to learn how to play a new trivia game. To fix the flat tire on your bike, you might follow directions in "Ten Easy Steps to Bike Repair." You memorize eight football plays before your first game. Every time you learn to do something new, follow directions, or memorize important information, you use study and test-taking skills.

This chapter will help you to develop good study and test-taking skills. You will learn to organize information, to skim and scan, and to use the parts of a book. You will learn how to memorize and how to use the SQ3R study method. Finally, you will learn about different types of test questions and how to answer each type.

1 Skimming and Scanning

Focus

Skimming and **scanning** can help you gather information quickly and easily.

In one day, you might read a chapter from a science book, part of a library book, and the ads on a cereal box. You do not read all of these in the same way. Sometimes you read slowly and carefully. Other times you read quickly to find specific information. Skimming and scanning are two types of fast reading that help you discover information quickly.

Skimming

Skimming is one way of reading fast. You skim to get a general idea of what a book, chapter, or article is about. You look for the main ideas and important details. When you skim, do not read every word. Pay special attention to the following.

Titles	Topic sentences	Pictures and captions
Headings	Key words	

Scanning

When you are looking for specific information, use a type of fast reading called **scanning**. When scanning, do not read every word. Skip words until you find what you want.

How would you use scanning in the following situations?

1. Your science teacher has given you an assignment. You are to read the chapter "Animal Life" in your textbook. Then you are to write the definitions of *vertebrate* and *invertebrate*.
2. Your school will be sending eight representatives to the National Student Olympics. The list has been posted on the bulletin board. You look at the list to see if you are on it.

Exercises Practicing Skimming and Scanning

A. Skim the following article. What are some of the topics you will learn about? Write them on your paper.

B. Scan the article. Find and write the answers to the following questions.

1. What is forked lightning?
2. How are sheet lightning and heat lightning different?
3. What is ball lightning?

Kinds of Lightning

All lightning strokes are basically about the same. However, they appear to have different forms, depending on the position of the observer.

Forked, zigzag, or chain lightning is a chain of brilliant light that appears to zigzag. It actually follows a winding path, like that of a river. The single streak of lightning often breaks into several branches or forks.

Sheet lightning has no particular form. It is usually a bright flash that spreads all over the horizon and lights up the sky. Sheet lightning is really light from a flash of chain lightning that takes place beyond the horizon.

Heat lightning, often seen on summer evenings, is the same as sheet lightning, but the flashes are fainter.

Ball lightning seems to consist of balls of fire, as small as walnuts or as large as balloons, that last about three to five seconds. They fall swiftly from the clouds until they strike the ground and explode. Sometimes they roll slowly along the ground and do not explode until they hit an obstacle. Ball lightning is the least understood of all forms of lightning. Many meteorologists even doubt that it exists. They think it may be an optical illusion. However, so many reliable witnesses have seen it that scientists have begun to study it. They have produced ball lightning in the laboratory. This lightning does not appear to be dangerous.

—*The World Book Encyclopedia*

2 The SQ3R Study Method

Focus

Use the **SQ3R study method** to learn and understand important information in your reading.

You cannot always read by skimming and scanning. Sometimes you must read more carefully so that you can understand and learn new material. Learning is easier and more effective if you use a study method. SQ3R is a five-step study method. *S* stands for *survey*. *Q* means *question*. The *3R*'s are *read*, *record*, and *review*.

The SQ3R Study Method

Survey	Skim the material to get a general idea of what it is about. Look at the title. It tells you what is included in the chapter. Look at pictures and graphs. Read the introduction and summary of the chapter.
Question	Discover what questions you should be able to answer when you finish reading. Are there study questions at the end of the material? Did your teacher give you things to look for? Look at maps, graphs, and pictures. Ask yourself questions about them.
Read	Read the material carefully. Look up unfamiliar words in a dictionary. Think about what you are reading.
Record	Write in your own words the answers to the questions you found earlier.
Review	Every few days, review what you have learned. Can you explain the subject without using your notes? Can you discuss the main ideas? If not, go over your notes again.

Exercise Using SQ3R

The following article explains food chains. Use the SQ3R method to study these paragraphs.

1. Survey the article.
2. Write three questions that you should be able to answer.
3. Read the article slowly and carefully.
4. Scan the article to find the answers to your questions. Write, or record, the answers.
5. Review what you have learned.

Understanding Food Chains

Forming Food Chains

When an animal eats a plant, it receives some of the plant's stored energy. That animal may be eaten by another animal. Energy flows from one living thing to another in a series of steps called a food chain.

All food chains begin with green plants, the food producers. Some food chains have only two steps or links, such as corn →human. Whenever you eat corn, a cookie (made from wheat flour), an apple, or any other food that came from a green plant, you are part of a simple food chain.

Losing Energy

Some food chains have several links: grass→mouse→ snake→hawk. As energy flows through a food chain it seems to disappear. Actually, energy can be changed but not destroyed or created. However, every time energy changes, some of it becomes heat energy which is given off into the air or water. So far as living things are concerned, this energy is useless.

—LAURENCE PRINGLE

Questions for Review

1. What is a food chain?
2. What is lost in a food chain?
3. What comes from lost energy?
4. Name a three-step food chain.

3 Using the Parts of a Book

Focus

Learn to use the parts of a book to find the exact material you need.

How can you decide if a nonfiction book is one that will be helpful to you? How can you use it to quickly find the information you need? There are three important parts of a book that can help you in both of these situations: the **table of contents**, the **index**, and the **glossary**.

A **table of contents** is in the front of a nonfiction book. It lists the chapters in the book. Some tables of contents also list the important topics in each chapter. The table of contents tells the first page of each chapter and chapter part.

By skimming the table of contents, you might be able to tell if the information you need is in the book. Look at the table of contents in this book. Would you be able to find information about poetry?

The **index** is at the end of a nonfiction book. It is more detailed than the table of contents. The index is an alphabetical listing of the topics in the book. Page numbers follow each index entry.

Look under several possible topics to find the information you need. For example, to find information on cacti, you might look at entries for *cactus*, *plants*, and *desert*. Look in the index of this book. On what pages can you find more information about note cards?

Some nonfiction books have a part called a **glossary**. Look for the glossary at the back of a nonfiction book. A glossary is a dictionary that gives the definitions of many words found in the book. Use the glossary to look up any unfamiliar words you may find as you read.

Exercises Using the Parts of a Book

A. Look at the table of contents on this page. Then answer the questions below.

Australia

Contents

In what chapter and part would you find answers to the following questions?

1. Two of Australia's territories are Queensland and Victoria. Name the other four territories.
2. Australia covers how many square miles?
3. Name four important Australian industries.
4. How many people live in Australia?
5. What is the most important form of transportation from Australian cities to the Outback?
6. Who were the first people in Australia?
7. What mountain range is near Australia's east coast?

B. Look at the index in this book. On what pages do you find information about the following topics?

stringy sentences
ZIP code
suffixes
metaphor
double negatives
Dewey Decimal System

4 How To Memorize

Focus

Good memorizing skills can help you learn material quickly and easily.

You often must memorize both in and out of school. In school, you might have to memorize a list of vocabulary words, science definitions, or history dates. Out of school, you may find yourself memorizing baseball statistics or a friend's telephone number.

Here are some hints that can make memorizing easier. Since people learn in different ways, try all of these methods. Find the ones that work best for you.

1. Recite out loud. Sometimes the sound of your own voice helps you remember. List the facts you want to learn. Then say the facts out loud. You can even turn them into a song or chant. Walking back and forth while reciting or singing the facts might also help you remember.

2. Write out the material. If you are studying in a quiet place, you may not be able to recite what you must memorize. Then, try memorizing by writing. Sometimes, the movement of your hand can help you remember. Seeing what you have written will also help.

3. Connect ideas. It is easier to memorize facts if they fit together in some pattern. Can the facts be arranged in alphabetical or time order? In your history class, for instance, you might try memorizing important dates in the order in which they happened. Can the items be grouped together in categories? For example, imagine that you want to remember what you must take on a camping trip. Group the items into categories: food, clothes, and equipment.

4. Use memory games. There are many tricks and games that will help you memorize. For example, draw a picture that includes everything on your list. When it is time to recall your list, just think of the picture. You will then be able to "see" the items on your list.

Here is a game that uses letters rather than pictures. Take the first letter of each word you need to memorize. Arrange these letters to form a word. For example, imagine that you must memorize the names of the five Great Lakes. The word *HOMES* contains the first letter of each lake: *H*uron, *O*ntario, *M* —. Can you finish the list?

5. Repeat and review the material. Repeat your list or memory game. Say it to yourself often, at different times of the day. In this way, you will easily call the facts to mind when they are needed.

Exercise Practicing Memory Skills

Review the five memory methods. Now read the four examples below. Which memory method do you think would work best in each of these situations? Why?

1. Kirsten must learn the thirteen original American colonies for history class.
2. Your computer science class must learn ten new computer terms. You must learn the correct spelling and definitions of these terms.
3. Your father has asked you to go to the corner grocery store to buy the following items: milk, lettuce, cheese, broccoli, mushrooms, yogurt, hamburger, and tuna. How will you remember this grocery list?
4. Fred wants to remember which states border the Gulf of Mexico. The states are: Florida, Alabama, Louisiana, and Texas. Can you help Fred?

5 Preparing for and Taking Tests

Focus

You can improve your test scores. Learn how to prepare for a test and how to take a test.

Test-taking is like any other school activity. You can plan and prepare for tests to improve your performance.

Preparing for a Test

1. Know what material you are responsible for. This will help you focus your studying on the important facts and information.
If you have any questions, ask your teacher before the day of the test.

2. Make a study plan. Decide how much time you will need to study for the test. Allow enough time. Plan your study time around homework, family chores, and other activities.

3. Look over your study materials. Skim the reading assignments and class notes. Review the questions you wrote when you used the SQ3R study method. Review any questions, worksheets, and study guides you received in class.

4. Memorize special facts. Make a list of important names, dates, events, or definitions. Use the tips you learned in part 4 of this chapter to memorize these important facts.

5. Review. Reread and study any difficult material.

6. Be rested and alert. Get plenty of sleep the night before the test. Eat a good breakfast.

Now you are ready to take the test. Follow the guidelines for taking a test on the next page.

Taking a Test

1. **Skim the test.** Look at the length of the test and the types of questions. Note any sections that may be more difficult and require extra time. This overview will help you plan your time more effectively.

2. **Plan your time.** Decide how much time you will need to complete each part of the test and to review your answers.

3. **Read or listen to all of the directions before you begin.** Make sure you understand the directions before you begin work. Do not be afraid to ask questions if you do not understand what you are supposed to do.

4. **Answer the easiest questions first.** Then, go back to the more difficult questions. Allow extra time for longer or more complicated questions.

5. **Review.** After you finish the test, look over your work. Answer any questions you may have skipped. Look over your answers to the more difficult questions.

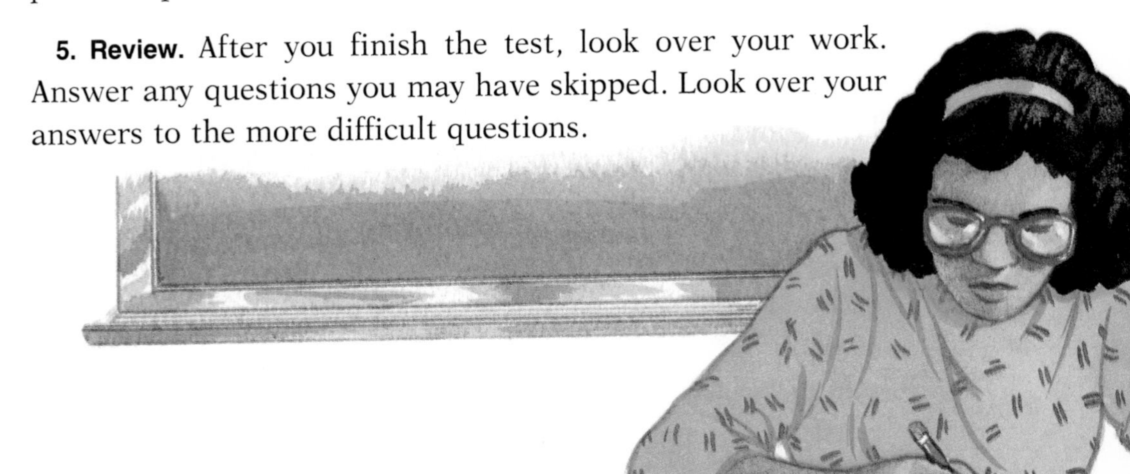

Exercise Preparing for and Taking a Test

Choose a test that you will be taking soon. Write out a study plan for this test. The guidelines on page 134 will help you in making your plan. Use your study plan to prepare for this test.

When it is time to take the test, follow the guide above.

6 Types of Test Questions

Focus

There are many types of test questions. Know how to answer each kind.

A test may have several kinds of questions. Improve your test scores by learning how to answer each type.

1. True-False A true-false question is usually written as a statement. You must decide whether the statement is correct or incorrect. If *any part* of a statement is false, the whole statement is false. Words such as *always, never, all,* and *none* often are in false statements. Words such as *some, a few, usually, often,* and *most* may be found in true statements.

2. Multiple Choice A multiple choice question has three or more possible answers. The choices are usually identified by small letters: *a, b, c.* Read all of the answers. Eliminate choices that you know are incorrect. Then choose the *best* answer from those remaining. Pay special attention to choices such as *all of the above* or *none of the above.*

3. Matching In this kind of question, numbered questions are listed in one column. Lettered answers are listed in a second column. Place the letter of the correct answer next to the question. You may use an answer more than once, or not at all.

4. Fill-in-the-Blank This kind of question asks you to add the missing word or phrase to an incomplete sentence. You may be given a list of answers to choose from. Always use proper capitalization and punctuation when completing the sentence.

5. Short Answer Write one or two sentences to answer the question. Answer in complete sentences, using proper capitalization and punctuation.

6. Questions for Standardized Tests. These tests are used to compare the progress of students in different school districts, states, or the country. They are usually multiple choice.

Standardized tests and some class tests may have separate answer sheets. You mark the correct answer by filling in small circles or boxes with pencil marks. Because these separate answer sheets are scored by machines, you must be very careful when marking answers. Fill in the circles or boxes completely. If you change an answer, erase it cleanly.

Exercise **Answering Test Questions**

Number your paper from 1 to 5. Write the letter of the correct answer to each of these multiple choice items.

1. Standardized tests often contain this type of question.
   a. true-false c. fill-in-the-blank
   b. multiple choice d. matching
2. A short answer question should be answered with
   a. an essay c. one or two sentences
   b. one or two words d. a paragraph
3. False statements often contain this word.
   a. often c. never
   b. always d. both b and c
4. In this kind of question, numbered questions are listed in one column. Lettered answers are in a second column.
   a. multiple choice c. matching
   b. true-false d. short answer
5. When answering a multiple choice question,
   a. read all of the answers before you choose one
   b. eliminate choices you know are incorrect
   c. choose the best answer
   d. all of the above

Using English in Science

In this chapter, you have learned many study skills, such as skimming, scanning, and the SQ3R study method. These study skills can help you learn new and complex information in science.

Exercise Learning About Solar Heat

Read the directions below for an experiment on storing solar heat. Skim to discover what you will be doing and what materials you will need. Then answer the questions that follow.

How To Test for Solar Heat Storage

This experiment tests how different materials store solar heat (heat from the sun). To perform the experiment, you will need the following: a cardboard box, five styrofoam cups, five thermometers, water, salt, crumpled paper, soil, and sand.

First, put a thermometer in each cup. Next, fill each cup with one of the five materials listed above (water, salt, paper, soil, sand). Then, put the cups in the box and close the lid. Put the box in the sun.

When the box is very warm, move it to the shade. Immediately, write down the temperature of each cup. Keep checking the thermometers every few minutes and record the temperatures. Which cup has the highest temperature for the longest time? The material in this cup is the best of the five tested for storing solar heat.

1. What is solar heat?
2. What five materials will be tested for their ability to store heat?
3. What other items do you need for the experiment?
4. How will you tell which material holds heat best?

Chapter 7 Review

A. Using the Parts of a Book The library has a new book on photography for beginners. You decide to examine the book to see if it would interest you.

1. Where would main topics of a book be listed in the order they appear?
2. Where would topics be listed alphabetically?
3. Where might you find the meaning of an unfamiliar word?
4. Where would you find the page number on which a chapter begins?
5. Which section lists more items: the table of contents or the index?

B. Understanding Good Study Skills Each of the following statements is incorrect. Write each statement correctly.

1. When skimming, pay special attention to the index, glossary, and table of contents.
2. When scanning, read every word carefully.
3. Do not read the chapter summary when you survey. It will only confuse you.
4. The *Q* of SQ3R stands for "Quickly read."
5. The *3R* of SQ3R means *Read, Recite, Reorganize.*

C. Reviewing Test-Taking Skills Read the following statements. Write *True* or *False* for each one.

1. Capitalization and punctuation are not important when you answer a fill-in-the-blank test question.
2. When you take a test, allow time to review answers.
3. When you answer a multiple choice question, eliminate the incorrect answers first.
4. You should be well rested before taking a test.
5. To save time on a test, do not read directions.

Chapter 8

Exploring the Dictionary and Thesaurus

Imagine that you read the word *hypersonic* in your science book. You do not know what *hypersonic* means. How do you find the meaning?

You are writing a letter to a friend about the new Ferris wheel at the state fair. You are unsure how to spell *Ferris*. What can you do?

The answers to these and other questions can be found in a dictionary. In this chapter, you will learn to use the dictionary to find information about words. You will discover everything from the definition of a word to its part of speech.

You will also learn to use a thesaurus. This book lists words along with synonyms and antonyms for those words. Using the dictionary and the thesaurus can make you a better writer.

1 Finding the Word You Want

Focus

All of the words in a dictionary are arranged in alphabetical order.

A dictionary is easy to use. Because words are listed in alphabetical order, you can quickly locate the information you are looking for.

Using Alphabetical Order

The words that are listed on each page of the dictionary are called **entry words**. They are usually listed in two columns. The words are in **alphabetical order**. The first part of the dictionary has words that begin with *a*. Then come words that begin with *b*, and so on.

Many words begin with the same letter. When that happens, they are alphabetized by the second letter. For example, the word *sand* is listed before the word *scale* because *a* comes before *c*. Many words have the same first and second letters. Then they are alphabetized by the third letter and so on. For example, the word *stamp* is listed before the word *steel* because *a* comes before *e*.

Here are some groups of words listed in alphabetical order.

Group 1	Group 2	Group 3
autumn	sail	the
eel	scale	their
pigeon	soap	them
zebra	sweater	then

Exercises Using a Dictionary

A. Write the words in each group in alphabetical order.

1	2	3	4
hoot	mountain	sandal	palace
whoop	ridge	sample	casement
howl	valley	thermos	cottage
squeal	meadow	lunchbox	castle
bellow	lagoon	sang	pad
screech	lake	traffic	cabin
yell	beach	tray	casting
yap	river	sandwich	wigwam

B. The numbered columns of words are in alphabetical order. Rewrite the words in each column. Insert the additional words in the correct place.

Words To Add

1. state, span, startle, speak, stalk
2. telephone, term, tablet, tadpole, tennis

1	2
stamp	telescope
standard	tell
stray	temper
subject	tender
syllable	tenor

2 Using Guide Words

Focus

Guide words are the two words in heavy black type at the top of a dictionary page. They tell you the first and last words on that page.

Look at the sample dictionary page on page 145. At the top of each column on the page, there is a word in heavy black type. This word is called a **guide word**. Guide words help you find the right page when you are looking for an entry word.

The guide words on the sample page are *rocky* and *Roman*. Now look at the entry words that are listed on that page. The first entry word is *rocky*. The last entry word is *Roman*. Guide words tell you that all the entry words on this page will be between *rocky* and *Roman* in the alphabet.

When you use a dictionary, learn to use the guide words. They will help you find your word. First look for guide words that begin with the same letter as your word. Then look at the second and third letters of the guide words. This will help you find guide words that are close to your word in the alphabet. Sometimes your word may even be a guide word. Most of the time, however, your word will come between two guide words.

rock·y (räk′ē), *adj.* **1.** tending to rock or sway; not steady [a *rocky* desk]. **2.** weak or dizzy: *slang in this meaning.* —**rock′i·er,** *compar.;* **rock′i·est,** *superl.* —**rock′i·ness,** *n.*

rocking horse

Rocky Mountains, a mountain system in western North America. It stretches from Alaska to New Mexico. Also called *Rockies.*

ro·co·co (rə kō′kō), *adj.* having rich decoration and many fancy designs, such as leaves, scrolls, etc. [*Rococo* architecture was popular in the 18th century.]

rod (räd), *n.* **1.** a straight, thin bar of wood, metal, etc. [a fishing *rod*]. **2.** a stick for beating as punishment. **3.** punishment. **4.** a measure of length equal to 5½ yards. **5.** a staff carried as a symbol of position or rank, as by a king. —**spare the rod,** to keep from punishing.

rode (rōd), past tense of **ride.**

ro·dent (rō′d'nt), *n.* an animal having sharp front teeth for gnawing. Rats, mice, rabbits, and squirrels are rodents.

ro·de·o (rō′di ō *or* rō dā′ō), *n.* **1.** a contest or show in which cowboys match their skill in riding horses, roping and throwing cattle, etc. **2.** a roundup of cattle. —**ro′de·os,** *pl.*

roe (rō), *n.* fish eggs.

roe (rō), *n.* a small, graceful deer found in Asia and Europe. —**roe** or **roes,** *pl.*

roe·buck (rō′buk), *n.* the male of the roe.

Roent·gen rays (rent′gən), same as **X rays.**

rogue (rōg), *n.* **1.** a dishonest or tricky person; scoundrel; rascal. **2.** a person who likes to have fun and plays tricks. **3.** an elephant or other animal that wanders apart from the herd and is wild and fierce.

ro·guer·y (rō′gə rē), *n.* the actions of a rogue; trickery or playful mischief. —**ro′guer·ies,** *pl.*

ro·guish (rō′gish), *adj.* **1.** dishonest; tricky. **2.** playful; mischievous. —**ro′guish·ly,** *adv.*

roil (roil), *v.* **1.** to make muddy or cloudy, as by stirring up stuff at the bottom [to *roil* a pond]. **2.** to make angry; vex.

roist·er (rois′tər), *v.* **1.** to be noisy and lively; revel. **2.** to brag or show off. —**roist′er·er,** *n.*

role or **rôle** (rōl), *n.* **1.** the part that an actor takes in a play [the heroine's *role*]. **2.** a part that a person plays in life [his *role* as scoutmaster].

roll (rōl), *v.* **1.** to move by turning over and over [The dog *rolled* on the grass. Men *rolled* logs to the river.] **2.** to move on wheels or rollers [The wagons *rolled* by. *Roll* the cart over here.] **3.** to wrap up or wind into a ball or tube [*Roll* up the rug.] **4.** to move smoothly, one after the other [The waves *rolled* to the shore. The weeks *rolled* by.] **5.** to move or rock back and forth [The ship *rolled* in the heavy seas. Sally *rolled* her eyes.] **6.** to spread, make, or become flat under a roller [to *roll* steel]. **7.** to say with a trill [He *rolls* his "r's".] **8.** to make a loud, echoing sound [The thunder *rolled.*] **9.** to beat with light, rapid blows [to *roll* a drum]. —*n.* **1.** the act of rolling [the *roll* of a ball]. **2.** a list of names for checking who is present. **3.** something rolled up into a ball or tube [a *roll* of wallpaper]. **4.** bread baked in a small, shaped piece. **5.** a roller. **6.** a rolling motion [the *roll* of a boat]. **7.** a loud, echoing sound [a *roll* of thunder]. **8.** a number of light, rapid blows on a drum. —**roll in, 1.** to arrive or come in large numbers. **2.** to have much of: *used only in everyday talk* [*rolling in* wealth]. —**roll out, 1.** to make flat by using a roller on. **2.** to spread out by unrolling. —**roll up,** to get or become more; increase [to *roll up* a big score].

roll call, the reading aloud of a list of names, as in a classroom, to find out who is absent.

roll·er (rōl′ər), *n.* **1.** a tube or cylinder on which something is rolled [the *roller* of a window shade]. **2.** a heavy rolling cylinder used to crush, smooth, or spread [A steam *roller* crushed the gravel on the road.] **3.** a long, heavy wave that breaks on the shore line. **4.** a canary that trills its notes. **5.** anything that rolls.

roller coaster, an amusement ride in which cars move on tracks that curve and dip sharply.

roller skate, a skate having wheels instead of a runner, for skating on floors, walks, etc.

roll·er-skate (rōl′ər-skāt′), *v.* to move on roller skates. —**roll′er-skat′ed,** *p.t.* & *p.p.;* **roll′er-skat′ing,** *pr.p.*

roller skates

rol·lick (räl′ik), *v.* to play in a gay, lively way; romp; frolic. —**rol′lick·ing,** *adj.*

rolling mill, a factory or machine for rolling metal into sheets and bars.

rolling pin, a heavy, smooth cylinder of wood, glass, etc., used to roll out dough.

rolling stock, all the locomotives and cars of a railroad.

ro·ly-po·ly (rō′lē pō′lē), *adj.* short and plump; pudgy [a *roly-poly* boy].

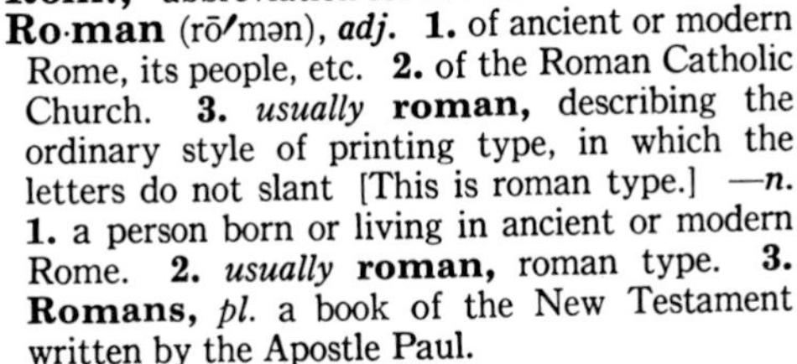
rolling pin

Rom., abbreviation for **Roman.**

Ro·man (rō′mən), *adj.* **1.** of ancient or modern Rome, its people, etc. **2.** of the Roman Catholic Church. **3.** *usually* **roman,** describing the ordinary style of printing type, in which the letters do not slant [This is roman type.] —*n.* **1.** a person born or living in ancient or modern Rome. **2.** *usually* **roman,** roman type. **3.** **Romans,** *pl.* a book of the New Testament written by the Apostle Paul.

Exercises Using Guide Words

A. Number your paper from 1 to 10. In the list below are ten sets of guide words. After each set of guide words is another word. Decide whether you would find that word on a page before the guide words, on the page with the guide words, or on a page after the guide words. Write *Before*, *With*, or *After* beside each number on your paper. Here is an example.

Guide Words		Other Word
able	animal	action

The word *action* comes between *able* and *animal* in the alphabet. Therefore you would find *action* on the page with the guide words *able* and *animal*. So *With* is the right answer.

	Guide Words		Other Word
1.	batter	bearing	bead
2.	root	round	route
3.	trillion	tropical	trouble
4.	may	mechanic	mattress
5.	baker	banana	balance
6.	luggage	lying	lunch
7.	home	hoof	hole
8.	fan	fat	fascinate
9.	burr	buzz	bystander
10.	top	touch	tooth

B. See how easily you can find the following words in your dictionary. Write each word. After the word, copy the two guide words from the page where you found it.

1. buffalo
2. shark
3. elk
4. walrus
5. butterscotch
6. raspberry
7. chocolate
8. vanilla
9. wood
10. plastic
11. glass
12. metal

3 Word Division and Pronunciation

Focus

A dictionary entry tells you how to divide a word into syllables and how to pronounce it.

Syllables

A dictionary entry shows how to divide each entry word into parts. Each word part pronounced with a single uninterrupted sound is called a **syllable**. In the sample dictionary page shown on page 145, there is a dot between syllables in the entry words. For example, the word *roller* is shown as **roll • er**.

Why does an entry show how to divide the word into syllables? One reason is to help you to develop better spelling skills. If you can think of a word broken into little parts, it will probably be easier to remember how to spell it.

There is another reason why the dictionary breaks entry words into syllables. Sometimes a word will not fit at the end of a line you are writing. Part of the word will have to be written on the next line. When that happens, always divide the word between syllables. Use the dictionary when you need to know how to divide a word into syllables.

Pronunciation

A dictionary entry also gives the **pronunciation** of a word. That is, it tells you how to say the word. The pronunciation appears in parentheses just after each entry word. For example, find the entry word *roll* on the sample dictionary page. Just after the entry word, you will see (rōl). This is the pronunciation of *roll.*

The sample dictionary page shown on page 145 has a **pronunciation key** at the bottom. You can use the pronunciation key to find out how to pronounce *roll* (rōl). Look at the pronunciation key. Find a word that has ō in it. The word is *go.* This tells you that the *o* in *roll* is pronounced like the *o* in *go.* It is not pronounced like the *o* in *confess.*

There is something else that you should notice about pronunciation. Words that have more than one syllable have **accent marks**. These accent marks look like this: ′. A dictionary uses accent marks to show how words are pronounced. When you say a word with more than one syllable, you pronounce one syllable more strongly than the rest of the word. For example, say the word *roller.* You said *ROLLer. Roller* has a stronger emphasis on the first syllable. The pronunciation of *roller* on the sample dictionary page shows an accent mark after the first syllable. This tells you that the first syllable is pronounced more strongly than the second syllable.

Exercises Mastering Pronunciation and Word Division

A. Rewrite each of the following words. Divide each word into syllables, leaving spaces between the syllables. Use your dictionary for help.

1. whirlpool
2. jewelry
3. overboard
4. potato
5. thirsty
6. unlimited
7. citizen
8. delivery
9. allowance

B. Here are nine groups of words. Use a dictionary to find the pronunciation of each word. First, write down each word. Next, write the correct pronunciation of each word. Then underline the words that rhyme in each group.

1. fluff
   through
   enough
2. dough
   though
   rough
3. freight
   height
   site
4. drought
   thought
   clout
5. trough
   dough
   scoff
6. sleight
   weight
   eight
7. vein
   ensign
   reign
8. bury
   cherry
   flurry
9. steak
   beak
   weak

4 Definitions and Parts of Speech

Focus

A dictionary entry tells the meaning and the part of speech of a word.

Definitions are the largest part of every dictionary entry. They explain the meanings of entry words. Sometimes a picture is shown to help explain the meaning of the entry word. Many words have more than one definition. If a word has more than one definition, the definitions are numbered. For example, look at the definitions for *rod* on the sample dictionary page on page 145. There are five definitions given for this word.

Many definitions are followed by a phrase or sentence in italics. This sentence shows a particular meaning of the entry word. It uses the word in a way that makes the meaning clear. For example, look at the entry for *roll* on the sample page. Look at definition 2.

"to move on wheels or rollers"

Now look at the words written in italics.

The wagons *rolled* by. *Roll* the cart over here.

The sentences give good examples of what *roll* means.

A dictionary entry also tells what **part of speech** a word is. If a word can be used as more than one part of speech, the dictionary will give definitions for each part of speech. Look again at the definitions on page 145. There are abbreviations before the definitions. Here are the meanings of some of these abbreviations.

n.	noun	*adj.*	adjective	*v.*	verb
pron.	pronoun	*adv.*	adverb		

Read the chart below. Notice the four parts of the dictionary entry for the word *roe*.

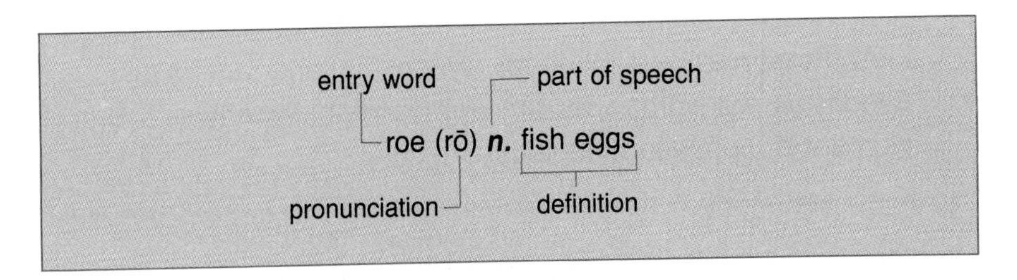

Exercises Finding Definitions

A. Each of the sentences below has a word that is in italics. Use your dictionary to find the meaning of this word. Write down the definition that fits best in the sentence.

1. Derek learned to speak German *abroad*.
2. At camp we told our favorite *yarns*.
3. Do you think you have lived long enough to write your *memoirs*?
4. Our teacher *primed* us before the test.
5. The outcome of the basketball game *hinges* on how well our team plays.
6. Ellen *leafed* through the book to find her place.
7. Could the new medicine be a *panacea*?
8. The airplane began to *yaw* as the storm winds became stronger.
9. At practice, our team *trounced* the other team.
10. He returned the missing wallet *intact* to its owner.

B. Each of the following words can be used as more than one part of speech. Look up each word in your dictionary. Write two sentences for each word. Each sentence should use the word as a different part of speech. Underline the word in each sentence. Then tell what part of speech the word is in that sentence.

ring dress model tack price fry

5 Using a Thesaurus

Focus

A **thesaurus** is a book of synonyms and antonyms. **Synonyms** are words with similar meanings. **Antonyms** are words with opposite meanings.

A **thesaurus** is a reference book that is helpful to writers. It is a list of words along with synonyms and antonyms for these words. A thesaurus can help a writer find words that are lively and specific to replace words that are dull or too general. The thesaurus at the back of this book is even more useful. It helps you decide when to use the different synonyms.

Many thesauri that you will use have entries that are arranged in alphabetical order, just like a dictionary. Other thesauri, however, have indexes that you must use to locate a word. The index lists every word and synonym in the thesaurus. The index also shows you where to find each word in the thesaurus. The thesaurus in this book contains an index.

When you are writing, you can refer to a thesaurus to help you find good word choices for a particular sentence. Imagine that you wrote the following sentence.

The deer *jumped* over the brook.

Suppose you wanted to find a better word than *jumped* to describe what the deer did. You could look up *jump* in a thesaurus. Here is what you might find.

JUMP—*N.* jump, leap, spring, bound, hop, skip, buck, canter, bob, gambade, somersault, upspring, vault, hurdle.

V. jump, leap, spring, bound, hop, lollop, skip, trip, buck, canter, curvet, somersault, hurdle, clear, jump over, vault, parachute, caper, frisk, cavort, dance, gambol, prance, frolic, romp, rebound, recoil, carom, ricochet, bounce, jounce, bob.

Adj. jumping, jumpy, frisky, skittish, resilient, buoyant, elastic, springy.

Notice that the entry gives many synonyms for *jump*. Some of these words mean the same thing as *jump* when it is used as a noun (*N.*). Some mean the same thing as *jump* when it is used as a verb (*V.*) or as an adjective (*Adj.*). In the sentence you wrote, *jumped* is a verb. So you would look at the synonyms after *V.* to find a better word for your sentence. You might choose *bounded, leaped*, or *sprang*. Which would you choose?

When you use a thesaurus, you must be careful. Synonyms do not always mean exactly the same thing. Always check your dictionary if you are in doubt about using a synonym. For example, another synonym for *jump* is *parachute*. However, the example sentence would sound silly with that word.

The deer *parachuted* over the brook.

Always study the meanings of synonyms carefully. Then select just the right word to say what you mean.

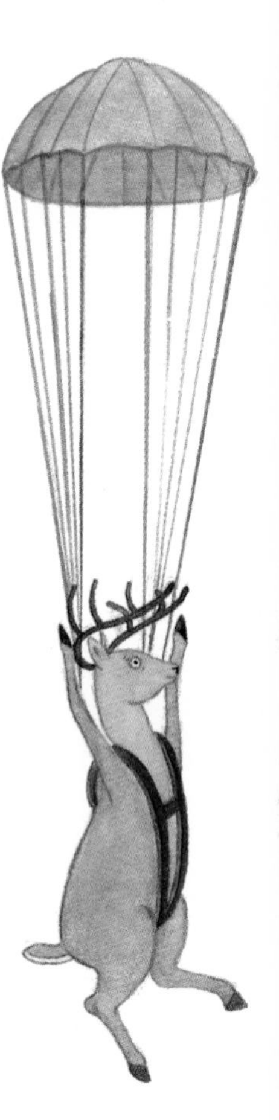

Exercises **Using a Thesaurus**

A. Read each sentence below. Then look up each word in italics in the special thesaurus at the back of this book. Find a good synonym for each word. Rewrite the sentences using the synonyms.

1. We were not *afraid* of the monsters in the movie.
2. The sculpture in the plaza is *big*.
3. The clowns at the circus were *funny*.
4. Our Glee Club will give the money it *gets* from the concert to the school for the deaf.
5. Mr. Wicket gets *angry* when things don't go his way.

B. Choose one of these words:

group beautiful bright see

Then read the synonyms listed for the word in the thesaurus at the back of this book. Select three synonyms for the word. Write a sentence for each synonym. Be sure to use the synonym correctly.

Using English in Other Subjects

You have learned how to use a dictionary and thesaurus to find information about words. Some dictionaries, however, do not give information about words. These special dictionaries have information about particular topics or subject areas. For example, did you know there are dictionaries of art, music, and geography? If you need to give a report on Michelangelo for your art class, or write about the Amazon River for your geography class, you can find the information in one of these special dictionaries.

Exercise Using Special Dictionaries

Go to your public library. Ask the librarian to help you find one or more of the special dictionaries from the following list. Then look through the dictionary to see what kind of information can be found in this book.

Write a paragraph that tells what kinds of information can be found in your special dictionary. Finally, choose one entry from the dictionary and write a paragraph about the entry from the information given in the dictionary.

Special Dictionaries

Webster's Biographical Dictionary
Webster's New Geographical Dictionary
McGraw-Hill Dictionary on Scientific and Technical Terms
Concise Oxford Dictionary of Music
Harvard Dictionary of Music
Dictionary of Mythology, Folk Lore, and Symbols
Dictionary of American History
Dictionary of United States History

Chapter 8 Review

A. Mastering the Dictionary Refer to the sample dictionary page on page 145 to answer the following questions.

1. Divide the word *rococo* into syllables. Which syllable is accented? What part of speech is the word *rococo*?
2. What word on the page can be used as both an adjective and a noun?
3. Which word on the page has two acceptable pronunciations? Write them out.
4. Use the word *rogue* in two sentences, each showing a different meaning of *rogue*.
5. What two words on the page are spelled differently but pronounced the same way?
6. What word on the page has two entries with two completely different meanings? What are those two definitions?

B. Using the Dictionary Each of the sentences below has an italicized word. Look up each word in your dictionary. Write the word in syllables, with a space between each syllable. Then write the definition that best fits the use of the word in the sentence.

1. The *silhouette* of the old tree stood out against the winter sky.
2. The hunter wore a *chamois* jacket.
3. The river is *navigable* only during part of the rainy season.
4. The bats looked like *phantoms* as they flew from the barn.
5. The *scull* moved swiftly across the glassy lake.

Chapter 9

Using Pronouns

Read the first four lines of this rhyme.

Little Bo-Peep has lost Little Bo-Peep's sheep.
  And can't tell where to find the sheep.
Leave the sheep alone, and the sheep will come home,
  Wagging the sheep's tails behind the sheep.

What seems strange about this verse? You probably noticed that the sentences are awkward and wordy. The verse does not have the rhythm of the original Mother Goose rhyme. One reason for these problems is that this verse contains no pronouns. Pronouns are words that take the place of nouns. Replacing nouns with pronouns can sometimes help writing flow more smoothly.

In this chapter, you will learn how pronouns take the place of nouns. You will also learn how pronouns show ownership, and how they help to make our speaking and writing smooth, clear, and interesting.

1 Substituting Pronouns for Nouns

Focus

A **pronoun** is a word used in place of a noun.

Suppose that each day for an entire month your lunch bag contained only a peanut butter and jelly sandwich. Imagine wearing only blue clothes or studying only math all week long. The same thing over and over is dull.

To keep our language from becoming dull, we use different types of words when we write and speak. **Pronouns**, for example, are words that can take the place of nouns. When you use pronouns, you do not have to use the same nouns again and again. Read these sentence pairs. Notice how the pronoun in each second sentence takes the place of the noun in italics in the first sentence.

Carmen pruned the rose bush. *She* cut the branches carefully.

A gusty *wind* beat against the window. *It* blew all night.

Armando's room needed cleaning. *His* clothes were scattered everywhere.

The farmer collected *gourds*. The farmer used *them* to make bird houses.

Pronouns help you in your writing and speaking. Here are three ways pronouns are used to replace nouns.

To refer to yourself:

I asked *my* mother to give *me* a ride.

To refer to the person you are talking to:

Did *you* bring *your* camera?

To refer to other persons, places, or things:

The people ran from the lion. *They* were afraid of *it*.

Like nouns, pronouns can be singular or plural.

Singular Pronouns

Person Speaking:	I	my, mine	me
Person Spoken To:	you	your, yours	you
Other Persons, Places, and Things:	he	his	him
	she	her, hers	her
	it	its	it

Plural Pronouns

Person Speaking:	we	our, ours	us
Persons Spoken To:	you	your, yours	you
Other Persons, Places, and Things:	they	their, theirs	them

Key to Writing and Speaking Nouns cannot always be replaced with pronouns. Sometimes the noun must be repeated so that the meaning is clear.

Confusing: When there are onions on hamburgers, Yvette won't eat *them*. (What won't Yvette eat, the onions or the hamburgers?)

Better: Whenever there are onions on hamburgers, Yvette won't eat the onions.

Exercises Using Pronouns

A. Copy the following sentences. Underline the pronouns.

1. Lenore strolled along the beach with him and me.
2. My favorite was the Mummy Room.
3. Look! You can see your reflection in the pool.

4. I took the lantern to our tent.
5. Zana will ride her unicycle in the parade.
6. The chimney sweep waved at us from our roof.
7. He returned the bleating lamb to its mother.
8. Your map is more recent than mine.
9. The colonists showed their feelings about the unfair taxes.
10. Will you hand me the egg rolls, please?

B. Copy the sentences below. Use pronouns in place of the words printed in italics.

1. Mark made a pet of a grizzly bear. *Mark's* bear was named Gentle Ben.
2. Sea elephants are not actually elephants. *Sea elephants* are seals.
3. Lorna wanted to be an author. *Lorna* wrote in *Lorna's* journal every day.
4. Cover the bottom of the aquarium with small rocks. Spread *the small rocks* around.
5. Tom and I looked through the telescope. *Tom and I* saw the "red planet."
6. Bess interviewed Dr. Tom Robinson. *Dr. Robinson* told *Bess* about medical school.
7. Pedro has a special lamp. *Pedro* grows plants under *the lamp's* light.
8. The green apples are tart. Use *the green apples* for apple crisp.
9. Freida said, "*Freida* will put the camera on a tripod."
10. Mr. Kim showed *Karana and me* how to feed the fish.

C. Writing You rubbed a magic lamp and have been granted three wishes. Two of the wishes must help someone else. Write a brief paragraph about what you wish for. Who will be helped? How will your life and the lives of these people be changed? Underline the pronouns in your paragraph.

2 Using the Subject Form of Pronouns

Focus

The **subject pronouns** are *I*, *you*, *he*, *she*, *it*, *we*, and *they*.

Use only subject pronouns as the subject of a sentence or after a state-of-being verb.

Using Pronouns as the Subjects of Sentences

Notice the subject of each of these sentences.

I visited my uncle.
He gave me a ride on his truck.
We drove along the river.

The subjects in these sentences are the pronouns *I*, *He*, and *We*. Four other subject pronouns are *you*, *she*, *it*, and *they*.

Most of the time, you will have no trouble using these pronouns as subjects. However, when there are two or more parts in a subject, you may sometimes get confused.

Look at both of these sentences. Which one is correct?

Faye and she painted the mural.
Faye and her painted the mural.

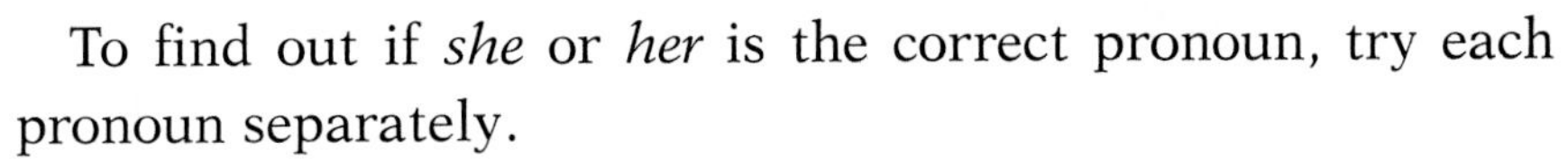

To find out if *she* or *her* is the correct pronoun, try each pronoun separately.

She painted the mural. Her painted the mural.

Obviously, the correct pronoun to use is *she*.

Faye and *she* painted the mural.

Use the same test when two pronouns are the subject. Which pronouns in this sentence are correct?

(He, Him) and (I, me) built a mobile.

Try each pronoun separately.

He built a mobile. Him built a mobile.
I built a mobile. Me built a mobile.

Clearly, the correct choices are *He* and *I*.

He and *I* built a mobile.

Notice that whenever *I* is used with another noun or pronoun as the subject of a sentence, *I* comes last.

Rachel and *I* were there. *She* and *I* brought a present.

Using Pronouns After State-of-Being Verbs

Read these two sentences.

The editor is she.
She is the editor.

The sentences mean the same thing. The state-of-being verb joins the subject to the pronoun. A pronoun that follows a state-of-being verb can be made the subject of the sentence without changing the meaning of the sentence. So, a pronoun that follows a state-of-being verb must always be a subject pronoun. Change each sentence below without changing the meaning of the sentence.

The best player was she.
The semi-finalists were Dan and I.

Key to Writing and Speaking Subject pronouns following state-of-being verbs may sound wrong. Don't trust what sounds right. Follow the rule.

Exercises Mastering Subject Pronouns

A. Choose the right answer from the two in parentheses. Write the correct answer on your paper.

1. Lydia and (I, me) started listening more carefully.
2. Elena and (she, her) demonstrated a front flip.
3. (I and Ingrid, Ingrid and I) tasted the tofu.
4. Uncle Jerry and (we, us) ate at Grandma's house.
5. Julena and (they, them) tried on the costumes.
6. (She, Her) and Carl caught two trout.
7. Josh and (him, he) shared the reward.
8. The sailors and (they, them) boarded the charter bus for the harbor.
9. Mary Ann and (she, her) picked okra.
10. Dad and (us, we) are learning a sign language.

B. Write the following ten sentences on your paper. Correct any pronoun usage that is incorrect. If the sentence is correct, write *Correct*.

1. Kit and him tried again to throw the boomerang.
2. I and Mom went to school last night.
3. The best cooks are Mr. Hogan and she.
4. Betty and him finished reading before everyone else.
5. Was it they who arrived early?
6. Me and Dad had some yard work to do.
7. Tom knocked on the front door and said, "Tim and me are here."
8. Had they boarded the train already?
9. The best gymnast in the school was her.
10. Him and I are repotting the plants.

C. Writing You are sending some friends on a scavenger hunt. Write out the directions you will give them. Include these phrases: *Pat and they, Eric and he, Renee and she, Toby and I*. Try to include some sentences with subject pronouns after state-of-being verbs.

3 Using Pronouns as Objects

Focus

The **object pronouns** are *me*, *you*, *him*, *her*, *it*, *us*, and *them*.

Use an object pronoun whenever the pronoun is not part of the subject. If the pronoun does not follow a state-of-being verb, use an object pronoun as well. The pronouns *you* and *it* may be used as both subject and object pronouns.

Read the following sentences. Which pronoun should be used in each sentence?

Sherlock Holmes suspected (they, them).

Did the puppy follow Rani and (she, her) home?

Stand between (we, us) on the stage.

Gloria helped (he and I, him and me) grease the pans.

Uri told (we, us) members about this year's dues.

Notice that in each of the examples above, the pronoun to be chosen is not the subject. Also, the pronoun does not follow a state-of-being verb. Therefore, the object pronoun is the correct choice in each sentence.

Sherlock Holmes suspected *them*.

Did the puppy follow Rani and *her* home?

Stand between *us* on the stage.

Gloria helped *him and me* grease the pans.

Uri told *us* members about this year's dues.

If you are not sure which pronoun to use in a sentence, first decide whether the pronoun is the subject or follows a state-of-being verb. If the pronoun is not the subject and does not follow a state-of-being verb, use an object pronoun.

Exercises Using Object Pronouns

A. Number your paper from 1 to 10. Choose the correct pronoun in the following sentences. Write it on your paper.

1. Ms. Rohr handed each of (they, them) a ball of yarn.
2. Mr. Ho showed Gina and (we, us) how to sand the board.
3. At the school recital, the jazz group performed after (they, them).
4. Corin's directions confused (he, him) totally.
5. The splashing dolphin drenched (she, her).
6. Above (we, us), the kite was snagged on a branch.
7. Gwen spotted (we, us) from across the field.
8. Insects scare (I, me).
9. At the art fair, an artist sketched (she, her) in pencil.
10. Indian pottery interested Samantha and (he, him).

B. Number your paper from 1 to 10. Choose the correct pronoun in the following sentences. Write it on your paper.

1. Carlotta made favors for the party and gave (they, them) to (we, us).
2. We broke (they, them) by accident.
3. Could Jerry take (we, us) to the ballet?
4. No one around here knows (he, him).
5. Larry asked (I, me) to answer the phone.
6. Can you help (we, us) with the heavy packages?
7. Nancy cooked (they, them) over an open fire.
8. Louise is coming for (he, him) at noon.
9. Ava showed (she, her) how to hold the marionettes.
10. Zack will meet (we, us) here at one o'clock.

C. Writing Your social studies class is studying genealogy, or family histories. Write a letter to an older member of your family. Ask for information that will help you draw your family tree. Find out about specific family members and what happened to each. Use at least three object pronouns in your letter.

4 Using *We* and *Us* with Nouns

Focus

The pronouns *we* and *us* are often used with nouns.

When you use phrases like *we girls* and *us boys*, you must be sure that you are using the right pronoun. You can tell which pronoun to use by dropping the noun and saying the sentence without it.

We girls went roller skating.
Dad drove *us* boys.

Both sentences are correct. In the first sentence, the pronoun is the subject of the sentence. The subject pronoun *we* is used with *girls*. In the second sentence, the pronoun is not the subject. That is why the object pronoun *us* is used.

Remember that a good way to decide which pronoun to use is to read the sentence without the noun. *We went roller skating* is correct. *Us went roller skating* is not correct. *Dad drove us* is correct. *Dad drove we* is not correct.

Notice the correct use of *we* and *us* in these sentences. *We students entered the auditorium.* (The pronoun is in the subject position, so *we* is correct.) *Cory took a picture of us Scouts.* (The pronoun is in the object position, so *us* is correct.)

Exercises Using *We* and *Us*

A. Copy these sentences. Choose the correct pronoun from those given in parentheses.

1. Climbing the rope was hard for (we, us) boys.
2. (We, Us) Americans have fifty stars on our flag.
3. Grandma told (we, us) children to wash our hands before starting to make bread.

4. Will she give (we, us) students our papers today?
5. (We, Us) chorus members will sing on Sunday.
6. Were (we, us) contestants standing in the right line?
7. Only (we, us) sailors knew how high the waves were.
8. Our rabbi got thank-you cards from several of (we, us) temple members.
9. Should (we, us) volunteers arrive early?
10. The money belonged to both (we, us) boys.

B. Decide whether the pronouns *we* and *us* are used correctly in the following sentences. If the sentence is incorrect, rewrite it correctly. If the sentence is correct, write *Correct* on your paper.

1. Us swimmers brought home another trophy.
2. The author wrote the play for us children.
3. Please tell we council members about the election.
4. We painters won the contest.
5. Us dancers were not on the program.
6. We baseball players got our new uniforms.
7. Will us farmers have another record corn crop?
8. Us girls could jump rope better than anyone else.
9. Two counselors made maps for we campers.
10. Every morning, us paper carriers make our deliveries.

C. Writing You are making a photo album with the pictures you took at the circus. A member from each of the performing groups has agreed to autograph your pictures. Each performer will also write a caption telling what is happening in the picture. On your paper, write five of the sentences the performers put in your album. Use some of the phrases listed below.

Example: The ringmaster chased us clowns out of the ring.

we jugglers	us performers
we acrobats	us bareback riders
we entertainers	us animal trainers
we musicians	us clowns

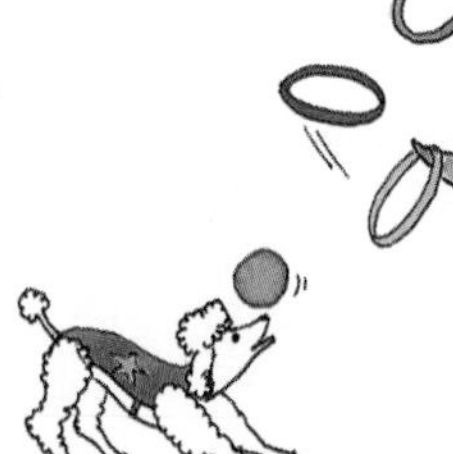

5 Possessive Pronouns

Focus

Possessive pronouns are used to show that someone or something owns something.

Just like nouns, pronouns can be used to show possession. Some possessive pronouns may be used before a noun: *my* dog. They show ownership of that noun. Other possessives may be used by themselves: The dog is *mine*. They show ownership of the nouns they follow.

You learned that to make the possessive form of a noun, you add an apostrophe or an apostrophe and *s* to the noun. Possessive pronouns do not use an apostrophe. Pronouns have special possessive forms.

Used Before a Noun	Used Alone
my	mine
your	yours
his, her, its	his, hers
our	ours
their	theirs

Notice the possessive pronouns in the sentences below.

Bedouins rode *their* camels across the desert.
The kayak is *mine*.

Using *Its* and *It's*

The possessive pronoun *its* and the contraction *it's* sound alike and look similar. Therefore, many people confuse them. Remember *its* without an apostrophe is the possessive form of *it*. *It's* (with an apostrophe) means "it is" or "it has."

> The salamander lost *its* tail. (The tail belongs to the salamander.)
> *It's* a library book. (*It is* a library book.)

Exercises **Using Possessive Pronouns**

A. Copy each of the following sentences. Where there is a blank, write a possessive pronoun. Use the information in the parentheses.

> Example: I found ______ notebook. (The notebook belongs to you.)
> I found your notebook.

1. ______ handwriting can be read easily. (The handwriting belongs to you.)
2. Did you see ______ faces? (The faces belong to them.)
3. Those keys are ______. (The keys belong to you.)
4. The dog lost ______ collar. (The collar belongs to it.)
5. The error is ______. (The error was made by her.)
6. The reward is ______. (The reward belongs to us.)
7. This is ______ chance. (The chance belongs to us.)
8. The fingerprints are definitely ______. (The fingerprints belong to him.)
9. That was ______ book. (The book belongs to me.)
10. The red car is ______. (The car belongs to them.)

B. Writing Pretend you and your friend are organizing a garage sale. You will sell items that belong to several family members. Write a paragraph describing what you will sell and who owns each item. Use possessive pronouns in your paragraph.

Exercises for Mastery

Chapter 9

Using Pronouns

A. Finding Pronouns Number your paper from 1 to 10. Copy the following sentences. Underline the pronouns.

1. We wrote a tall tale about a helpful giant.
2. She organized her shell collection.
3. I forgot my lines.
4. Will it work on this computer?
5. Dede, are you wearing jeans to the picnic?
6. If you have an umbrella, I won't bring mine.
7. Isaac tried to protect his dog from the bear.
8. They warned us about the poison sumac.
9. He checked our car's engine.
10. I went on the Ferris wheel with them.

B. Choosing Subject Pronouns Copy the sentences below. Choose the right pronoun.

1. (We, Us) went on a hayride.
2. Wes and (I, me) mow lawns.
3. The finalists were Paula and (he, him).
4. (Wilson and I, I and Wilson) traded baseball cards after school yesterday.
5. Will (she, her) buy toe shoes or ballet slippers when she goes shopping?
6. The guilty ones are Nathan and (we, us).
7. Bonita and (them, they) work at an ice rink in their neighborhood.
8. (She, Her) gathered acorns.
9. The next batters will be Sammy and (she, her).
10. The new stage managers for our annual school play are (they, them).

C. Choosing Object Pronouns Choose the right pronoun from the two in parentheses. Write it on your paper.

1. Bees stung both of (they, them).
2. Meg introduced Allan and (I, me).
3. Dad called (they, them) from Toledo.
4. The weaver showed her loom to Pat and (we, us).
5. The bird house was made by (him, he) and Sally.
6. A family of raccoons followed Lars and (he, him).
7. Chad played against (she, her) in the tournament.
8. Randi brought Andrea and (I, me) presents.
9. Astronomy interests my brother and (I, me).
10. The miniature railroad was constructed by Vinnie and (she, her).

D. Using Possessive Pronouns Copy the following sentences. Where there is a blank, write a possessive pronoun, using the information in parentheses.

1. ______ smile always cheers me up. (The smile belongs to him.)
2. I changed ______ school clothes. (The clothes belong to me.)
3. One mitten is ______. (The mitten belongs to you.)
4. They bathed ______ dog. (The dog belongs to them.)
5. This is ______ lunchtime recess. (The lunchtime belongs to us.)
6. That locker is ______. (The locker belongs to her.)
7. The antique clock is ______. (The clock belongs to them.)
8. The spider spun ______ web. (The web belongs to it.)
9. Proofread ______ paper. (The paper belongs to you.)
10. The ferret is ______. (The ferret belongs to me.)

Using Grammar in Writing

A. Diaries are fun to keep and interesting to read. Pretend that you are writing a page in your diary. Tell about an important or exciting day in your life. It can be true or imaginary. Use pronouns to avoid repeating names or to show ownership.

B. Notice how the following chain is built:

I like him. He likes her. She likes us. We like them. They like me. *I like him.*

Every sentence begins with a subject pronoun and ends with an object pronoun. The object pronoun that ends one sentence is changed to its subject form to start the next sentence.

Beginning with the pronoun *you*, make your own chain of ten different pronoun sentences. For fun, see how long you can make your chain without repeating a pronoun.

C. Using Pronouns in Health Choose a person who has helped in public health. You might choose someone like Jonas Salk, who developed the polio vaccine. You might also choose Florence Nightingale, the founder of modern nursing, or Louis Pasteur, who perfected pasteurization. Do some research on the person you choose. Write a paragraph about this person's accomplishment. Use pronouns in your paragraph.

Chapter 9 Review

A. Identifying and Using Pronouns Number your paper from 1 to 10. Choose the correct pronoun for each sentence. Identify your choice as *Subject Pronoun* or *Object Pronoun*.

Example: The fastest runner was (he, him).
he, Subject Pronoun

1. Jake and (he, him) watched the rodeo.
2. Sylvia and (I, me) went ice skating.
3. Jorge sat with Anita and (she, her).
4. Don't give (he, him) the present now.
5. Will (they, them) fly or drive home?
6. Jussi held the trophy proudly in front of (he, him) and John.
7. I bought high-top gym shoes because I like (they, them) the best.
8. The joke made (we, us) laugh.
9. Martha and (she, her) left an hour ago.
10. Will (we, us) see any Indian relics at the burial mounds?

B. Choosing the Correct Pronoun Number your paper from 1 to 10. Choose the correct pronoun. Write it on your paper.

1. A pod of whales swam past (we, us).
2. The gorilla protects (its, it's) young.
3. Mom took (we, us) girls to the hockey game.
4. Tom and (I, me) went to the museum.
5. Mr. Li showed (we, us) rock hounds some amber.
6. (Its, It's) always interesting to study the stars.
7. (We, Us) coin collectors meet once a month.
8. Those skates belong to Kelly and (she, her).
9. The cat got (its, it's) tail caught in the door.
10. The laundry detergent ad said, "(Its, It's) new and improved."

Chapter 10

The Process of Narrative Writing

When you were a young child, you probably enjoyed hearing stories. There were stories about a sleeping princess, an old woman who lived in a shoe, a lost glass slipper, and many more. A good story can take you to a new world, one filled with sights and sounds and people you might otherwise never have met.

Writing that tells a story is called narrative writing. You have probably written many narratives. When you write a letter to a friend and tell about a trip, that is narrative writing. When you write a composition about the day you took your kitten to the veterinarian, that, too, is a narrative.

In this chapter, you will use the process of narrative writing to write a story of your own. It might be a real story, or it might be an imaginary one. You will also learn skills that will help you to tell a story orally.

1 Thinking About Narrative Writing

Focus

Writing that tells a real or imaginary story is a **narrative**.

Imagine that your class has just finished reading Shirley Jackson's story, "Charles," about a little boy who is always getting into mischief. Your teacher asks you to write a story about a time when you, or someone you know, got into mischief. What would you write?

Example 1

Read and Think. Paul wrote the following story. Think about what makes this story interesting.

> The electricity had been off for two days since the blizzard began. There was nothing to do. I wandered into the kitchen.
>
> My two-year-old sister, Amy, sat in the middle of the floor surrounded by bits of paper. She had taken all the labels off all of the cans in the cupboard. "What are you doing?" I yelled.
>
> Just then, Mom came through the door. At first, she looked angry. Then, she started to laugh. "Well, meals around here are certainly going to be an adventure!" she said.
>
> That night we ate canned pears, cranberry sauce, peas, and ripe olives for dinner. After the blizzard, we continued to open one "surprise can" each night until they were gone.

Think and Discuss. Read Paul's story again. Discuss the following questions with your classmates.

1. Who are the people or characters in Paul's story?
2. Where does the story take place?
3. What happens first? What happens next? What is the conclusion of the story?
4. Is the story based on a real or an imaginary event?

Example 2

Read and Think. Here is another example of narrative writing. It was written by Joy Adamson, a writer who lived and worked in Africa. The narrative describes a real experience with Elsa, a lioness Joy Adamson raised.

> Whenever I sat down, Elsa wanted to play. One day I sat with my back against a tree and started reading a huge bundle of letters. Suddenly I was squashed by Elsa. As I tried to free myself from her three hundred pounds, the letters were scattered all over. I finally got to my feet and began to collect them. Elsa bounced onto me every time I bent down to pick one up, and we rolled together on the ground. Elsa's cubs thought this was great fun. They dashed around after the fluttering paper. I thought that the writers would have enjoyed seeing how much their letters were appreciated. —JOY ADAMSON

Think and Discuss. Discuss these questions in class.

1. Who are the characters in the narrative?
2. What is Elsa like? How do you know?
3. How are the details that tell the story arranged?

Now It's Your Turn

You have just read two examples of narrative writing. Both narratives have characters. Each one has a setting, where the story takes place. The events in each narrative are told in time order—what happened first, what happened next, and so on.

In this chapter, you will learn how to write your own narratives. Keep these two stories in mind as you work. They will help you plan and write your own stories.

2 The Parts of a Narrative

Focus

Every narrative has three important parts: a **setting**, **characters**, and a **plot**.

The writer of a story creates a special world. Sometimes this world is imaginary. At other times it is real. To create this special world, the writer must give his or her story a setting, some characters, and a plot.

Setting The setting of a story is where and when the story takes place. A story might take place in the city of Santa Fe, at a park, in your house, on the beach, or in the Kingdom of the Leprechauns. The story might happen in the present time, at some time in the past, or far into the future.

Characters Every story has one or more characters. The characters can be real or imaginary people. The characters can also be animals, birds, fish, or talking trees.

Plot The plot is what happens in a story. If you made a list of all of the events in a story, in the order that they happen, that list would be the plot of the story.

Exercise **Understanding the Parts of a Narrative**

Read the narrative below. Answer the questions that follow.

from J. P. SOUSA

Lots of folks around Kildugan Creek thought Uncle Jerry was crazy. Instead of selling his rickety little farm after years of dry weather and ruined crops, he stayed on and kept preaching about how there was going to be tons of rain soon. All the rest of the people, except those who stayed, sold their farms and moved to California. Old Jerry wouldn't budge. Day after day he'd sit on his porch playing his harmonica. "Old Jerry's a harmonica-playing fool," his neighbors said. But they admitted that he was very good at it.

One hot afternoon, along about sundown, Uncle Jerry was playing a concert for his bony chickens and his two or three skinny cows. He liked to play marching tunes, especially "The Stars and Stripes Forever," by the great bandmaster, John Philip Sousa. He was blowing away at the piece when suddenly he glanced down and saw a big, black diamondback rattler coiled up at his feet. Uncle Jerry's false teeth almost fell out and the harmonica almost fell in, but he managed to keep on playing because that seemed the sensible thing to do. He played everything he knew and then started over again. When he swung into "The Stars and Stripes Forever" once more, he noticed the snake got kind of a happy look and swayed back and forth with the music.

Uncle Jerry kept playing until he ran out of breath. The sun had gone down and the moon was floating around overhead when, finally, he gave up. "You'll have to go ahead and bite me," he told the snake, "if that's what you're hankerin' to do. I'll be blasted if I'm going to entertain you any more."

The snake seemed to nod as if it understood, and it looked completely satisfied. Then it gave its rattlers a few shakes as if it were applauding, and crawled meekly away.

—ADRIEN STOUTENBERG

1. What is the setting of the story?
2. Identify the characters.
3. How are the events arranged?
4. What is the climax of the story?
5. Tell the plot in your own words.

3 Prewriting: Finding Ideas for a Story

Focus

You can find story ideas in your experiences, your reading, and your imagination.

Finding a Topic

Before you can write a story, you need an idea. To find a story idea, think about the world around you. Use your imagination.

Discovering Stories in Your Experiences Sometimes the best place to look for story ideas is your own life. Think about the places you have gone and the interesting experiences you have had. Think about the vacation your family took last year. Is there some story from that trip just waiting to be told? Think about the day you finally went off the high dive. Wouldn't that make an interesting story? Think about your family and friends. You might write about the day your best friend moved to another state.

Discovering Stories When You Read You can find story ideas in your reading. Sometimes an item in a newspaper or magazine may suggest a story to you. Sometimes, you may find a story idea in a journal entry you wrote or in a letter you received.

Discovering Stories in Your Imagination Your imagination is a great place to find story ideas. You might think about an ordinary animal, like a cat, and imagine what would happen if that cat had magical powers. Would it turn all dogs into mice? Would it fly? Maybe you saw a lonely-looking man on a bus. What do you suppose his story is? You can use your imagination to create one. Think about that crumbling, old house you pass on the way to school. What spooky things happened there last Halloween? Anything can happen in your imagination.

Developing Your Ideas

Once you have an idea for a story, you have to develop your idea by deciding on a setting, characters, and a plot. The best way to develop a story is to ask questions about your idea. Ask *Who? When? Where? What Happened? Why?* and *How?*

Write down the thoughts that you have as you think these questions through. These are your prewriting notes. Look at these notes often as you write your story.

Cassie decided that she wanted to write a story about the day she thought her family had forgotten her birthday. She asked herself some questions and came up with the following prewriting notes.

> **Who?** Me, Mom and Dad, Ned
> **When?** My birthday, Dec. 7, last year
> **Where?** Our house
> **What Happened?** I woke up expecting a great day—things were strange.
> I didn't get any presents.
> No one wished me a happy birthday.
> Mom and Dad went off to work, and Ned left for baseball practice.
> I was really down.
> That night, I had the best surprise party of my life.

Exercises Finding and Developing Story Ideas

A. Finding Ideas Many writers carry a notebook at all times. Then they can record story ideas whenever they think of them.

For the next two or three days, write down in your journal any story ideas that come to you. Share your ideas with your classmates.

B. Developing an Idea Choose the story idea you like the best from Exercise A. You might also find a story idea in the **Power Handbook.** Your idea might be for a real story or an imaginary one. Then ask questions to develop your idea. Write down as many details as you can think of.

4 Prewriting: Organizing a Story

Focus

Organize a story by writing a **plot outline.**

Suppose you have discovered an idea for a story. You have decided on characters and chosen a setting. Now you can continue developing your story.

Making a Plot Outline

Your next step is to organize what will happen in your story. You can do this by making a plot outline. You learned in part 2 that plot is the series of events that tells what happens in a story. When you make a plot outline, you list those events in the order that they happen. This order is called **time order**.

The plot outline below was made by one writer, Alex, as he was getting ready to write a story about getting lost at the circus. Look at his thoughts as he studied his outline.

1. I got to go to the circus on my own.
2. I get lost.
3. ~~2.~~ I go backstage.
4. ~~3.~~ I meet Fuego, the Fire-eater.
5. ~~4.~~ Fuego was so big and scary.
6. ~~5.~~ Fuego helps me find my seat.
7. ~~6.~~ I'm scared to tell him I'm lost but I do.

~~7. I like to read books about the circus.~~

I forgot to say I got lost.

I have to change the order of these two.

The last detail isn't important to my story.

As Alex worked on his plot outline, he noticed some problems. He left out some important information. He also included some information that he did not need in the story. Some of his information was not listed in correct time order. So, Alex fixed his outline. Whenever you organize information for a story, or for any kind of writing, be sure to reread your outline. You might want to change it just as Alex changed his.

Exercises **Organizing the Events in a Story**

A. Organizing Events Imagine that you are writing a story about learning to ride a horse. Your plot outline is shown below. Put it in correct time order.

1. I was excited and scared the first time I rode a horse.
2. Brownie looked gentle and kind, but I was still very nervous.
3. The riding teacher suggested I feed Brownie some sugar cubes.
4. The riding teacher took me to the stables.
5. My horse's name was Brownie.
6. Brownie nibbled the cubes from my hand and looked at me as if she knew I was a friend.
7. She showed me which horse would be mine.
8. That's when I realized Brownie and I would get along just fine.

B. Making a Plot Outline Choose one of the story ideas you developed on page 181. Make a plot outline for it. Remember to record your outline and change it if you have to.

5 Drafting a Story

Focus

Follow your plot outline as you write your rough draft. Use time words to make the order of events clear to the reader.

Drafting Your Story

Now you are ready to write the first draft of your story. As you write, remember that every good story has an introduction, a body, and a conclusion.

The **introduction** is the beginning of a story. It usually tells where and when the story takes place. The introduction also presents most of the major characters in the story.

The **body** is the middle part of the story. This part is where most of the action takes place.

In the **conclusion**, the writer brings the story to a close.

Alex has written a draft of his circus story. Here is the introduction. Notice that he made some changes as he drafted. His reasons for each change are shown in blue on the side.

I should say how much fun the circus was.

Last Tuesday, I finally convinced Mom that I could go to the circus on my own. *The circus was as much fun as I thought it would be.* There was just one thing I hadn't expected. I'd made a wrong turn on the way back ~~to my seat~~ *from buying popcorn*. Suddenly, I was backstage, lost. I was face to face with *the circus's star attraction—the one and only* Fuego *the Fire-eater*.

I forgot to say where I was going when I got lost.

I'd better add a bit more about Fuego.

You can see how Alex thought out his draft. Later you will see how he improved it further.

Using Time Words

Using time words in your story can help the reader follow the order of events. Time words let the reader know when things happened. Look again at Alex's introduction. The phrase "Last Tuesday" tells you when the story took place.

Here are some time words that you can use in your narrative writing.

Time Words and Phrases

next, tomorrow, later, soon, first, just then, suddenly, after dinner, that afternoon, long ago, the last time

Exercises Drafting a Story

A. Adding Time Words Rewrite the following draft. Add time words to make the order of events clear. Then underline the time words that you added.

I had to care for my little sister while Mom and Dad painted the living room. She spilled her cereal all over the kitchen floor. She painted herself with mustard and ketchup. I tried to dress her in her playsuit and she bit me. Mom and Dad asked me if I would baby-sit for her again. What do you think I said?

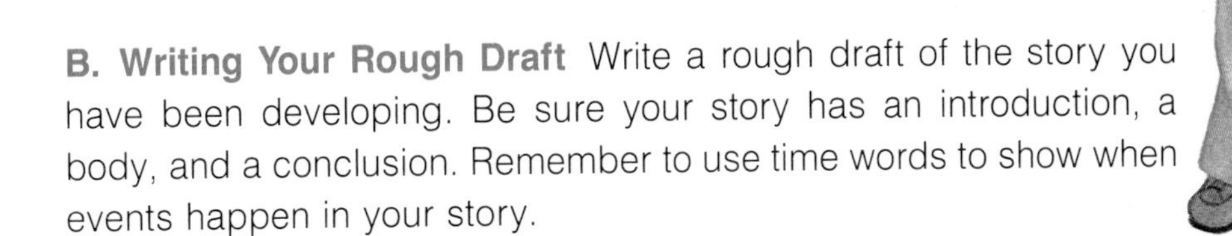

B. Writing Your Rough Draft Write a rough draft of the story you have been developing. Be sure your story has an introduction, a body, and a conclusion. Remember to use time words to show when events happen in your story.

6 Drafting: Using Description and Dialogue

Focus

Use **description** and **dialogue** to make your story more interesting.

Using Description

When you write a story, you may want to describe what a character looks like. You also may want to tell about the setting. Description is an important part of story telling. Good description appeals to the senses of sight, sound, touch, taste, and smell. Good description makes the reader feel almost as if he or she is part of the story.

When Alex was drafting his story, he first described Fuego like this.

> Fuego was a big, scary man.

Alex decided to improve his description so that his readers could get a better picture of the fire-eater. His revised description appeals to the sense of sight.

> Fuego seemed as tall as a tree. He was dressed in purple. In each huge hand, he carried a torch, ready for eating.

To learn more about how to write good description, see Chapter 15.

Using Dialogue

One way you get to know people is by talking with them. In a story, a reader gets to know the characters by "listening" to the dialogue. Dialogue is the conversation between characters in a story. Use dialogue to tell your readers about your characters and to keep the action moving in your story.

Look again at Alex's draft of his story. First he had written this sentence.

> Fuego asked me why I was backstage.

Alex then decided he did not want just to tell his readers what happened. He wanted to show them. He needed to add some dialogue. He changed his draft in this way.

> His voice shouted down at me, "What are you doing back here?"

Now Alex's readers both see and hear Fuego. By using description and dialogue, Alex has made Fuego seem more real. Alex has also made his story more interesting.

Exercises Using Description and Dialogue

A. Writing a Description Here are five subjects. Choose one, or select a subject of your own. Describe the subject in detail. Try to appeal to some or all of the five senses.

1. a totem pole
2. a pizza
3. a park in spring
4. a float in a parade
5. a clown

B. Adding Description and Dialogue Add description, dialogue, or both to the rough draft of your story.

7 Revising a Narrative

Focus

Revise your story carefully before making a final copy.

After you finish the draft of your story, put it away for a while. Then reread it and ask yourself the following questions.

Guidelines for Revising a Narrative

1. Are the characters, plot, and setting clear?
2. Do the events in my story follow time order? Does my story have an introduction, a body, and a conclusion?
3. Can I add description or dialogue to make my story seem more real to the reader?

Sample Revision

Here is the body of Alex's story. Notice how he has started to revise his narrative.

More descriptive words needed here.

Fuego seemed as tall as ~~a~~ an oak tree. He was dressed in shiny purple. In each huge hand, he carried a flaming torch, ready for eating.

He scared me. He looked angry. His booming voice shouted down at me, "What are you doing back here?"

I should describe Fuego's voice.

I said I was lost. The circus band was playing ~~a song.~~ "Waltzing Matilda."

I should tell what song the band was playing.

As Alex continued to work on his draft, he noticed several problems. Then he thought about how he could correct them.

Problem: The second paragraph is boring. I need to describe what happened.

Result: Alex added these lines: *He scared me so much that I spilled my bag of popcorn all over the floor. Fuego's face got red and angry.*

Problem: I need more dialogue.

Result: Alex changed the third paragraph. *My knees began to shake. "I'm lost," I whispered.*

Problem: The circus band really has nothing to do with this story.

Result: Alex left out the last sentence.

Read the final copy of Alex's story on page 191. Notice how his revisions helped to make his story more interesting.

Proofreading Your Narrative

Before you can make a final copy of your revised narrative, you must proofread it. Look for any mistakes you might have made in grammar, capitalization, punctuation, or spelling. Carefully correct any mistakes you find.

As you proofread, give special attention to the way you wrote dialogue. When you write a character's exact words, you are writing a direct quotation. There are special rules for capitalizing and punctuating direct quotations. You can learn more about capitalizing and punctuating quotations by looking at the **Power Handbook**. There you will find rules and examples to help you proofread your narrative.

Exercises **Revising a Narrative**

A. Adding the Correct Punctuation Read the following conversation from a story. Copy it on a separate sheet of paper, using the correct punctuation for dialogue.

> Hi, Greg, Ann said. Did you pick up the corn chips and salsa? Yes, but I forgot to bring the records you asked for, Greg said. Don't worry. Tony is bringing a radio, Ann answered. As they put the food away, she asked, Are you sure Alice knows what time the party begins? Greg smiled and said, I'm sure. I reminded her this afternoon.

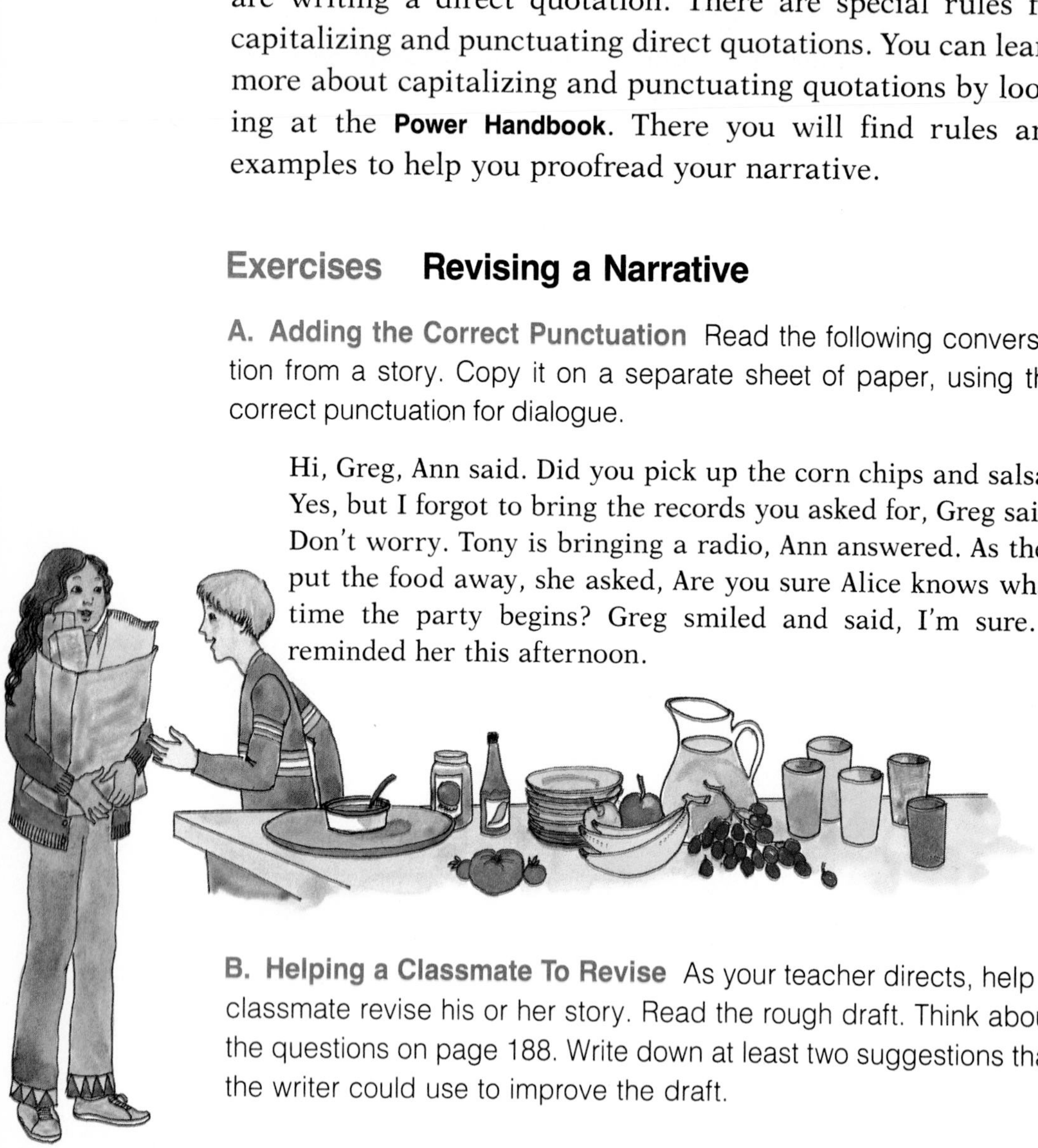

B. Helping a Classmate To Revise As your teacher directs, help a classmate revise his or her story. Read the rough draft. Think about the questions on page 188. Write down at least two suggestions that the writer could use to improve the draft.

8 Making a Final Copy

Focus

After you have proofread your story, give it a good title. Then make a final copy.

Your final copy should be neat and easy to read. It should also include an interesting title that hints at what the story is about. Write your title on the line above the first line of your story. Here is the final copy of Alex's story.

Where There's Smoke, There's Fuego

Last Tuesday, I finally convinced Mom I could go to the circus on my own. The circus was as much fun as I thought it would be. There was just one thing I hadn't expected. I'd made a wrong turn on my way back from buying popcorn. Suddenly, I was lost backstage. I was face to face with the circus's star attraction—the one and only Fuego the Fire-eater.

Fuego seemed as tall as an oak tree. He was dressed in shiny purple. In each huge hand, he carried a flaming torch, ready for eating.

He scared me so much that I spilled my bag of popcorn all over the floor. Fuego's face got red and angry. His booming voice shouted down at me, "What are you doing back here?"

My knees began to shake. "I'm lost," I whispered.

Fuego smiled, and somehow he didn't seem quite so big anymore. He said, "I got lost, too, the first time I went to the circus. It was so much fun, I decided to join it!"

Fuego showed me back to my seat. We even stopped along the way, and Fuego bought me a new bag of popcorn.

Exercise Making a Final Copy and Sharing

Make a final copy of your story. Include a title. When you are done, proofread your story one more time. Exchange stories with your classmates. Read and enjoy one another's work.

Speaking and Listening

Storytelling

Before people could write stories, they told stories. Stories became a special tradition. They were handed down from one generation to the next.

A good storyteller knows how to bring a story to life. The listeners feel the excitement. The suspense grips them. They listen to every word, eager to find out what happens next.

Here are some storytelling tips.

Guidelines for Good Storytelling

1. Choose a story with plenty of action and good dialogue.
2. Know the story well.
3. Practice telling your story. See page 199 for tips on practicing.
4. Use your voice to bring the story to life. When a character whispers, you whisper. If a door creaks, let your voice creak, too.
5. Use hand gestures and facial expressions that will help you tell the story.

Exercises Telling and Listening to Stories

A. Telling a Story Practice telling the story you wrote for this chapter. Then tell the story to your classmates.

B. Listening to a Story Ask an older person to tell you a special story about when he or she was your age. Listen especially to the way the storyteller uses his or her voice. Try to picture the story in your imagination.

Creative Writing

Choose one of the pictures below. Create a story, using the picture you choose as your idea starter. Use the writing process that you have learned in this chapter when writing your narrative.

Using English in History

Narration can be used to make history come to life. Many writers choose people, places, and events from history when they write stories. Irene Hunt, for example, used the Civil War as the setting for a book she wrote called *Across Five Aprils*. It is a story about how the war affected a young boy. Hazel Krantz wrote a story called "They Ride Like the Wind" about a rider for the Pony Express. Here is part of that story.

> Leading his exhausted mustang pony and clutching the mochila filled with mail, the sixteen-year-old boy staggered through the blizzard to an isolated cabin. After warming him with coffee and a good meal, the kindly settlers begged, "Stay the night. This is no weather in which to ride."
>
> "No, thanks," the boy said, shaking his head. "This is the Pony Express. The mail has to go through."

Exercise Telling a Story from History

Read more about the Pony Express. Look for information in your social studies book, encyclopedias, and other books in the library. Then write a story in which you are a rider for the Pony Express. Who else is in your story? What happens? How does your story turn out? Your class might want to publish a booklet of all the stories. You could call it *Tales from the Pony Express*.

Chapter 10 Review

A. Using Time Order Read the following sentences. Put them in correct time order.

1. She thinks of good and bad things about being invisible.
2. The orange man gives Blanca a tiny bottle of orange liquid.
3. She drinks the green liquid and is visible again.
4. She decides she does not want to be invisible.
5. She becomes invisible.
6. Blanca is bored and wishes that something interesting would happen.
7. This time, the orange man gives her a bottle of green liquid.
8. She drinks it.
9. Suddenly, a little orange man appears.
10. The orange man appears again.

B. Writing Dialogue Change each statement below to a line of dialogue. Be sure to capitalize and punctuate each line of dialogue correctly.

Example: Rob said that we should call home.
"We should call home," Rob said.

1. JoAnn asked us if that was a robin.
2. Dennis urged us to make up our minds.
3. He announced that he finished the puzzle.
4. The zookeeper warned us not to disturb the panda.
5. She asked us to point out the North Star.
6. Lauren asked Mom what causes a thunderstorm.
7. Jeff said that Mr. Anderson raises bees.
8. Terri noted that a chameleon changes color.
9. Dad suggested we find a quieter place to study.
10. Mr. Owens asked us to sing that verse again.

Chapter 11

Improving Speaking and Listening Skills

Have you ever lost your voice? You probably had to write down everything you wanted to say. You may have noticed for the first time how much of your day is spent speaking.

Speaking is a very natural activity. In fact, it is sometimes hard to remember that speaking is a skill. However, you can learn more about speaking and improve your skill. You can also learn how to improve the closely related skill of listening.

In this chapter, you will learn about speaking and listening in some special situations. This chapter will show you how to prepare and deliver a talk. You will also learn how to listen carefully to someone else's talk. Finally, you will find out how to take part in and lead a discussion.

1 Preparing a Talk

Focus

Prepare a talk by using the process of writing. Then make note cards and practice.

You learned about the stages in the writing process in Chapter 6. You do not always express your ideas in writing. Sometimes you will have to talk in front of a group. You might be making an announcement, giving a report, or telling about something that happened to you. Much of what you learned about the writing process can be used in preparing a talk. Choosing a topic and purpose, gathering ideas, and organizing your thoughts are all part of preparing a talk. However, you will not write your talk out word for word. Instead you will make note cards and practice your talk out loud.

Using Note Cards

Certainly, you do not want to read your talk word for word. Therefore, you prepare note cards. Note cards, such as the one below, help you remember ideas and stay on the subject.

II. Ramses II was a famous Egyptian pharaoh

A. Reigned from 1290 to 1224 B.C.
B. Came to the throne at an early age
C. Was co-ruler with his father

Each note card needs only enough information to jog your memory. A fact or two, written on a 3″ × 5″ note card, will work well. The cards are easy to hold and each one may be set aside after it is used.

Practicing Your Talk

Once you have prepared your talk, practice presenting it out loud. Here are some guidelines.

Guidelines for Practicing a Talk

1. Read through your notes several times.
2. Practice your talk in front of a mirror. Notice your posture, the expression on your face, and your hand movements.
3. Practice your talk aloud several times. Record yourself on a tape recorder if possible. Does your voice sound natural?
4. Present your talk to family members or friends. Use their suggestions to make your talk better.
5. Practice until you feel relaxed. You will learn more about delivering your talk in part 2 of this chapter.

Exercises Preparing and Practicing a Talk

A. You will be giving a three-minute talk. You will be talking about a hobby of interest to you. First narrow this topic by choosing a particular hobby. Gather facts on your topic. Prepare the notes you will use. Include information about what equipment or supplies are needed for your hobby. Also tell why this hobby is fun. Write your notes on 3″ × 5″ note cards. Remember, you need only enough material on each card to jog your memory.

B. Practice your talk before two or three of your classmates. Discuss their ideas for improving your talk. Make any necessary changes. Use the guidelines in this lesson and in part 2.

2 Delivering a Talk

Focus

How you look and how you sound are important to the success of your talk.

The way you present a talk is important to your audience. You are presenting your ideas, but you are also presenting yourself. These guidelines will help you make a good impression when you deliver a talk.

Guidelines for Delivering a Talk

1. **Stand tall.** Your posture is important. Stand still, but do not stand stiffly. Take a deep breath to help you relax.
2. **Keep your eyes on your listeners.** Look directly at your audience. This is called eye contact. Each person in the audience will feel you are talking directly to him or her. Keep your expression pleasant. Look at your notes only when necessary.
3. **Speak loudly.** Your audience wants to hear what you are saying. Be sure your voice is loud enough, but not too loud. Try to keep your voice natural. Speak clearly and slowly.
4. **Use gestures when you speak.** Your face and hands can help you make a point. Keep your gestures, or body movements, natural. Use only gestures that will emphasize an idea. Do not distract your listeners from what you are saying.
5. **Use visual aids.** If they would help, use visual aids, such as maps, charts, and pictures. Be sure any visual aids you use are large enough to be seen. Hold or point to your visual aids so that you can also be seen.

Exercises Delivering a Talk

A. In part 1, you planned and practiced a talk. Now give your talk in front of the class. Review the guidelines in this lesson before you present your talk.

B. Study the situation below. Answer the questions that follow. Write the answers on your paper.

> Diego was explaining how to make a piñata. First, he read several facts from his paper to the class. Then, he showed a very large piñata he had made. He pointed to it as he told about the materials he used. He began to speak so softly that it was hard to hear him. Finally, he looked at the students and smiled. He told them they would enjoy making their own piñatas.

1. Name two things Diego did that helped when he gave his talk.
2. Name two things that could be improved.

3 Listening to and Judging Talks

Focus

Good listening is a skill. Only a good listener can fairly judge a talk.

Knowing how to listen to a talk is just as important as knowing how to give one. A good listener gets more out of what is being said. Here are some guidelines for becoming a better listener.

Guidelines for Listening to a Talk

1. Sit where you can easily see and hear the speaker.
2. Pay close attention to the speaker. Do not allow yourself to be distracted.
3. Keep eye contact with the speaker. Show that you are interested.
4. Try to pick out main ideas. Listen for key words that the speaker uses. These signal that the speaker is giving important information. For example, important ideas follow words like *first*, *next*, *for example*, *most importantly*, and *let me point out*.

Sometimes you will be asked to evaluate or comment on someone else's speech. To do this, you must listen carefully. Then you can make a fair judgment about the speaker. Here are some guidelines for judging a talk.

Guidelines for Judging a Talk

1. What was the main point of the speech? Did the speaker make it clear?
2. Was enough information presented about the subject? Was any information unnecessary? Did the facts seem correct?
3. Did the speaker's ideas fit together well?
4. Did the speaker stand tall? Did the speaker appear relaxed?
5. Did the speaker look directly at the audience?
6. Was the speaker easy to hear and understand?
7. Were the speaker's gestures helpful and natural?

Exercises **Listening to and Judging a Talk**

A. Listen to the evening news on television. Pay attention to how the newscaster speaks and looks. Notice how many of the guidelines he or she follows. Write a brief paragraph telling about the newscaster's presentation.

B. Use the guidelines in this lesson to make an evaluation form for judging a speaker. Make one heading *Content*. Under that list: *Clear topic*, *Clear purpose*, *Enough information*, *Organized information*. Make another heading *Presentation*. Under that put: *Eye contact*, *Posture*, *Voice*, *Gestures*. Use the form to judge the speeches of two classmates. Mark *Good*, *Fair*, or *Needs Work* next to each category.

4 What Is a Group Discussion?

Focus

A **discussion** is a good way to share ideas. You can help a discussion run smoothly.

Sometimes you share your thoughts with others about an idea or a problem. This is called a **discussion**. You can use discussion to plan an event, solve a problem, or study for school. Follow these guidelines for a group discussion.

Guidelines for Taking Part in a Discussion

1. Be informed. Be sure you have done any necessary reading and research. Add any new information you have.
2. Stay on the subject.
3. Ask questions
   a. to clarify a point.
   b. to get information.
   c. to help the discussion move forward.
4. Listen carefully to others.
5. When you disagree, say so. However, be polite.

Leading a Discussion

If you are the leader of a discussion, you have some special jobs to do.

Guidelines for Leading a Discussion

1. When you begin the discussion, state the problem.
2. Ask questions when a point is not clear.
3. Keep order. Make sure everyone takes turns talking.
4. At the end of the discussion, sum up what has been decided or discussed.

Exercises Talking in Groups

A. Read the following statements about a group discussion. Write *True* or *False* on your paper for each one. Then rewrite each false statement so that it gives correct information.

1. In a discussion, you talk with others about an idea.
2. The discussion leader's only job is keeping the discussion moving forward.
3. The discussion leader should do most of the talking.
4. Participants in a discussion should not ask questions.
5. The discussion leader should be sure everyone has a chance to express his or her ideas.
6. Participants in a discussion should ask questions only to get information.
7. It is important for a participant in a group discussion to listen to what others say.
8. People in a discussion should never disagree.
9. One of the discussion leader's duties is to keep order.
10. Even a disagreement should be stated politely.

B. Pretend that a scout troop wants to collect old newspapers and glass from the neighborhood. The group discusses this problem: How should the troop organize the collection? During the discussion, the following comments are made. Which comments move the discussion forward? Which seem out of place?

1. I think we should collect the papers and glass on Saturday morning.
2. What are we going to do with the money we get at the recycling center?
3. The recycling center says that colored glass should be separated from clear glass.
4. Old newspapers are a fire hazard. We will have to store them carefully.
5. My sister cut her hand on a piece of broken glass and had to have five stitches.

5 Examining Group Discussions

Focus

Both the participants and the leader must follow the guidelines for a good discussion.

The discussion that follows took place at a meeting of a student committee. Susan, Carmen, Jason, and Nan had been asked by the P.T.A. to suggest ways to improve the school playground. Nan is the leader of the discussion. You learned the guidelines for group discussion in part 4. Think about those guidelines as you read the discussion.

NAN: We have been asked to decide how we want the playground area used. We also need to decide what equipment should be added or removed. Any ideas?

JASON: I don't like that playground. There's too much stuff for the little kids.

CARMEN: I think we should talk about safety. The merry-go-round is dangerous.

JASON: C'mon, Carmen. What are you, a traffic cop? You don't know anything about safety.

SUSAN: Excuse me, Jason. Maybe Carmen should tell us why she thinks the merry-go-round is dangerous.

CARMEN: I do know about safety. I went to the playground before this meeting and watched for awhile. The big kids push it too fast and scare the little ones. The other problem is that the little kids can be pulled under it.

SUSAN: I have another idea. Do you think the playing field should be made any larger?

JASON: Super! Maybe the sliding board and swings could be moved closer together to give the older kids more room. We need some climbing bars, too.

NAN: What about the merry-go-round?

CARMEN: Maybe we should talk to someone who knows more about the equipment.

NAN: Good thinking. Now let's see. So far we think we should have two areas, right? We want a playground for the little kids near the building. We'd like a larger playing field for the older ones farther away. I think we've reached a good stopping point. We can talk again tomorrow.

Exercise Evaluating a Discussion

Review the guidelines for discussion in part 4. Evaluate the sample discussion. On your paper, answer these questions.

1. As discussion leader, how does Nan get the discussion off to a good start?
2. Do Jason's first two comments follow the guidelines? Explain your answer.
3. Why is Susan's first comment important?
4. How does Carmen show that she is an informed participant?
5. How does Susan's second comment help the discussion move along?
6. Does Jason's third comment more closely follow the guidelines for discussion than his first did? Explain.
7. What topic does Nan steer the group back to?
8. How is Carmen's last comment useful for the meeting that will take place the next day?
9. Does the way Nan ends the meeting follow the guidelines for leading a discussion? Explain.
10. What should Nan do first at tomorrow's meeting?

Using English in Science

Now you know how to prepare a talk and deliver it. You will have many opportunities to give talks in other classes.

Sometimes in science you will be asked to show how to do something. This is one kind of oral report. It is called a demonstration speech. In a demonstration speech, you show and tell at the same time. Here are a few guidelines to help you prepare your demonstration.

1. Do the demonstration several times yourself. Practice until you feel sure of yourself.
2. Make notes as you practice. Your notes should list the purpose of the demonstration, the materials you use, each step you will go through, and the results.
3. Do not put your notes on 3″ × 5″ cards. Instead, write the same information you would put on a card, a fact or two, on a sheet of paper. Write in very large letters. You will be able to place your notes so that you can read them, but your hands will be free to do the demonstration.
4. Practice doing the demonstration and telling about it at the same time. Use your notes to tell the audience about the purpose, materials, steps, and results.
5. Do one step at a time. Go slowly and speak clearly. Be sure your audience can follow what you are doing.

Exercise Giving a Demonstration Speech

Give a demonstration of a science experiment. Choose a simple experiment from your science book, or ask your teacher to help you choose one that ties in to what you will be learning in science class. Use the guidelines above and on page 200 to help you practice. When you feel ready, present the experiment to your class.

Chapter 11 Review

Giving Talks and Participating in Group Discussions Read the following statements. Number your paper from 1 to 15. Write *True* or *False* on your paper.

1. Do not practice what you will say in a talk. You might not sound natural.
2. It is better not to disagree with other participants in a group discussion.
3. Slouching when you give a talk makes a bad impression on your audience.
4. Note cards should contain all the information that can be written on them.
5. It is the group leader's job to keep everyone on the subject.
6. Listening is a skill and can be improved.
7. It does not matter if one or two group members remain silent during a discussion.
8. You can evaluate a talk fairly only if you listened to the talk very carefully.
9. Take care to look at your notes, not at the audience. Otherwise, you may lose track of your ideas.
10. Keep your hands quietly by your sides while you give a talk.
11. Deciding whether or not the information in a talk is accurate is not part of evaluating a talk.
12. Never ask questions during a discussion.
13. If you are a listener, you do not need to look at the person speaking.
14. Discussion may be used only for problem solving.
15. Giving a talk involves more than knowing what to say about your subject.

Cumulative Review

Unit 2

Composition

Writing Narratives Look at the following groups of words. Use some of these words to write a story. Remember to include characters, plot, and setting.

explorer—ocean—storm
huge—bear—terror
noisy—amusement park—scary
favorite—vacation—exciting

Grammar

Pronouns Number your paper from 1 to 15. Choose the correct form of the pronoun from the parentheses. Write it on your paper.

1. Rebecca and (me, I) dug for clams.
2. The decathlon finalists were Alex and (she, her).
3. A frog hopped by the other campers and (he, him).
4. (We, Us) two cleaned out Aunt Lena's gutters.
5. The gerbil made a nest in (its, it's) cage.
6. The citizenship award was given to (us, we) scouts.
7. (Lauren and I, I and Lauren) listened to the crickets chirping loudly.
8. The cowboy did rope tricks for (they, them).
9. I flew (my, mine) kite in the Chinese New Year parade.
10. Please repair Brenda's skates and take (they, them) to (she, her).
11. Can the dog find (its, it's) bone?
12. (We, Us) cousins had a picnic at the park.
13. Jonathan and (she, her) planned the class party.
14. Give the folders to Jana and (he, him).
15. The mime presented a show for (us, we) students.

Related Skills

A. Study Skills The following five statements are incorrect. Rewrite each statement so that it is true.

1. A short answer test question should be answered with one or two words.
2. SQ3R stands for *survey, question, read, research,* and *repeat.*
3. The glossary lists the chapters in a book.
4. Always answer the hardest questions on a test first.
5. To find the definition of *cumulus* in a science book, look in the index.

B. Speaking and Listening Skills Read the speaking situation described below. List the things the speaker did well. List the things that could be improved.

In social studies class, Rita gave a report on the pyramids of Egypt. Then she showed a model of a pyramid. At first, she stared at her notes a great deal. As she talked, she pointed out parts of the pyramid. At first, she spoke very quickly, but she slowed down as she went along. Everyone in the room could hear her very well.

C. Dictionary Skills On your paper, write short answers to the questions below. Write in complete sentences.

1. What do the guide words in a dictionary tell you?
2. How many syllables does *dromedary* have?
3. Name two things, besides the definition, that the dictionary entry tells you.
4. Where can you find help if you do not understand the symbols for the pronunciation of a word?
5. How can a thesaurus help you?

UNIT 3

Dreams and Descriptions

Unit 3 will help you to see and describe your world more carefully. You will learn to use adjectives and adverbs to tell about how something looks, sounds, tastes, smells, and feels. You will see how you can tell about everyday things in a new, different way with the special language of poetry. Finally, you will learn to explain how something works or how something is done.

The skills you learn in this unit will help you in all of your school subjects. In social studies, you will be better able to describe a foreign country. In science, you will be able to explain how a battery works.

These skills are not just for school. No matter where you are, you will be able to share your ideas and dreams with others.

TO DARK EYES DREAMING

Dreams go fast and far
these days.
They go by rocket thrust.
They go arrayed
in lights
or in the dust of stars.
Dreams, these days,
go fast and far.
Dreams are young, these days,
or very old,
They can be black
or blue or gold.
They need no special charts,
nor any fuel.
It seems, only one rule applies,
to all our dreams—
They will not fly except in open sky.
A fenced-in dream
will die.

—ZILPHA KEATLEY SNYDER

Chapter 12

Adjectives for Strong Description

Imagine that someone put this ad in your local newspaper:

> Bicycle. With fenders, seat, handlebars.
> Call for information.

What do you know about this bicycle? Is it old, new, or free? Does it have tan fenders, or a leather seat? Does it have shiny handlebars or a flat tire?

The answers to all these questions can be found by adding adjectives to the ad. Adjectives are words that modify nouns and pronouns.

In this chapter, you will learn how to use adjectives correctly. You will discover how adjectives can help you do the *most interesting*, *accurate*, *entertaining*, and *colorful* writing you have ever done.

1 What Are Adjectives?

Focus

An **adjective** is a word that modifies a noun or pronoun.

What do you imagine when you read this sentence?

I saw a dog.

This sentence expresses a complete idea. However, words may be added that describe *dog* more exactly.

I saw a *huge* dog.
I saw a *lovable* dog.

Words like *huge* and *lovable* are called adjectives. **Adjectives** are words that modify, or change, the idea expressed by a noun or pronoun. Adjectives usually come before the word they modify. Adjectives can also come after the word. Sometimes a state-of-being verb stands between a noun or pronoun and the word describing that noun or pronoun.

Dark clouds rolled across the sky.
The decorations are *colorful*.
She seems *happy*.

Sometimes more than one adjective modifies the same word. Usually, adjectives used together are separated with commas. Adjectives telling number, shape, and color often do not follow this rule.

Large, noisy crows flew over the field.
Three noisy crows flew over the field.

Key to Writing and Speaking Adjectives make your writing and speaking more exact and more interesting.

Example: *Many huge* alligators live in *that warm*, *murky* pond.

Exercises Finding and Using Adjectives

A. In each of the following pairs of sentences, only the adjectives have been changed. Number your paper from 1 to 5. For each pair of sentences, list each noun that is modified. After the noun, write the adjectives that modify it.

Example: a. The tall man lifted the heavy box.
b. The strong man lifted the enormous box.
man—tall, strong   box—heavy, enormous

1. a. The small girl ran through the grassy field.
   b. The careless girl ran through the muddy field.
2. a. Twenty clowns wore silly costumes.
   b. Wacky clowns wore huge costumes.
3. a. Many fairgoers won different prizes.
   b. Lucky fairgoers won valuable prizes.
4. a. Soft music played on an old radio.
   b. Classical music played on a nearby radio.
5. a. The newborn puppies were frisky and playful.
   b. The spotted puppies were wet and muddy.

B. Rewrite the following five sentences. Add one adjective for each noun in each sentence. Underline the adjectives you have used.

Example: The boy read a book.
The young boy read a funny book.

1. The wind blew down the barn.
2. The man painted a picture of the sunset.
3. Boys fished in the pond behind the barn.
4. The tiger slept in a cage.
5. Bicyclists ventured into the tunnel.

C. Writing Using words only, create your own self-portrait in a paragraph. Describe yourself so well that a classmate could recognize you from just your "word picture." Have your teacher collect all the paragraphs and pass them back at random. Try to guess who wrote the description that is given to you.

2 Adjectives Tell *What Kind, How Many*, or *Which One*

Focus

An **adjective** tells *what kind, how many*, or *which one* about the noun or pronoun it modifies.

Some Adjectives Tell *What Kind*

Many adjectives tell *what kind* about a noun or pronoun. Here are some of those adjectives.

furr*y*	play*ful*	lov*able*
color*ful*	vici*ous*	rest*less*

The five endings in italics are often found on adjectives: *-y, -ful, -ous, -able,* and *-less*.

Some Adjectives Tell *How Many*

Some adjectives tell *how many* about a noun. The adjectives in italics tell *how many* about the noun they modify.

six animals   *several* people   *few* lions   *more* insects

Some Adjectives Tell *Which Ones*

Adjectives can also tell *which one* or *which ones* about the nouns they modify. These adjectives that point to a noun always come before the noun.

this koala	*these* squirrels
that kangaroo	*those* rabbits

Exercises Using Adjectives That Tell *What Kind*, *How Many*, or *Which One*

A. Number your paper from 1–10. Write the adjective in each sentence. Next to the adjective, write the noun it describes.

1. There were joyful shouts from the stands.
2. Eight children raced past.
3. Sam had collected speckled stones.
4. Jed wore a warm jacket.
5. Curt climbed several hills.
6. We sang funny songs on the trip.
7. The bag contains some sandwiches.
8. The question has many answers.
9. Mr. Chalmers is a capable carpenter.
10. Several swans swam past the boat.

B. Supply the kind of adjective asked for in the parentheses.

Example: __________ trees fell into the ravine. (how many)
Four trees fell into the ravine.

1. Put these __________ boxes on that shelf. (what kind)
2. We had __________ sheets of green paper. (how many)
3. People crowded into __________ room. (which one)
4. Look at __________ silver tray of cheeses. (which one)
5. We bought these __________ pears. (what kind)

C. Writing In this exercise, you will write your own story using adjectives that tell *what kind*, *how many*, or *which one*. The following list gives twelve nouns with an adjective modifying each noun. Use at least five of these combinations to write a one-paragraph story.

brave captain	many planets	dangerous trip
fearless crew	this adventure	purple skin
this spaceship	that crater	single antenna
six creatures	rocky ground	poisonous air

3 Articles

> **Focus**
>
> The words *a*, *an*, and *the* are special adjectives called **articles.**

The words *a, an,* and *the* form a special group of adjectives. They are called **articles**.

You may use the word *the* before singular or plural nouns beginning with any letter.

the alphabet   *the* sentences

You may use the words *a* and *an* before singular nouns only. Follow these rules in choosing the correct article.

1. Use *a* before words beginning with consonant sounds.

a person   *a* fresh egg
a story   *a* crisp apple
a glass   *a* good idea

2. Use *an* before words beginning with vowel sounds.

an average person   *an* egg
an impossible story   *an* apple
an enormous glass   *an* idea

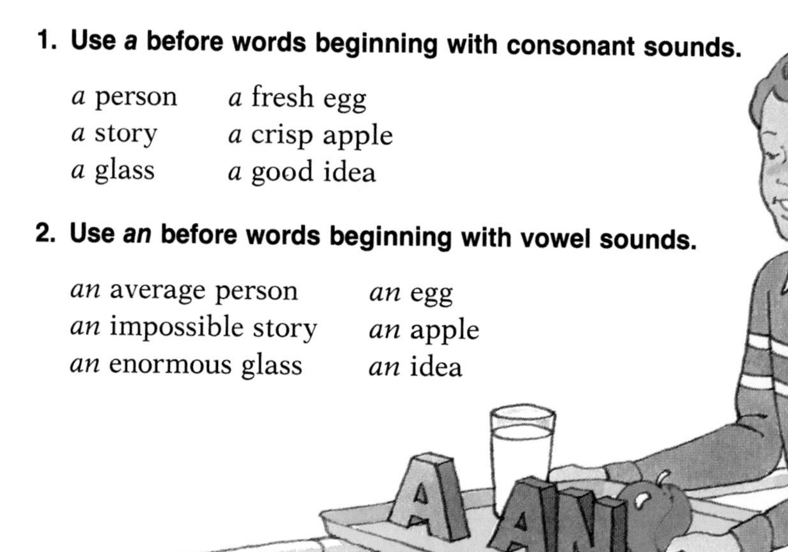

Some words begin with a silent *h*. In these words, you do not say the *h* sound. Instead, you pronounce the word with the sound of the vowel after the *h*. Therefore, you use *an*.

an honor   *an* hour   *an* honest child

Exercises Using Articles

A. Copy the following sentences. Fill in the blanks with *a* or *an*.

1. Do you keep ______ diary?
2. Mr. Jones is ______ honorable judge.
3. Sarah held ______ brush and ______ comb.
4. Gordon got ______ haircut.
5. The train left ______ hour ago.
6. ______ dachshund has ______ long body.
7. Diana tossed ______ horseshoe.
8. ______ old woman opened ______ umbrella.
9. I had ______ nightmare last night.
10. The woodsman carried ______ ax and ______ saw.

B. Number your paper from 1 to 10. In each sentence, decide whether *a* or *an* could be used to replace *the*. Write your choice.

1. The iceberg floated out to sea.
2. We took a tour of the new home.
3. Captain Pete kept his boat in the harbor.
4. The idea came quickly to him.
5. Every morning, the rooster wakes us.
6. The egg in that bowl has a cracked shell.
7. Our health class visited the city hospital.
8. Jerry found his first answer in the atlas.
9. Seven actors came through the entrance.
10. Sean made the agreement yesterday.

C. Writing Write five sentences, using two of the nouns below in each. Place an article and another adjective before each noun.

Example: ringmaster, audience
A tall ringmaster greeted the eager audience.

1. circus
2. elephant
3. clown
4. tricks
5. act
6. audience
7. acrobat
8. lions
9. man
10. woman
11. children
12. ringmaster

4 Using Adjectives Correctly

Focus

This, *that*, *these*, and *those* are adjectives used to point out specific people, places, things, and ideas.

This, that, these, and *those* tell *which one* or *which ones*. They point out specific nouns and pronouns.

This book is more interesting than *that* one.
These pencils are sharper than *those* pencils.

Them and *Those*

The word *them* is not an adjective. Never use *them* to modify a noun.

Incorrect: Al filled *them* bottles.
Correct: Al filled *those* bottles *or* Al filled *them*.

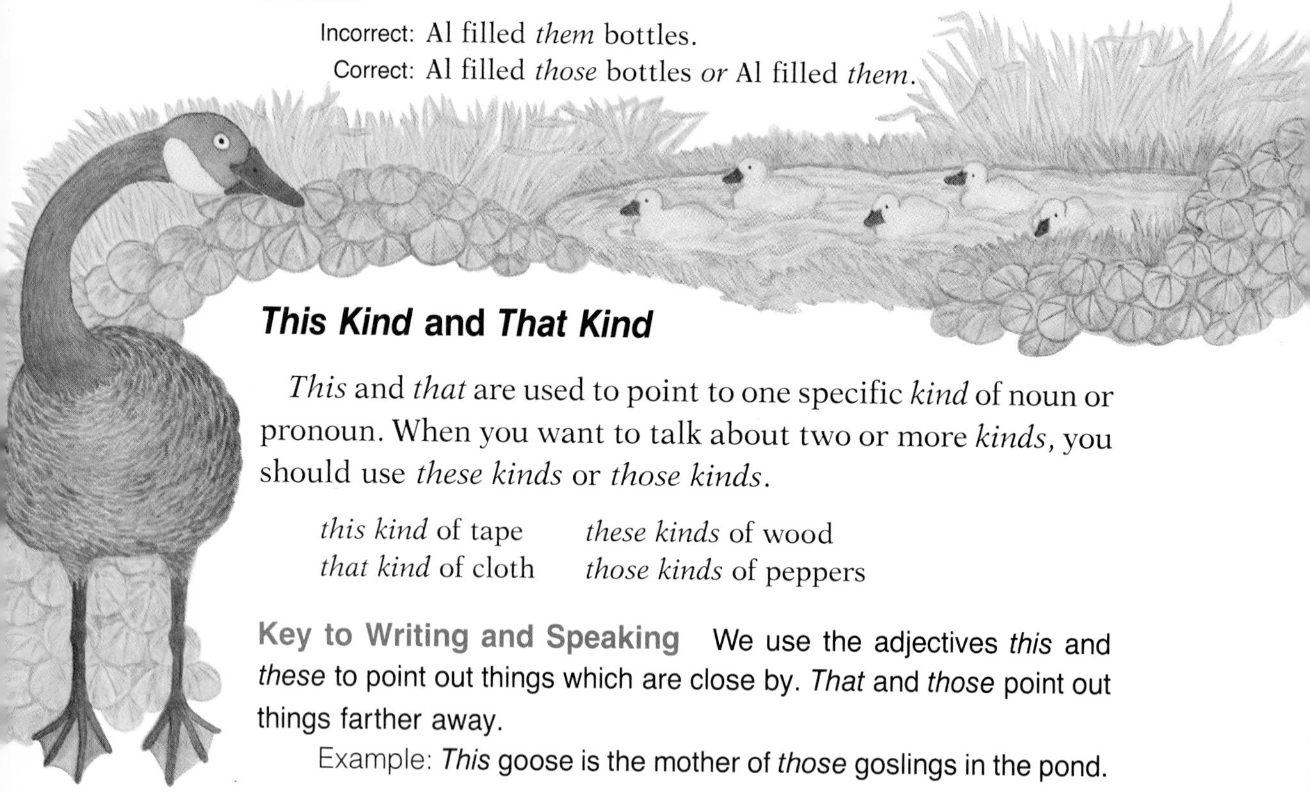

This Kind and *That Kind*

This and *that* are used to point to one specific *kind* of noun or pronoun. When you want to talk about two or more *kinds*, you should use *these kinds* or *those kinds*.

this kind of tape	*these kinds* of wood
that kind of cloth	*those kinds* of peppers

Key to Writing and Speaking We use the adjectives *this* and *these* to point out things which are close by. *That* and *those* point out things farther away.

Example: *This* goose is the mother of *those* goslings in the pond.

Exercises Using Adjectives Correctly

A. Choose the right word for each sentence. Write your choice on your paper.

1. (Those, Them) firecrackers exploded.
2. (That, Those) kind of dog biscuit is nutritious.
3. Does (this, these) kind of ski mask keep you warm?
4. Alethia always uses (this, these) kind of paper for her watercolor paintings.
5. (That, Them, Those) kind of bee stings.
6. Many farmers grow (this, these) kinds of vegetables.
7. A queen wore (them, those) jewels.
8. Terry likes (this, these) kinds of projects.
9. (Those, Them) reins control the horse.
10. Marietta built (that, those) kind of model airplane.

B. Copy each sentence on your paper and correct the words in italics that are wrong. Four sentences contain no error. Write *Correct* for these.

1. Lauren liked the mittens but never wore *them*.
2. I got *those* kind of braces, too.
3. *Those* are her favorite school shoes.
4. *Them* boys jumped into the pool.
5. *That* kinds of trumpets are the loudest.
6. Walter bought six sheets of *them* kind of paper.
7. Mother didn't like *those* kind of juice.
8. Hanna mailed seven of those pictures to *them*.
9. *Them* are the best tasting tomatoes.
10. *Those* kinds of rules make traffic safer.

C. Writing You are showing your garden to a visitor from the city. Standing at the edge of your garden, you point out and identify plants near you and some farther away. Your garden contains beans, corn, broccoli, cabbage, and tomatoes. Write a paragraph about your garden. Use some of the adjectives you have just studied.

5 Making Comparisons with Adjectives

Focus

An adjective can be used to **compare** people, places, things, and ideas.

Adjectives have a different form when they are used to compare.

Here are the rules to follow for using short adjectives in comparisons.

1. When you compare two people, places, things, or ideas, you usually add *-er* to the adjective.

tall + er = taller	large + er = larger
thin + er = thinner	funny + er = funnier

Note that if the adjective ends in a single consonant following a single vowel, you double the final consonant before adding the ending. If the adjective ends in silent *e*, you drop the final *e* before adding the ending. If the adjective ends in *y* following a consonant, change the *y* to *i* before adding the ending.

2. When you compare three or more people, places, things, or ideas, you usually add *-est* to the adjective.

tall + est = tallest	large + est = largest
thin + est = thinnest	funny + est = funniest

Using *More* and *Most* in Comparisons

Some adjectives add *-er* or *-est* to make a comparison. Other adjectives use the words *more* or *most* instead of *-er* or *-est.* Long adjectives and adjectives ending in *-ful,* like *beautiful,* are words that use *more* or *most* in making comparisons.

Here are the rules for using long adjectives in comparisons.

1. Use *more* when comparing two persons, places, things, or ideas.

more careful	more difficult
more terrible	more dangerous

2. Use *most* when comparing three or more persons, places, things, or ideas.

most careful	most difficult
most terrible	most dangerous

Use only one form of comparison at a time. If you use *-er* or *-est,* do not use *more* or *most* in the same comparison. You would not say, "I'm more hungrier than I thought." You also would not say, "My cat has the most meanest face."

The Forms of *Good* and *Bad*

A few adjectives change to completely new words when they are used in comparisons. Here are two important adjectives of this kind.

good	better	best
bad	worse	worst

Aunt Sally is a *good* cook, but Uncle Bill is *better.*
Grandma makes the *best* Christmas dinner.

The second show was *worse* than the first.
While it wasn't the *worst* storm this year, it was a *bad* one.

Exercises Using Adjectives To Make Comparisons

A. Some of the following adjectives add *-er* and *-est* when they are used in comparisons. Others are used with *more* and *most*. Number your paper from 1 to 12. Copy each adjective. Then write the two forms it uses in comparisons.

Example: slow, slower, slowest
colorful, more colorful, most colorful

1. helpful
2. dark
3. pretty
4. handsome
5. dangerous
6. intelligent
7. wide
8. hard
9. wonderful
10. great
11. silly
12. curious

B. Number your paper from 1 to 10. Choose the correct adjective form for each sentence. Write it on your paper.

1. Jeff is the (more athletic, most athletic) of the twins.
2. Which of the two pails is (larger, largest)?
3. I picked the (thinner, thinnest) of the four books.
4. This piece of cloth is the (biggest, bigger) of the two.
5. Pat is (carefuler, more careful) than Tom.
6. Darren is the (fastest, most fast) runner of all.
7. The lake is (more deep, deeper, more deeper) than it was last year.
8. Your house is the (more colorful, most colorful) one on our block.
9. The last arithmetic problem on the test was also the (most hard, hardest).
10. This is the (most delicious, deliciousest) peach pie I have ever eaten.

C. Writing Think about your three favorite TV stars, singers, or sports figures. Write five sentences that compare the three people you have chosen. Underline all the adjectives you use to compare your favorites.

Exercises for Mastery

Chapter 12

Adjectives for Strong Description

A. Finding Adjectives In each of the pairs of sentences below, only the adjectives have been changed. Number your paper from 1 to 5. For each pair of sentences, list each noun that is modified. After the noun, write the adjectives that modify it. Do not include articles.

1. a. We swam in a large, clear lake.
   b. We swam in a warm, shallow lake.
2. a. Tiny birds perched on the bare branches.
   b. White birds perched on the dark branches.
3. a. The powerful speaker talked to a joyous crowd.
   b. The fearful speaker talked to a rowdy crowd.
4. a. A hot, gusty wind swept the area.
   b. A fierce, cold wind swept the area.
5. a. Six old horses lived in the dirty stall.
   b. Young, spotted horses lived in the other stall.

B. Identifying Kinds of Adjectives Number your paper from 1 to 10. Write all the adjectives in each sentence. Beside each adjective you list, write if it tells *Which One*, *What Kind*, or *How Many*.

Example: Grandpa planted six bushes.
six—how many

1. These mice have long, skinny tails.
2. Did you make this wonderful bread?
3. I'll buy these four colorful fish and that big fishbowl for Janice.
4. Several close neighbors visited the new family on this block.
5. Those boys and girls went to the first game.
6. Cool, clear water is the best drink.

Exercises for Mastery Continued

7. That report was interesting to read.
8. I broke the green vase when I washed it.
9. When did the new students buy those pens?
10. At the game, Anna saw one boy and two girls she knew from camp.

C. Using Articles Copy these sentences. Fill in the blank with *a* or *an*.

1. Do you have _____ extra sweater?
2. The rock made _____ big splash.
3. I smelled _____ odd odor.
4. Our town has _____ outdoor pool.
5. Amy wore _____ plaid skirt and _____ yellow sweater to the dance.
6. It's _____ honor to meet you.
7. Did you get _____ answer to the letter you sent to the White House?
8. _____ lifeguard sat on _____ high seat.

D. Choosing the Right Word Choose the right word for each sentence. Write your choice on your paper.

1. A lumberjack cut down (them, those) trees.
2. (This, These) kinds of cereal are not sugared.
3. Pam collects (this, them, these) kinds of stamps with pictures of endangered animals.
4. (Those, Them) scary stories are true.
5. What's in (them, those) boxcars?
6. Mom wears (that, those) kind of perfume.
7. (This, These) kind of game takes too long.
8. Special blacksmiths make (them, those) horseshoes that are worn by racehorses.
9. We build fires with (this, these) kind of wood.
10. I topped the salad with (them, those) nuts.

E. Making Comparisons with Adjectives Choose the right word for each sentence. Write your choice on your paper.

1. Angel's lunch is the (gooder, better, best) of all.
2. Tammy told the (difficulter, more difficult) riddle.
3. Cats make the (wonderfullest, most wonderful) pets.
4. Hand me the (softer, softest) of the four pillows.
5. This plant is (healthier, healthiest) than that one.
6. "Washing dishes is (easier, more easier) than drying them," said my little brother.
7. Carey's story was (funnier, more funny) the second time she told it.
8. One spy in the movie was (carefuller, more careful) than the others.
9. Of the two reports, Charla's is (better, best).
10. Saturday always seems like the (shorter, shortest) day of the week.

Using Grammar in Writing

A. Unicorns and dragons are creatures that we learn about from folk tales. Imagine that you are a knight on an adventure. You come across a very strange, never-before-seen creature. As you ride back to the castle, you think about how you will describe what you have seen. Write a brief paragraph giving all the details of this unusual beast.

B. Use some of the following twelve adjectives to write a paragraph about a day in the life of one of the seven dwarfs. Underline each adjective as you use it.

beautiful	more hopeful	wrinkled	poor
seven	sillier	most wonderful	sad
smartest	worse	curious	best

C. Using Adjectives To Write About Art Visit a museum or use an art book to look at several paintings. Choose your favorite painting. Write a brief paragraph that describes it.

Chapter 12 Review

A. Finding Adjectives That Tell *What Kind, How Many,* and *Which One* On your paper, label three columns *What Kind, How Many,* and *Which One.* Find adjectives in the following sentences. Put each adjective in its proper column.

1. She saw an old friend at the new park.
2. Good news came this morning.
3. Samantha always does the best job she can.
4. Seventy pounds of potatoes fell from a truck.
5. These apples are tart and juicy.
6. Last night, all the better players practiced.
7. Don't you have an aqua sweater?
8. We folded the clean towels on the wobbly table.
9. Jade can be green or pink.
10. Few animals were outside during the bitter cold.

B. Choosing the Correct Adjective Number your paper from 1 to 10. Choose the correct adjective form for each sentence.

1. Shawn's cold was (worse, more worse) than Ed's.
2. The second time she got a (closer, closest) look.
3. Her job was (difficulter, more difficult) than his.
4. Of the ten masks we saw, the gorilla was the (uglier, ugliest) one.
5. Which fish is the (colorfulest, most colorful)?
6. We picked the (more beautiful, most beautiful) of the two roses.
7. Lu has the (better, best) time in the marathon of all.
8. He wasn't the (worse, worst) hurdler in school.
9. Between Jenny and Greg, Jenny was (hopefuller, more hopeful) about her chances of winning.
10. Do the leaves of a maple or an oak turn (browner, brownest) in the fall?

Chapter 13

Adverbs for Exact Meaning

Imagine that you are a newspaper reporter who is covering the Olympic trials in your city. You wait to see which athletes will jump *highest* and run *fastest*. You watch gymnasts tumble and vault *skillfully*. *Yesterday* you saw swimmers race. Without adverbs, you would not be able to write precisely about what you see.

An adverb is a word that tells you more about a verb, an adjective, or another adverb. Adverbs brighten your speaking and writing. In this chapter, you will learn how to recognize adverbs and how to use them correctly. You will discover that adverbs can add detail to your speaking and writing. You will also learn how to use adverbs in comparisons.

1 What Are Adverbs?

Focus

An **adverb** is a word that modifies a verb, an adjective, or another adverb.

You have already learned about one kind of modifier, the adjective. You will now learn about another modifier called the adverb.

An adverb modifies a verb, an adjective, or another adverb.

The girls have searched *everywhere*. (*Everywhere* modifies the verb *have searched*.)

That box is *very* heavy. (*Very* modifies the adjective *heavy*.)

Dale goes skating *quite* often. (*Quite* modifies the adverb *often*.)

An adverb tells *how, when, where,* or *to what extent* about the word it modifies.

Heather swam *quickly*. (*Quickly* tells *how* Heather swam.)

The corn was harvested *yesterday*. (*Yesterday* tells *when* the corn was harvested.)

You may play table tennis *downstairs*. (*Downstairs* tells *where* you may play table tennis.)

This chili is *too* spicy. (*Too* tells *to what extent* the chili is spicy.)

Here are some words that are frequently used as adverbs.

How	When	Where	To What Extent
well	now	here	very
hard	never	there	almost
fast	often	inside	too

Many other adverbs are formed by adding *-ly* to adjectives.

quick—quickly	happy—happily	tight—tightly
slow—slowly	sad—sadly	careless—carelessly

Exercises **Using Adverbs**

A. In these sentences, the words in italics are adverbs. Write the verb, adjective, or adverb that each adverb tells more about.

1. Carlos *very* carefully counted the coins.
2. We are *so* happy about our move to Iron Mountain.
3. The band will *soon* march in the Rose Bowl parade.
4. Lara *nearly* lost her balance on the uneven bars.
5. Big red Delicious apples *completely* filled the box.
6. We stared at the *brightly* colored rainbow.
7. We barbecue on the outdoor grill *quite* often.
8. The chef *lightly* steamed the vegetables.
9. The sky diver looked *down*.
10. The dog barked *wildly* at the burglar.

B. Number your paper from 1 to 10. Write the adverb in each sentence. Then tell what word the adverb modifies.

1. The hurdlers waited impatiently for the race to begin.
2. The pirates never found the buried treasure.
3. This watch always keeps the correct time.
4. The carpenter carefully measured the ceiling beams.
5. The scouts left yesterday for the jamboree.
6. Debbie tugged hard on the rope.
7. Leroy soon learned to speak Swahili.
8. My canteen is almost empty.
9. The gust of wind scattered the leaves everywhere.
10. Monica usually keeps score for the volleyball team.

C. Writing Imagine that you and a friend are exploring a dark cave. Suddenly you spot a brilliant gold treasure chest. Write directions for opening the chest, using these word pairs.

turn around	hardly ever	tap everywhere
sing softly	very gently	extremely dangerous
laugh silently	blink now	look inside

2 Making Comparisons with Adverbs

Focus

Adverbs, like adjectives, can be used in comparisons.

Read these sentences.

John Henry worked *harder* than the steam engine.
Of all the men, he worked *hardest*.

Notice that John Henry's action is being compared to the action of something or someone in each sentence. The word that shows the comparison in each sentence is an adverb.

There are three ways adverbs change to show comparison.

1. When you compare two actions, add *-er* to most short adverbs. When you compare three or more actions, add *-est*.

hard	harder	hardest
fast	faster	fastest

2. When you compare two persons or things, use the word *more* with most adverbs that end in *-ly*. When you compare three or more actions, use *most*.

carelessly	more carelessly	most carelessly
quickly	more quickly	most quickly

3. Change some adverbs completely when you use them in comparisons.

well	better	best	much	more	most
badly	worse	worst	little	less	least

Never use the *-er* ending with the word *more* or the *-est* ending with the word *most*.

Incorrect: Evan ran *more faster* than Sam.
Correct: Evan ran *faster* than Sam.

Exercises Making Comparisons with Adverbs

A. Number your paper from 1 to 12. Copy each adverb. Then write the two forms it uses in comparisons.

Example: much
much, more, most

1. rapidly
2. little
3. happily
4. hopelessly
5. fast
6. carefully
7. brightly
8. badly
9. loudly
10. well
11. slowly
12. hard

B. Number your paper from 1 to 10. Write the correct adverb form from the two in parentheses.

1. Of the eight skaters, Katie performed (more skillfully, most skillfully).
2. Louise worked (more hard, harder) than Dan.
3. The squirrel came (more near, nearer) to us.
4. The new trampoline works (more well, better) than the old one.
5. Of the two girls, Anna jumped (higher, highest).
6. Colin runs (more fast, faster) than I can.
7. Janie pitched the softball (farthest, farther) than Anita.
8. Of the two quarterbacks, Roy passes (better, best).
9. Of the three cereals, I like corn flakes (less, least).
10. The angelfish ate (more greedily, most greedily) of all.

C. Writing Pretend that you are competing in the Summer Olympics. Think about which event you would enter. Would it be basketball, volleyball, swimming, track, gymnastics, cycling, boxing, judo, or wrestling? Make a list of some of the highlights of the competition. Use this list to write a paragraph about this special event. Use four of the following adverbs to compare your performance to others:

fast	long	easily	high
quickly	hard	much	smoothly

3 Adjective or Adverb?

Focus

An **adjective** describes a noun or pronoun.

An **adverb** tells about, or modifies, a verb, an adjective, or another adverb.

Many adjectives and adverbs look similar. Read the adjectives and adverbs in the following list. Notice that many adverbs are formed by adding *-ly* to the adjective form.

Adjective	**Adverb**
soft	softly
quiet	quietly
beautiful	beautifully

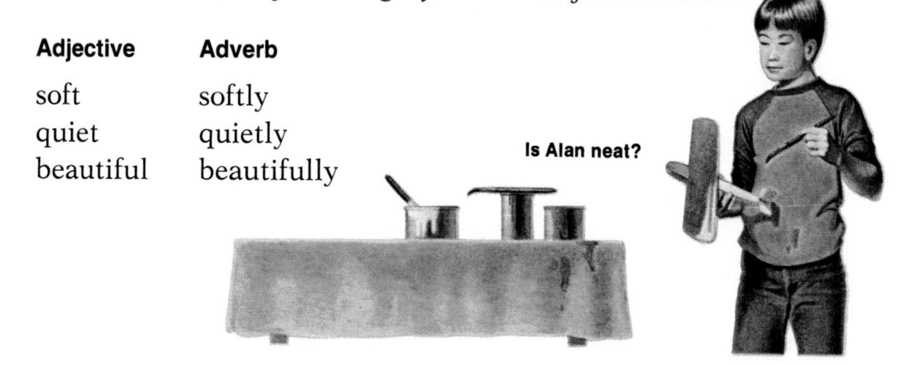

Is Alan neat?

Does he paint neatly?

Now read this sentence.

Karen hummed (quiet, quietly) as she finished her drawing.

Should you use *quiet* or *quietly* in this sentence? To discover the answer, ask yourself what word is being modified. Does the word modify a noun? If so, use the adjective *quiet*. Does the word modify a verb, an adjective, or another adverb? If so, choose the adverb *quietly*.

In the sentence above, the word modifies *hummed*, a verb. Therefore, use the adverb *quietly*. Read this sentence.

Marianna plays the violin (beautiful, beautifully).

What word is being modified by the choices in parentheses? *Plays* is the word being modified. *Plays* is a verb. Because an adverb modifies a verb, choose the adverb *beautifully*.

Using *Good* and *Bad*, *Well* and *Badly*

Sometimes you may have trouble deciding whether to use *good* or *bad*, or *well* or *badly* in sentences. Follow these rules to find the correct form.

The words *good* and *bad* are adjectives. Use them to describe nouns and pronouns. *Good* and *bad* tell *what kind*.

This is a *good* sandwich. I have a *bad* cold.

The words *well* and *badly* are adverbs. Use them to tell *how* something is done.

Pat sings *well*. Paul acts *badly*.

Key to Writing and Speaking There is an exception to the rule about using *good* and *well*. When referring to a person's health, use *well*. Write or say: *Catelin is not well today.* Do not write or say: *Catelin is not good today.*

Exercises Choosing the Right Word

A. Number your paper from 1 to 10. Write the correct modifier from the two given in parentheses. Next, write the word it modifies.

1. The old turtle moved (careful, carefully) through the tall, green grass.
2. Because Jill had a cold, she did not feel (good, well).
3. Greg is a (real, really) fast swimmer.
4. Jane can see (well, good) without glasses.
5. The racer turned the corner (sharp, sharply).
6. Helen played the game (good, well).
7. Mark waited (eager, eagerly) for his dinner.
8. Concrete expands (slow, slowly) in high temperatures.
9. Wild cats stalk their prey (silent, silently).
10. The doctor is trying to help you get (good, well).

B. Each sentence has one error. An adjective is used in place of an adverb. Number your paper from 1 to 10. Find the usage error in each sentence. Correct it.

1. The tractor moved rapid across the field.
2. Did you eat good at breakfast?
3. Your costume is near complete.
4. Angela spoke soft on the phone.
5. The guard searched the area careful.
6. We should get to the theater punctual.
7. These old jeans fit bad.
8. If you are not good by tomorrow, we will call the doctor.
9. Paul saw a real interesting display at the Museum of Science and Industry.
10. The guide dog was trained good.

C. Writing Do you remember this old nursery rhyme? "There once was a girl, and she had a little curl right in the middle of her forehead. When she was good, she was very, very good, but when she was bad, she was horrid."

Write a paragraph that tells what the little girl did when she was good and what she did when she was bad. Use adverbs to make your action verbs very clear and specific. Underline the adverbs in your paragraph.

Exercises for Mastery

Chapter 13

Adverbs for Exact Meaning

A. Using Adverbs Write every adverb used in each of the following sentences.

1. Otters swim swiftly and silently.
2. The fullback almost scored a touchdown today.
3. This mystery book is quite enjoyable.
4. Ruthie never rides her bike too far.
5. Dennis cut the grass very short.

B. Making Comparisons with Adverbs Write the correct adverb form from the two in parentheses.

1. Of the four, Sue finished her chores (faster, fastest).
2. Recite your lines (more clearly, clearer).
3. Of the two girls, Pam sewed (better, best).
4. Of all the team swimmers, Van swims (more strongly, most strongly).
5. We laughed (most hard, hardest) at the last joke.
6. This baby cries (more often, oftener) than that one.
7. Of all the children, Drew cares (more, most) for the family farm.
8. This castle is (more heavily, heavier) guarded than the one on the hill.
9. Judy works (more hard, harder) than Estelle.
10. The rain came (more soon, sooner) than predicted.

C. Choosing the Right Word Write the correct modifier for each sentence. Next, write the word it modifies.

1. Drive (slow, slowly) in school zones.
2. Ilona dresses (neat, neatly).
3. Skip acted (bad, badly) on the trip.
4. Ms. Rossi is (real, really) patient with her class.
5. The soloist sang (good, well).

Using Grammar in Writing

A. Imagine that you are at a state fair. At the fair, you see livestock shows, a Ferris wheel, quilt displays, the latest farm equipment, and a fantastic grandstand show. Write a paragraph in which you describe what you see and hear at the state fair. Be sure to use adverbs in your paragraph to describe how everything sounds and looks. Use adverbs to compare the sights and sounds at the fair and to tell where and when exciting things happen.

B. Pretend that you are an adventurer of long ago. You are exploring an area near your home. Make a list of what you see and hear. Use it to write a paragraph about a discovery.

In a second paragraph, compare this place of long ago to the same area today. How is it different? Which do you like better? Use adverbs to compare the past and the present.

C. Using Adverbs in Social Studies Archaeologists are scientists who study past civilizations. They study the tools made by ancient civilizations. They also study bones, houses, and tombs to learn what life was like many years ago.

In an encyclopedia, look up *Inca*, *Maya*, *Pompeii*, or *Troy*. Write a brief report telling what archaeologists have learned about these people and places. Use adverbs to tell *when*, *where*, *how*, and *to what extent*. Underline the adverbs.

Chapter 13 Review

A. Finding Adverbs Number your paper from 1 to 10. Write all of the adverbs in each sentence below. Then write the word each adverb modifies.

1. The squeaky door made so much noise!
2. Padraic's speeches are often quite long.
3. "That videocassette recorder is far too expensive," Holly sighed.
4. We will have a really fantastic dinner later.
5. Cautiously, gracefully, the deer entered the glen.
6. It was very nice outside yesterday.
7. Crocuses usually bloom early.
8. "Come here, now!" the officer commanded sternly.
9. The old truck always backfires loudly.
10. Maria restlessly paced back and forth.

B. Choosing the Correct Modifier Number your paper from 1 to 10. For each sentence, write the correct modifier. Next, write the word or words it modifies.

1. Tom's tooth hurts (bad, badly).
2. Jenny is a (real, really) careful worker.
3. At the end of the game, Christopher limped (slow, slowly) away from the football field.
4. Harry works (harder, more hard) than Ed.
5. My kite flies (more high, higher) than yours does.
6. Alex dressed (quick, quickly) so that he wouldn't miss the bus.
7. Jeremy was not hurt (bad, badly) when he fell from the tree in our neighbor's yard.
8. Rhonda did not feel (good, well) yesterday.
9. Of all fruits, I like grapefruit (less, least).
10. Karen's science experiment was the (more, most) accurate one in her class.

Chapter 14

Increasing Sentence Power

Before putting two pieces of wood together, a carpenter will make sure each one is just right. If necessary, the carpenter will throw out a bad piece, sand a rough spot, or trim an edge. One bad board might spoil the whole project.

A writer takes the same care with sentences. Each one must be just right. A sentence must say exactly what the writer wants it to say. A poorly written sentence can confuse the reader. This chapter will show you how to improve your writing by improving your sentences. You will learn to combine related ideas to make your writing flow smoothly.

1 Avoiding Run-on and Stringy Sentences

Focus

Avoid **run-on** and **stringy sentences** in your writing.

In Chapter 2, you learned that a sentence is a group of words that expresses a complete thought. Sometimes, however, a writer puts too many thoughts into a sentence. This results in a **run-on sentence** or a **stringy sentence**.

Avoiding Run-on Sentences

Read this group of words.

Evan is sitting at the window he is waiting for his friend.

In the example, two complete thoughts are run together. No period marks the end of the first idea. No capital letter marks the beginning of the second idea. This kind of sentence is called a **run-on sentence**. It should be written as two sentences.

Evan is sitting at the window. He is waiting for his friend.

Avoiding Stringy Sentences

Read this sentence.

We built a fire on the beach, and we cooked hot dogs and hamburgers then we ate.

This kind of sentence is called a **stringy sentence**. It strings too many ideas together with the word *and*. A stringy sentence should be written as several sentences.

We built a fire on the beach. We cooked hot dogs and hamburgers. Then we ate.

There are times when it is correct to join sentences or sentence parts with *and*. For instance, in the example, *and* is correctly joining two sentence parts that are alike: *hot dogs* and *hamburgers*. In parts 2, 3, and 4, you will learn how to use *and* to join sentences and sentence parts correctly.

Exercises Recognizing Run-on Sentences and Stringy Sentences

A. Read the following sentences. Write what kind each is: *Run-on Sentence*, *Stringy Sentence*, or *Correct*.

1. Jeff answered an ad in the paper he got a kitten.
2. Terry ice skates well and spins without effort and he does figure eights.
3. Lillian and Darren raced around the playground.
4. It rained on the Fourth of July we ate inside.
5. I have two younger brothers they are twins.

B. Rewrite the following sentences. Each sentence should contain only one complete thought.

1. Vera hit a slap shot and the puck suddenly shot off the ice and the referee called for a face-off.
2. My cousins write to me it's fun hearing from them.
3. Luis likes corn he doesn't like broccoli.
4. Keith catches fireflies he keeps them in a jar.
5. John went to Disney World and he thought it was great fun and he wants to go back next year.
6. We played baseball yesterday Judy scored three runs.
7. Lisa's pets are a chicken and a monkey and they live in her backyard and she takes good care of them.
8. Rick knows the capital city of every state ask him.
9. Teresa and Stacy went to the Sears Tower in downtown Chicago then they went shopping on State Street.
10. Last year we planted a maple tree it's in the back yard.

2 Joining Sentences with *and*, *but*, or *or*

Focus

Sentences or sentence parts can be joined together by conjunctions. The words **and**, **but**, and **or** are conjunctions.

Run-on and stringy sentences join ideas incorrectly. They must be separated into shorter, good sentences. However, ideas can be joined correctly to form good sentences.

Joining Complete Sentences

Sometimes two sentences show two ideas that are alike. These sentences can be joined by a comma and the word *and*.

Larry washed one dog. Grace washed the other.
Larry washed one dog, **and** Grace washed the other.

Sometimes two sentences show two ideas that are different. These may be joined by a comma and the word *but*.

The paint looked dry. It was still wet.
The paint looked dry, **but** it was still wet.

If two sentences show a choice between ideas, they may be joined by a comma and the word *or*.

Students worked on the mural. They practiced for the play.
Students worked on the mural, **or** they practiced for the play.

Joining Sentence Parts

Sometimes two sentences are so much alike that words are repeated. If the sentences are combined, the repeated words can be left out. Notice that no comma is needed before the conjunction when sentence parts are combined.

Sentence parts that show ideas that are alike can usually be joined by *and*. Here is an example.

> Paul collects stamps. *Paul collects* coins.
> Paul collects stamps **and** coins.

Sentence parts that show ideas that are different can usually be joined by *but*.

> Anne can help on Friday. *She can*not *help* on Saturday.
> Anne can help on Friday **but** not on Saturday.

Sentence parts that show a choice between ideas may be joined by *or*.

> You may glaze your pottery. *You may* leave it plain.
> You may glaze your pottery **or** leave it plain.

Exercises **Combining Sentences**

A. Join the following pairs of sentences by following the directions in parentheses.

1. Penny brought records. Ted brought a record player. (Join with **, and**.)
2. The team must arrive on time. They will forfeit the game. (Join with **, or**.)
3. The bus was ready to leave. Half the team wasn't on board. (Join with **, but**.)
4. The jar of strawberry jelly was open. A spoon lay nearby. (Join with **, and**.)
5. Liz heard a cat. She couldn't see it. (Join with **, but**.)

B. Join the related parts of the sentences in each pair. Follow the directions. Leave out the words in italics.

1. Carl bought tickets. Dot *bought tickets*. (Join with **and**.)
2. You may use tempera paints. *You may use* finger paints. (Join with **or**.)
3. The players were tired. *However, they were* happy. (Join with **but**.)
4. Gordon clapped. *He* cheered. (Join with **and**.)
5. The puppy chewed my shoes. *It chewed* Linda's wallet. (Join with **and**.)

3 Combining Sentences by Adding Words

Focus

Sometimes you can combine two sentences by adding a word from the second sentence to the first sentence.

Sometimes two sentences that work well together can be joined into one sentence. The new sentence may express an idea more clearly and smoothly than two separate sentences do. Read these sentences.

Jean bought a notebook. It was purple.

The only word in the second sentence that adds any information is *purple*. *Purple* can become part of the first sentence.

Jean bought a **purple** notebook.

Read these sentences. Notice how the important word from the second sentence has become part of the first sentence.

Alex studied for the test. *He studied* hard.
Alex studied **hard** for the test.

Lydia rubbed her fingers. *They were* chilled.
Lydia rubbed her **chilled** fingers.

In each example, only the important word in the second sentence was added to the first sentence. The words in italics were left out.

Sometimes you can combine words from more than two sentences. The sentences must all work together. One sentence must tell the main idea. Each of the other sentences must add one important word to the main idea.

A koala clung to a branch. *The koala was* sleeping. *The branch was* sturdy.
A **sleeping** koala clung to a **sturdy** branch.

Exercises Combining Sentences by Adding Words

A. Combine each set of sentences into one sentence. Leave out the words in italics. Write the new sentence on your paper.

1. The lemon is a fruit. *The fruit is* sour.
2. Al slid down the hill. *Al slid* quickly.
3. The Mustangs tried to win the championship game. *The Mustangs tried* hard.
4. Cut the tomato into slices. *Cut it* carefully.
5. Detective Johnson thoughtfully studied the clues. *The clues were* strange.
6. Ellen spotted the dog. *It was* lost.
7. Mr. Ogami drew a face on the paper I turned in yesterday. *The face was* smiling.
8. Lola and Molly waded in the stream. *The stream was* bubbling. *The stream was* little.
9. Julius unfolded the letter. *The letter was* important. *He unfolded it* slowly.
10. Rosa took off her jacket. *Her jacket was* new. *Her jacket was* corduroy.

B. Combine the sentences in each group. Add important words from the second and third sentences to the first. Write the new sentence on your paper.

1. Dad chopped the celery. He did it quickly. The celery was fresh and crisp.
2. Rosa's hat drooped in the rain. The hat was straw. The rain was heavy.
3. The horses raced through the streets. The horses were frightened. The streets were dark.
4. The car left a spot on the garage floor. It was a large spot. It was a greasy spot.
5. Three coins were inside the box. The coins were silver. The box was locked.

4 Adding Groups of Words

Focus

Sometimes groups of words from one sentence can be added to another sentence.

You may find that one sentence contains a group of words that adds important information to another sentence. You can combine the two sentences into one.

Read the examples below. Certain words in the second sentence have been added to the first.

I saw a small, black dog. *It was* sleeping in the shade.
I saw a small, black dog **sleeping in the shade**.

Trevor made apple crisp. *The apple crisp was* covered with chopped nuts.
Trevor made apple crisp **covered with chopped nuts**.

Notice that there are words in each second sentence that tell more about a person or a thing that was mentioned in the first sentence. These words are added near the name of that person or thing.

When the words tell something about an action, add them near the words that show the action.

Ruth was studying. *She was* in the living room.
Ruth was studying **in the living room**.

Some words may be added to more than one place in the new sentence.

I played soccer with the Jets. *I played* after school.
After school, I played soccer with the Jets.
I played soccer **after school** with the Jets.
I played soccer with the Jets **after school**.

Some words, however, may be added in only one place to make a clear and sensible sentence. Study these sentences.

> Our family visited the place where U. S. Grant is buried *on several occasions*. (Was Grant buried on several occasions?)
>
> Nancy saw a herd of goats coming over the hill *through her binoculars*. (Could the goats fit through the binoculars?)

When you combine two sentences into one, always read the new sentence. Be sure it is clear and sensible.

Exercises **Adding Groups of Words**

A. Combine the sentences in each pair. Add a group of words to the first sentence. Leave out the words in italics.

1. Anna bought some wrapping paper. *The paper was* covered with silver glitter.
2. The jar is full of grape juice. *The jar is* near the sink.
3. The gray-haired man is my piano teacher. *He is* standing behind Alex.
4. Those plants are weeds. *They are* beside the mailbox.
5. I saw a small, brown bat hanging upside down. *It was hanging* from a branch.

B. Combine the sentences in each pair by adding important words from the second sentence to the first sentence.

1. The black clouds looked threatening. The clouds were appearing on the horizon.
2. The tunnel leads to a dungeon. The tunnel is beneath this castle.
3. Flight 505 is arriving at Gate 16. The flight is from Atlanta.
4. That was Mr. Perkins. He was in the lobby.
5. The rain caused heavy flooding. The rain was from Hurricane Margaret.

Exercises for Mastery Chapter 14

Increasing Sentence Power

A. Avoiding Run-on and Stringy Sentences Number your paper from 1 to 10. If the sentence is correct as it is, write *Correct*. If it is a run-on or stringy sentence, rewrite the sentence. Each sentence should be one complete thought.

1. The firefighters arrived they put out the blaze.
2. At night, my brother and I played Clue or Probe.
3. The classroom gerbil escaped from its cage.
4. Dolores broke her leg and she had a cast for a long time and everyone signed the cast.
5. Atlanta and Savannah are two of the largest cities in Georgia.
6. That pitcher throws slow curve balls.
7. I added two fish to the aquarium both are goldfish.
8. Tony had a Halloween party and everybody wore costumes and I was Dracula.
9. Marla drew plans and she built a birdhouse and now it's outside.
10. My dog barks fiercely he frightens strangers.

B. Joining Sentences and Sentence Parts Number your paper from 1 to 10. Combine each set of sentences. Follow the directions in the parentheses. Leave out any words in italics.

1. John might bring his sleeping bag. He might bring my brother's. (Join sentences with **, or**.)
2. No one ate the toast. *The toast was* burnt. (Add only the important word.)
3. Rebecca doesn't like skating. I love it! (Join sentences with **, but**.)
4. Grandma read my report card. *She read it* eagerly. (Add only the important word.)

5. The weather forecast predicted rain today. *The weather forecast predicted rain* tomorrow. (Join the sentence parts with **and**.)
6. Arthur hit a long fly ball. *It went* over the fence. (Add a group of words.)
7. We finished making the puppets and scenery. *We did* not *finish making* the costumes. (Join sentence parts with **but**.)
8. The television picture was blurred. The sound was not working at all. (Join sentences with **, and**.)
9. These ants build nests from dirt. *The ants are* tiny. *The nests are* huge. (Add only important words.)
10. Mr. Dennis arrived. *He arrived* after breakfast. (Add a group of words.)

Chapter 14 Review

A. Correcting Run-on and Stringy Sentences Read the following run-on and stringy sentences. On your paper rewrite each sentence as two or three sentences.

1. Martha is in the school orchestra and she plays the violin and plays it well.
2. Jack caught the football and he ran twenty-nine yards and he made the first touchdown.
3. We made salad for lunch today it tasted delicious.
4. Kevin won the spelling bee his prize was a trip to Washington, D.C.
5. Carol rushed to her locker and she found her books under her coat and suddenly the bell rang.

B. Combining Sentences Read the following sentences. Combine each pair into one sentence. You will be joining related parts or whole sentences. Follow the directions in parentheses. Leave out the words in italics.

1. Chris works on Saturdays. *Chris does* not *work* on Sundays. (Join sentence parts with **but**.)
2. Katie will play soccer. Danny *will play soccer*. (Join with **and** or **or**.)
3. Tomorrow night at the school circus, I will be the clown. *I will be* the lion tamer. (Join sentence parts with **and**.)
4. The President of the United States is elected. The Justices of the Supreme Court are appointed. (Join sentences with **, but**.)
5. The fruit looked real. It was made of wax. (Join sentences with **, but**.)
6. Lauren might read chapter one of the book aloud. Kurt *might read chapter one aloud*. (Join sentence parts with **or**.)

Chapter 15

Description and the Process of Writing

Maria has just returned home from a weekend camping trip. Read these lines from her journal entry describing her trip.

> Before the others woke up, I walked from the pines to the lake. The air felt crisp and cold on my face. The lake was glassy. Heavy fog hung over the water, hiding the opposite shore. Soon a blazing yellow sun rose. The fog disappeared, and the birds began singing.

Maria has used description to make her journal entry more vivid. Descriptive writing is often an important part of other types of writing. Good description can make the characters and setting in a story come to life. For example, good description in a social studies report on the colonists will make the reader feel as if he or she were there.

In this chapter, you will learn how to write good descriptions. You will discover how you can make description a part of all your writing.

1 Thinking About Descriptions

Focus

Use descriptive writing to create a clear picture of your subject.

You are often asked to describe how something looks or feels or tastes. Imagine that you are writing a story about a pioneer. You want to show your readers what this character looks like. How would you do that?

Example 1

Read and Think. Ruth wrote this paragraph describing the main character in her story. Look for vivid words and phrases as you read.

> Tom Hurley was a big, gentle man. He stood six feet, six inches tall. His long blonde hair and curly beard were golden like the sun. Cool blue eyes twinkled beneath his bushy brows. His voice was deep and warm. His faded plaid shirt and dusty overalls smelled like the pine forest where he lived.

Think and Discuss. Read Ruth's paragraph again. Then discuss the following questions with your classmates.

1. What three senses does this paragraph appeal to? Give an example of each. How do these details help you picture Tom Hurley?

2. In the third sentence, the writer makes a comparison. What things are compared? What does this comparison tell you about Tom?

3. In her paragraph, Ruth uses adjectives like *gentle, curly, blue,* and *warm*. She also uses verbs like *twinkled* and *smelled*. Why are these words important to Ruth's description?

4. How are the details in this paragraph organized? Where does the description start? Where does it end?

Example 2

Read and Think. Here is a passage from a story by James Thurber. In it he describes a grocery store that he remembers from his childhood. What descriptive words and phrases does the author use to present a clear picture of his setting?

> It was an old store even then, forty-five years ago, and its wide oak floorboards had been worn pleasantly smooth by the shoe soles of three generations of customers. The place smelled of coffee, peppermint, vinegar, and spices. Just inside the door on the left, a counter with a rounded glass front held all the old-fashioned penny candies— —JAMES THURBER

Think and Discuss. Think about these questions. Discuss your ideas with your classmates.

1. What sensory details has James Thurber included in his description? Which senses do these words appeal to?

2. How do the words *pleasantly smooth, smelled of . . . peppermint,* and *old-fashioned penny candies* make you feel about this place?

3. How do phrases like *just inside* and *on the left* help you to see what the writer is describing?

Now It's Your Turn

You have read and thought about two different kinds of descriptive paragraphs. Both use vivid words and phrases to create a clear picture for the reader. Both also create a mood. Now you are ready to learn how to write descriptions.

2 Gathering Details for a Description

Focus

Begin a description by looking for details that appeal to the senses.

How do people learn about the world around them? They use their senses. They look, listen, touch, taste, and smell. That is why it is so important to include sensory details in a description. Sensory details help your readers to learn about the person, place, or thing you are describing.

Gathering Sensory Details

There are three ways you can gather sensory details for a description: observation, memory, and imagination.

Observing Your Subject Suppose you want to describe the tree house in your back yard. By observing that tree house, you would notice that it is made of light-colored wood put together with shiny metal nails. You would know that the wood feels rough and that the boards creak when you walk on them. You would see that the doorway is covered with a red-and-white blanket. You might even notice that the breeze seems cooler up in your tree house and that you can often smell the neighbor's roses. Observing is a good way to gather sensory details.

Using Your Memory Imagine that you want to describe your first attempt at ice-skating three years ago. You can try to remember what that day was like. You might remember that you could hear your teeth chattering and that your legs felt a little rubbery. You might also remember that you were wearing bright red pants and heavy mittens. Perhaps you remember the smell of burning wood from the chimneys of nearby houses. You can gather many sensory details by using your memory.

Using Your Imagination Suppose that you are writing an imaginary story. You will need to describe imaginary people, places, and things. Where can you find the details for your story? Use your imagination. Draw a picture of the person, place, or thing in your mind. You may even wish to draw it on a piece of paper.

By using your imagination, a character can look and sound just the way you want. A horse can have two heads. A house can float in the clouds. Paint your word picture with whatever colors suit the mood of your story.

Creating a Mood

The types of details you choose will depend on the **mood**, or feeling, you want to create. If you want to describe the fun-filled atmosphere of a state fair, use colorful details that picture the fun and activity. Choose words like *laughing*, *bright*, and *swirling*. On the other hand, if you are describing an old, abandoned building, use details that create an empty, eerie feeling. Choose words like *dreary*, *gray*, and *creaking*.

Exercises Gathering Details

A. Imagine a place that does not really exist, but could be real. Make a list of all the sensory details that would describe this imaginary place. Include details that appeal to as many senses as possible. Write the sense each detail appeals to.

B. Choose the person, place, or thing that you like best about your neighborhood. Make a list of sensory details that describe your subject. You might want to select a different topic from the **Power Handbook**. Save your notes. You will use them later in this chapter.

3 Organizing Details for a Description

Focus

To make your description clear, organize details in a logical order.

Once you have a list of sensory details, you need to organize them in a logical way. You want your readers to picture clearly what you are describing. Here are three good ways to organize details in a description.

Natural Order One of the most common ways to arrange details is to use natural order. When you use natural order, you arrange details according to the way you would notice them. For example, you might look at a tall tree by starting at the trunk and working your way to the top branches and leaves. To describe the street where you live, you might start with the houses at one end and work your way to the houses at the other end of the block.

Read the following paragraph. It is arranged in natural order. Notice that details are arranged in the order you would most likely notice them. The man is described from the top of his head to his feet.

> A slouched leather cap half hid his face, tanned by the sun and wind. He wore a coarse yellow shirt, open at the neck; shabby blue trousers, white on one knee and with holes in the other. . . . Upon his back was a well-filled knapsack, strongly buckled and quite new. In his hand he carried an enormous knotted stick; his stockingless feet were in hobnailed shoes; . . . —VICTOR HUGO

Order of Importance Another way to organize your description is to begin or end with the most important details about your subject. If you are describing a person with bright green eyes, that could be your starting point. If you were describing a cozy room on a cold winter night, the blazing fire in the fireplace might be the most important detail. You could save it for the end of the description.

Grouping by Senses A third way to organize a description is to describe with one sense at a time. Suppose you wanted to describe a Fourth of July parade in your town. You might begin by using all of the details that appeal to the sense of sight. Then you might add the sounds of the parade, followed by the smells, and so on. Notice the arrangement of sensory details in this paragraph.

> Spring came early that year. The odor of decaying leaves and wet earth mixed with the fresh green smell of new grass. As I walked into the garden, splashes of color greeted me. Tiny white lilies of the valley crowded under their waxy green leaves, and purple lilacs swayed gracefully in the warm breeze. In the background, sparrows and squirrels chattered noisily.

Exercises **Organizing Details**

A. Arrange the following list of details in natural order.

A Skyscraper

surrounded by brightly-colored iron benches
an American flag flying in the wind on the roof
windows on the top floors giving a view of the city
high spires of radio antennae reaching toward the clouds
display windows of elegant shops greeting passers-by

B. Use the details you wrote for Exercise B in part 2 to write a descriptive paragraph. First, organize the details according to natural order, order of importance, or the different senses. Then, write the first draft of your paragraph.

4 Revising Language To Improve Description

Focus

You can improve a description by carefully revising the language you have used.

Using Adjectives and Adverbs

Adjectives and adverbs are words that describe. Adjectives describe nouns and pronouns. Adverbs describe verbs, adjectives, and other adverbs. Read the story that Rick wrote about pirates. He wanted to give his readers a better picture of the pirate, so he added some adjectives and adverbs.

> slowly ... dirty red
> Blackeye went ^ up the ramp. He had a ^ scarf around his
> golden ... purple
> forehead. ~~An~~ ^ earring hung down from his ear. A ^ scar was across
> right ... horrible
> his cheek. Where his ^ eye should have been was a ^ black patch.

Notice that Rick did not add too many adjectives and adverbs to his description.

Using Strong Verbs and Precise Nouns

There are two kinds of verbs. Action verbs are words like *raced*, *bounce*, and *leap*. State-of-being verbs include words such as *was* and *seems*. Action verbs are stronger and more specific than state-of-being verbs. In a description, try to use as many strong action verbs as you can.

Nouns are important to descriptive writing as well. Some nouns are general. Words such as *dog*, *hat*, and *game* are general nouns. Other nouns give a more exact picture such as *beagle*, *beret*, and *checkers*.

Rick continued to revise his description. He replaced state-of-being verbs with action verbs, weak action verbs with strong action verbs, and general nouns with precise nouns.

> Blackeye ~~went~~ *hobbled* slowly up the ~~ramp.~~ *gangplank.* He ~~had~~ *wore* a dirty red ~~scarf~~ *bandana* around his forehead. A golden earring ~~hung down~~ *dangled* from his ear. A purple scar ~~was~~ *stretched* across his cheek. Where his right eye should have been ~~was~~ *sat* a horrible black patch.

Using Similes and Metaphors

Similes and metaphors compare one thing to another. Similes and metaphors can make a description clearer and more interesting. Rick added this simile to his description.

> Blackeye hobbled slowly up the gangplank *like a man on his way to the gallows*.

Here is Rick's revised description.

> Blackeye hobbled slowly up the gangplank like a man on his way to the gallows. He wore a dirty red bandana around his forehead. A golden earring dangled from his ear. A purple scar stretched across his cheek. Where his right eye should have been sat a horrible black patch.

Exercise Using the Language of Description

Reread the description you wrote in part 3 of this chapter. How can you improve your description? Try adding some adjectives and adverbs. Replace weak action verbs and state-of-being verbs with strong, specific action verbs. Replace general nouns with precise nouns. Add a simile or metaphor if that will make your description clearer. Use the Thesaurus on pages 464–476 to improve your word choice. When you have finished revising, make a final copy of your improved description and share it with your classmates.

Speaking and Listening

Making Introductions

Introductions help people get acquainted with one another. A good introduction should include some description.

For example, imagine that your cousin Tony has come from California to visit you. He will be going to school with you and meeting your friends. You know it will be difficult for Tony to remember everyone, so you have thought of a way to help him. You will include a short, descriptive phrase with every introduction. The description can tell what someone does or is, not just what someone looks like. For example, you might say, "Tony, this is Angela. She is the fastest runner in our class."

When you introduce people, remember these guidelines.

Guidelines for Introductions

1. Say both names clearly.
2. Tell something about each person you introduce.
3. Introduce an older person or a person in authority first.
4. Smile and show interest in both people.

Exercises Using Description in Introductions

A. Imagine that you are introducing three friends to your parents. Write a descriptive phrase you might include in the introduction. Make sure it is something that makes that person special.

B. Write a short introduction for someone you and your classmates know. Do not use the person's name. See if others can guess whom you are introducing by the descriptive phrases you use.

Creative Writing

A. Find an unusual picture in a newspaper or magazine. You might choose a photograph from a news article or a glossy magazine advertisement. List all the details about the unusual person, place, or thing in the photograph. Use your list to write a descriptive paragraph about this person, place, or thing.

B. Imagine that you have a room in your house all to yourself. What would this room look like? What would be in it? Write a description of your room. Be sure your description is well thought out. Try to help your readers see this room as clearly as you do.

C. Use sensory details and descriptive language to write about each of the numbered items below. Write your descriptions in riddle form. See how many your classmates can guess.

Example: I crunch when you munch me. I'm green as a lettuce leaf. My top is quite leafy, my body quite stringy. I'm a dieter's best friend. What am I?

1. spider
2. peanut butter
3. sand
4. raisins
5. lemon
6. clock

Using English in Science

In this chapter, you have learned how important observing is to describing. Scientists know the importance of observing, too. Some scientists observe through microscopes. Other scientists observe through telescopes. Scientists can even "observe" by carefully studying the information on computers. In all cases, scientists write descriptions of what they see.

In your science class, good describing skills can help you to describe what all or part of a plant or animal looks like. You can use your skills to describe the materials for an experiment. When you write descriptions for science class, remember what you have learned in this chapter. Use good adjectives and adverbs, strong action verbs, and precise nouns. Give your readers a clear picture of what you are describing.

Exercise Observing and Describing

Below are two photographs. These pictures were taken through an electron microscope. An electron microscope enlarges objects to thousands of times their normal size. Choose one picture and use your describing skills to write what you see. When you have finished your description, look on page 488 to find out what each object is.

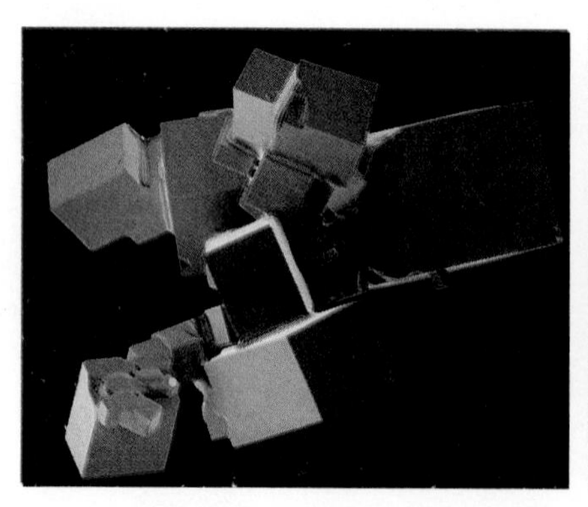

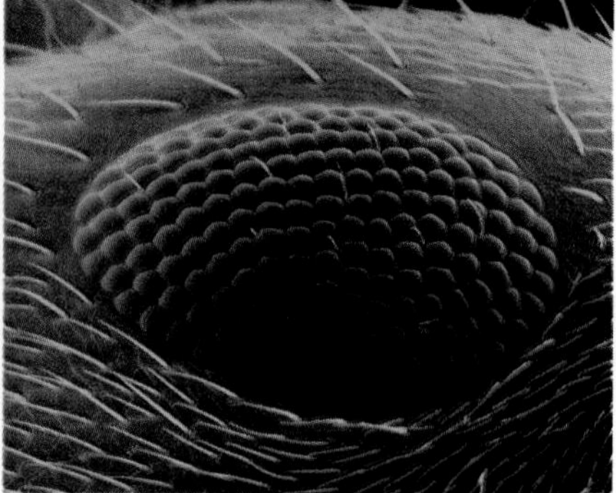

Chapter 15 Review

A. Using Sensory Details To Create Mood Read the following details that may be used to describe a house. Number your paper from 1 to 8. Then write *Dark and Dreary* or *Light and Happy* to tell the mood of each phrase.

1. an angry lion's-head knocker on the huge door
2. a round-eyed calico cat curled on the windowsill
3. damp, musty odor fills the air
4. pretty red geraniums lining the steps of the walk
5. dead tree branches tapping against glass from broken window panes
6. white lace curtains hanging in a bay window
7. children splashing in water from a lawn sprinkler
8. a massive dog growling from behind closed doors

B. Organizing Details Read the following list of details. Organize these details into a paragraph about pyramids. Write them on your paper in the order you would use them.

concrete blocks stacked one on top of another to the peak
built on hot sands of Egyptian desert
inside small rooms on lower level contain mummies and treasures of the past
final stone block may rest as high as the top of a forty-story building
base is larger than full city block

C. Using Descriptive Language Improve the following paragraph. Add good adjectives and adverbs, strong action verbs, and precise nouns.

The bear was on his hind legs. He smelled the air. His tongue licked his muzzle. His paws were in the air. The claws were sharp. The bear looked at us. We stayed where we were.

Chapter 16

Enjoying the Language of Poetry

Poetry is an invitation to play with language. When you write poetry, you can choose words that appeal to your senses. You can arrange the words so that they sing and dance in your ear. You can make them into a pleasing shape on the page. You can use them in special ways to help you explain what you see and feel.

In this chapter, you will study ways that you can shape language into poems. You will learn how to blend sounds, pictures, and ideas to create something special for your readers. Then you can take the things you learned to do in writing poetry and use them to make your stories and descriptions more exciting, too.

1 Shape in Poetry

Focus

Poetry is language arranged in lines and stanzas.

Writing poetry is a way for writers to express a great deal of meaning in few words. A poem looks different from other kinds of writing. The words are arranged in **lines.** The lines are often grouped into one or more units called **stanzas.**

How many stanzas make up the following poem? How many lines are in each stanza?

THE BAT

By day the bat is cousin to the mouse.
He likes the attic of an aging house.

His fingers make a hat about his head.
His pulse beat is so slow we think him dead.

He loops in crazy figures half the night
Among the trees that face the corner light.

But when he brushes up against a screen,
We are afraid of what our eyes have seen:

For something is amiss or out of place
When mice with wings can wear a human face.

—THEODORE ROETHKE

Notice that the poem is made up of complete sentences. When reading this kind of poem, stop at the end of a line only if a sentence also ends there.

Concrete Poems

A **concrete poem** takes on the shape of its subject. For example, a concrete poem about a kite might look like a kite.

The poem below is a concrete poem about poetry. Notice the different shapes of its parts.

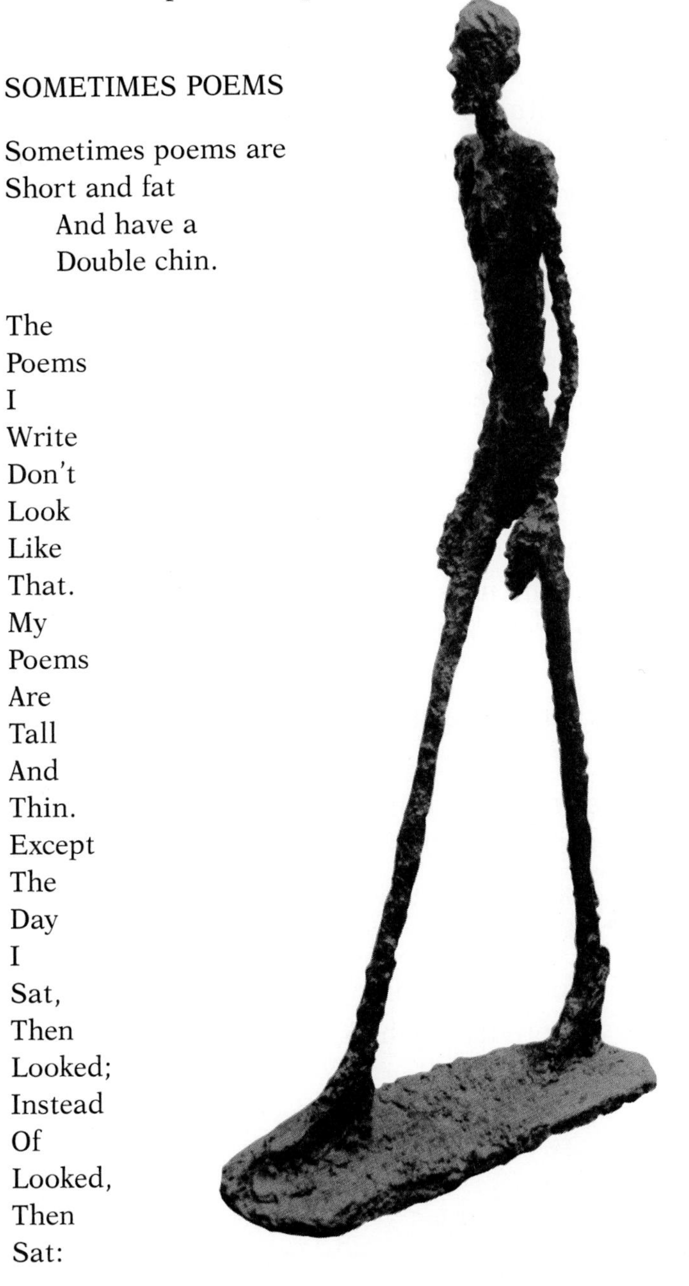

SOMETIMES POEMS

Sometimes poems are
Short and fat
    And have a
    Double chin.

The
Poems
I
Write
Don't
Look
Like
That.
My
Poems
Are
Tall
And
Thin.
Except
The
Day
I
Sat,
Then
Looked;
Instead
Of
Looked,
Then
Sat:

And squashed one flat.

—JUDITH VIORST

The subject of the first stanza of "Sometimes Poems" is short, fat poems with double chins. The stanza is shaped just like the subject. It is wider than it is long. The third and fourth lines tuck under the first two. The subject of the second stanza is skinny poems with very short lines. The shape of the stanza shows this. The third and last stanza shows how the poem looked when it got squashed.

Exercises Looking at the Shape of a Poem

A. Read "Sometimes Poems" on page 275. Then answer these questions about the poem.

1. How many stanzas are in the entire poem?
2. How many lines are in each stanza?
3. Is this poem written in sentences?
4. How many sentences are there in the poem?
5. How does the shape of the second stanza fit its subject?
6. How does the shape of the third stanza fit its subject?

B. Choose a subject for a poem, either one of the following or your own. Then write a poem in which the shape fits the meaning.

1. a word, such as *boring, rip,* or *downhill*
2. an animal, such as a worm, a bird, or a dog
3. an object, such as a train, a balloon, or a book
4. a career or activity, such as acrobatics, barbering, fishing, skiing, or sailing

2 Rhythm and Rhyme

Focus

Sound and **rhythm** can be used to add meaning to a poem.

When you read a poem, either aloud or silently, you hear the sounds of the words and phrases. Sound helps to bring out the meaning of a poem. Sound also helps to tell about the mood, or feeling, of a poem. Poets create sounds through patterns of **rhythm**, **rhyme**, and **alliteration.**

Rhythm

The words of a poem combine to create a **rhythm.** Rhythm is based on the strong beats in each line. In the following nonsense poem, the strong beats are marked. Read the poem aloud, stressing the marked words and parts of words.

A MAN IN THE WOODS SAID:

Fish with a spinner, fish with a fly,
Fish when the water is low or high,
But don't try to fish when the lake runs dry.

—JOHN CIARDI

The poem you just read has a strong, regular rhythm. You can hear clearly the four strong beats in each line.

Some poems do not have regular rhythm. The pace of the poem, or number of strong beats, may change from line to line.

Rhyme

Words whose endings sound alike are words that **rhyme**. In some poems, rhyming words fall at the ends of lines. In "The Bat" on page 274, the two lines in each stanza rhyme.

A **limerick** is a five-line poem with a pattern of rhyme. See if you can discover the pattern in this limerick.

DOGGEREL

There once was a sleeping hound, Si,
Who said in his sleep, "I can fly."
What he said wasn't true,
But you've heard, haven't you,
You're supposed to let sleeping dogs lie.

In a limerick, the first, second, and fifth lines rhyme. The third and fourth lines rhyme. A limerick has a quick, light rhythm. The long lines each have three strong beats. The shorter lines each have two beats. This rhythm fits the light-hearted subjects of these poems.

Alliteration

Alliteration is the repetition of consonant sounds at the beginning of words. This repetition can add rhythm and meaning to a poem. Here are some examples.

With curved claw Cat raked a furrow

—MARY CALHOUN

This example is about a cat. The sound made by the three *c*'s brings to mind the scratching movements of a cat.

Thirty thirsty thistles
Thicketed the green
Growing in a grassy swamp.

—KARLA KUSKIN

In the second poem, the *th* sound emphasizes the thickness of the thistles. The *gr* sound emphasizes their toughness.

Exercises Working with Sounds in Poetry

A. Read this poem. Then answer the questions.

THE TOASTER

A silver-scaled Dragon with jaws flaming red
Sits at my elbow and toasts my bread.
I hand him fat slices, and then, one by one,
He hands them back when he sees they are done.

—WILLIAM JAY SMITH

1. Tap out the beat of this poem. How many strong beats do you hear in each line?
2. What lines in this poem rhyme? Do the rhyming words form a pattern?

B. Reread the limerick "Doggerel." Review the rhythm and rhyme pattern of this poem. Does the poem contain alliteration?

Choose another animal as a subject. Write a limerick about the animal. Use the same rhythm and rhyme patterns as the sample limerick.

C. Choose one kind of food as a subject. Think about how it looks, feels, and tastes. Then write a poem about eating the food. Shape the poem to fit the subject. Use alliteration, if possible. You do not have to use regular patterns of rhythm and rhyme, although you may.

3 Pictures in Poetry

Focus

Poetry uses language to create pictures in the reader's mind.

When you read a poem, you see life through another person's eyes. A poet makes this possible by painting pictures with words. The pictures help to communicate the mood and the meaning of a poem. Three kinds of word pictures are **sensory images, similes,** and **metaphors.**

Sensory Images

A **sensory image** is a word or phrase that appeals to the senses. Images appeal to the senses of sight, hearing, smell, taste, and touch. For example, the image "polished puddles" appeals to the sense of sight. "Bees droning a sleepysong" appeals to the sense of hearing. "Purple velvet" appeals to both sight and touch.

Read the following lines from a poem by Robert Frost. To which senses do the images appeal?

> The buzz-saw snarled and rattled in the yard
> And made dust and dropped stove-length sticks of wood,
> Sweet-scented stuff when the breeze drew across it.

Simile and Metaphor

Both **similes** and **metaphors** compare unlike things that have something in common. Every simile includes the word *like* or *as*. Metaphors do not include these connection words. Read the similes and metaphors on the following page. What two things are compared in each? How are these two things alike?

The sun poured in like butterscotch.

—JONI MITCHELL

The moon had been lighted
and was hung in a treetop.

—STEPHEN CRANE

Your spoken words are roses fine and sweet,
The songs you sing are perfect pearls of sound.

—PAUL LAURENCE DUNBAR

The picture language of poetry can be used in other kinds of writing. You can use sensory images to make the people and places in stories and descriptions more real. You can use similes and metaphors to add a touch of imagination to description.

Exercises Creating Pictures in Poetry

A. Read the following poem. Then answer the questions.

BROKEN SKY

The sky of gray is eaten in six places,
Rag holes stand out.
It is an army blanket and the sleeper
slept too near the fire.

—CARL SANDBURG

1. What two things are being compared in this poem?
2. How are the two things alike?
3. Is the comparison a simile or a metaphor?

B. Choose a subject for a poem. List images that the subject brings to mind. Then arrange the images into a poem. Try to use a simile or metaphor in your poem.

Using English in Music

You have tried your hand at creating concrete poetry. You may also like to try creating concrete music. Concrete music is music made up of sounds in the environment. It is created by tape-recording sounds that have a special theme or that tell a story. For example, a composition of concrete music about sounds in the woods might begin with the sound of wind in the trees. It might continue with the sound of a brook gurgling over stones, the sound a squirrel makes scampering up a tree, bird songs, and the sound of a woodpecker tapping. It might finish with the sound, again, of wind in the trees.

Concrete music should have a beginning, a middle, and an ending. The beginning and the ending might be the same sound—the wind in the treetops, for example.

Exercise Creating Concrete Music

Below are some suggestions you can use to create concrete music. You can also think of your own idea.

1. At the Zoo—an Animal Symphony
2. Morning at Home (Use bits of talk if you like.)
3. Music Students Practicing
4. The Song of Garbage Collection Day

Choose a place with sounds you like. Experiment with a few sounds first. Record them and play them back, just to get a feeling for how they will sound on tape. Then create your composition of concrete music. You don't need to record all your sounds on one day. When you have finished, play your concrete music for your class.

Chapter 16 Review

Understanding Poetry Read this poem and answer the questions. Write the answers on your paper.

RAINY NIGHTS

I like the town on rainy nights
When everything is wet—
When all the town has magic lights
And streets of shining jet!

When all the rain about the town
Is like a looking-glass,
And all the lights are upside-down
Below me as I pass.

In all the pools are velvet skies,
And down the dazzling street
A fairy city gleams and lies
In beauty at my feet.

—IRENE THOMPSON

1. How many stanzas are in the poem? How many sentences are in the poem?
2. Is there a definite rhythm to the poem?
3. What lines rhyme? Do the rhyming words form a pattern?
4. Find an example of alliteration.
5. Look up the word *jet* in the dictionary. Which meaning has the poet used? Why do you think she chose this meaning?
6. Can you find a sensory image that appeals to both sight and touch?
7. What is the simile in the second stanza?
8. Find the metaphor in the third stanza. To what are the reflections in the pools compared?

Chapter 17

The Process of Writing To Tell *How*

Have you ever read the instructions for using a simple computer program? Have you ever read an encyclopedia article that explained how a volcano erupts? Have you ever checked out a "how-to" book from the library—*How To Make Paper Sculptures* or *How To Build Kites*? Each of these pieces of writing explains *how*.

In this chapter, you will learn to use the process of writing to explain *how*. You might tell how to do something. You might also tell how something happens or works. You will learn to write explanations that are easy to follow as well as interesting to read.

1 Thinking About Explanations

Focus

Writing that tells *how* explains how to do something or how something works or happens.

You are often asked to explain how something is done or how something works. In science class you might be studying ways to make science equipment from simple household materials. Your teacher might ask you to write about how to make a compass. How would you do this?

Example 1

Read and Think. Rick wrote these directions telling how to make a compass. Notice how he explains the process.

A compass that works can be made from items usually found around the house. First, collect a magnet, a sewing needle, a knife, a cork, a nonmetallic dish of water, and a teaspoon of detergent. Next, magnetize the needle. To do this, rub the needle with a magnet several times in the same direction. Then, make a groove on the flat side of the cork with a knife. Put the magnetized needle in the groove. Place the cork and needle in the nonmetallic dish of water. Finally, add one teaspoon of detergent to the water. This last step will stop any surface tension on the water. Surface tension causes the needle to drift to the side of the dish or to wobble. Now your compass is finished. Your needle should be pointing north!

Think and Discuss. Think about the following questions.

1. Are the steps for making a compass presented in any special order? What is that order?
2. What might happen if some of the steps were switched around or left out?

Example 2

Read and Think. Rick's paragraph explained how to do something. Now read a paragraph that tells how something works. The writer explains how braces straighten teeth.

> Chances are you know someone with braces. Four million people in the United States wear them to move out-of-line teeth back to where they belong. Braces do their job by gently pushing or pulling teeth. The orthodontist—a dentist who fits braces—hooks wires to holders that cement on to each tooth. The doctor adjusts the wires to move the teeth slowly in the right direction. Each tooth—all the way to the root—shifts in the jawbone. When the teeth get to the correct spot, off come the braces. The jawbone grows around the root and holds it in the new position.
>
> —from *3-2-1 CONTACT*

Think and Discuss. Read and answer these questions. Talk about your ideas with your classmates.

1. In what order are the steps given that tell how braces work?
2. Is each step stated simply and clearly?
3. After reading this explanation, were you able to understand how braces work?

Now It's Your Turn

You have now read and thought about two paragraphs that tell *how*. Each paragraph uses clear steps to explain how to do something or how something happens or works. Each presents these steps in time order—the order that they happen—to help the reader follow the explanation. In this chapter, you will learn to share your knowledge and interests. You will write an explanation that tells *how*.

2 Prewriting: Gathering Ideas

Focus

To start the writing process, decide exactly what you want to explain. Next, list all the steps and information needed to explain your topic.

Choosing a Topic

Often the topic for an explanation is chosen for you. A friend sees your go-cart. He asks you how you made it. Your class is studying volcanoes. Your teacher asks you to report on how a volcano erupts.

Sometimes, however, you can select your own topic to tell *how*. You might choose a process that you already know well. For example, if your hobby is building models, you might explain how to put together a working model rocket. You can also select a topic that you do not know well but that you want to find out more about. For example, you might want to know how the northern lights happen or how radar works.

Gathering Information

Once you have your topic, you have to make some notes about what you want to include in your explanation. If your topic is one you know well, the information in your notes will come from your own knowledge. However, if you do not know your topic well, your information will have to come from outside sources. You could get information from newspapers, magazines, and encyclopedias. You could also talk to a person who is an expert on your topic. To learn more about getting information from outside sources, see Chapter 21, "Sharpening Library and Research Skills."

Listing Important Steps

After you make notes about your topic, list all the steps involved in the process. State each step simply and clearly. If you are telling how to do something, imagine yourself going through the process. If you are explaining how something happens or works, pretend you are writing for people who know nothing about your topic. Be sure to include every step.

When you explain how to do something, your list of important steps should include gathering all the necessary materials such as tools, ingredients, or other supplies.

Exercises Finding a Topic

A. Thinking of Topics Do the activities below. They will help you think of topics for an explanation that tells *how*. Keep your ideas in your writing folder.

1. Write "I know how to . . . ." on your paper ten times. Then complete the sentence in ten different ways.
2. Ask ten questions about everyday objects in your home. Ask how your refrigerator stays cold, how a camera takes pictures, or how a microwave oven cooks.
3. Imagine you have been asked to produce a television show. The purpose of this show is to explain to people your age how the world around them works. What topics do you think your audience would like to know more about? Try to think of five topics. Begin each one with "How . . ." or "How to . . . ."

B. Choosing a Topic Select a topic for the explanation you are going to write. Choose your ideas from Exercise A or from the topics listed in the **Power Handbook** on pages 412-414. Then, begin your prewriting notes. Gather the information you need to explain your topic. Write down all the steps in the process. If you are explaining how to do something, include any necessary materials.

3 Prewriting: Ordering Details

Focus

The steps in an explanation that tells *how* should be arranged in time order.

To understand how something works, your reader needs to know what happens first, second, and so on. To follow directions successfully, your reader must complete each step in the right order. To help your reader understand your explanation, arrange the steps in the order in which they happen. This is called step-by-step order, or **time order**.

Arranging Your Details

Look over your notes. What happens first? Write a 1 beside this step. Put a 2 beside the second step and continue until all your steps are numbered. This list of numbered steps is called a **writing plan**. When you are telling how to do something, your first step will include gathering any materials you need for the project. Your last step will state the final product or result.

After you have numbered all your steps, look over them again. Have you left out any steps? If so, add them to your notes at this time.

A Sample Writing Plan

Anne's hobby is performing magic tricks. She decided to explain how to do one of her tricks. Below is her writing plan for explaining how to turn a full glass of water upside down without spilling a drop. Notice how she numbered her steps. Look at her thoughts as she studied her notes. The thoughts are shown in blue.

2. fill the glass with water
1. materials needed—(water) glass, water, paper
3. place paper across glass
4. press hand down on paper
7. ~~6~~. take your hand away
6. ~~5~~. press the paper a little longer
5. *turn glass upside down*

I should say what kind of glass.

I forgot an important step.

Exercises Arranging Details

A. Organizing Steps Imagine that you want to explain how a bee makes beeswax for a hive. Your prewriting notes are shown below. Finish numbering your details in step-by-step order.

1. a gland in the bee's abdomen makes wax
3. wax forms tiny white flakes
   wax becomes soft as chewed
2. wax oozes to the outside of bee's abdomen
   bee chews on the waxy flakes
   bee picks off flakes on abdomen with legs
   bee adds wax to honeycomb of hive

B. Making a Writing Plan Look over the list of steps you wrote in part 2 for your paragraph telling *how*. Number your details in time order. Then read over your organized notes. Add any missing details. Take out any details that are not needed.

4 Drafting an Explanation

Focus

Use your writing plan as a guide to draft your explanation.

A good writing plan is like a good map. Both tell you where to go next. Use your writing plan when you write your first draft. Continue to think about your topic as you write. Does each step follow smoothly from the step that came before it? Is each step written simply and clearly? If you need to, make changes as you draft. However, do not try to make your draft perfect at this time. You will have a chance to make your explanation even better when you revise it.

A Sample Draft

Anne used her writing plan to write the first draft of her explanation of a magic trick. Notice her thoughts as she worked on her draft.

I'd better be specific about how much water is needed.

To begin this trick, you will need a water glass, paper, and water. Fill the glass to the ^*very* top with water. Put the paper across the top of the glass. Press your hand down on the paper. Turn the glass upside down. Press the paper for a minute more. ^*Finally,* Take your hand away.

I should signal that this is the last step.

Anne thought more about her explanation as she drafted it. She will make more changes as she continues to use the writing process.

Signal Your Steps

Certain words and phrases can be used to "signal" a new step. These signal words can also show a time relationship between steps. Anne used *finally* as a signal word in her draft. Here are some common signal words that are helpful in telling how to do something or how something happens or works.

> **Signal Words**
>
> first, second, next, last, finally, then, now, when, while, until, as, after that, at the same time, the next step

Use these signal words or others like them as you draft and revise. They will help a reader follow the steps more easily.

Exercises Drafting an Explanation

A. Using Signal Words Add signal words to this draft to help the reader follow the steps.

> Panning for gold is easy and can be profitable! You'll need a good guidebook, an old pie pan, a small shovel, a pair of tweezers, and a jar with a lid. Use your guidebook to find a likely stream. Shovel gravel into the pan. Fill the pan with water. Slosh the watery gravel from side to side. Hold the pan over the stream. Wobble the pan up and down. The water will start to swirl around. Let the dirty water wash over the rim of the pan. Small pebbles, heavy black sand, and gold are left in the pan. Use tweezers to pick out the flecks of gold. Drop the gold into a jar with water.

B. Writing Your First Draft Write a first draft of your explanation. Follow your writing plan. If necessary, add ideas or rearrange them.

5 Revising an Explanation That Tells *How*

Focus

As you revise your first draft, make sure your explanation is simple, clear, and complete.

Writing that tells *how* must be easy to follow. When you revise, think about the questions in the box below.

Guidelines for Revising a *How* Explanation

1. Did I include all the required materials and any other necessary information?
2. Have I stated all the steps of the process?
3. Are my steps stated simply and clearly?
4. Have I used signal words to make my explanation easier to follow?

Ask one or two friends to read your draft. See if they can follow your directions and understand your explanation. Their comments can help you to revise your explanation.

A Sample Revision

A friend of Anne's read her draft. She tried to do Anne's trick. After Anne's friend dried off, she had these questions.

"What is the outcome of the trick? You never really say."

"Do you keep your hand on the paper as you turn the glass upside down?"

"How much paper do you need?"

Anne did not want any more friends to get wet. She thought about her friend's suggestions and then revised her paragraph. Notice her thoughts as she worked.

I need a good topic sentence.

I should add signal words.

I must make these instructions clearer.

I need to tell the outcome of the trick.

With this special magic trick, you can defy gravity! To begin ~~this trick~~, you will need a water glass, *one piece of* paper, and water. *First,* ~~F~~fill the glass to the very top with water. *Next,* ~~P~~put the *piece of* paper across the top of the glass. Press your hand down on the paper. *Keep pressing down with one hand as you* ~~T~~turn the glass upside down *with your other hand*. Press the paper for a minute or more. Finally, take your hand away. *The paper will seem to hold the water in the glass.*

Proofreading Your Explanation

Before you can make a final copy of your explanation, you must proofread it carefully. Look for mistakes in grammar, capitalization, punctuation, and spelling. Neatly correct any errors you find. For a review of proofreading symbols, turn to page 112.

Study the lines below from an explanation telling *how*. Notice how the writer has used proofreading symbols to correct the mistakes.

> ¶ Building a model rocket is fun and educational. First, take the parts out of the kit. Check them against the instructions to make sure you have ~~got~~ all the parts. Then start reading the instructions. Read all the instructions before you start building the rocket.

Exercises Revising an Explanation

A. Helping a Classmate Revise As your teacher directs, help a classmate revise his or her explanation. Read the rough draft. If the paragraph is telling how to do something, try to follow the directions in your mind. If the paragraph is telling how something happens or works, try to understand the process. Think about the questions in the box on page 294. Make at least two suggestions that the writer could use to make the draft clearer.

B. Revising Your Explanation Use the questions on page 294 to revise your explanation. Also, use the suggestions of a friend or classmate who has read your draft.

6 Writing and Sharing a Final Copy

Focus

Proofread your writing a final time. Choose an interesting title that hints at the process you are explaining. Then make a final copy of your work.

You want to be proud of your final copy. Make it clean and neat. Choose a title for your explanation. The title of an explanation often names the subject being explained.

Here is the final copy of Anne's paragraph. Notice how she used the ideas from page 294.

The Water Trick

With this special magic trick, you can defy gravity! To begin, you will need a water glass, one piece of paper, and water. First, fill the glass to the very top with water. Next, put the piece of paper across the top of the glass. Press your hand down on the paper. Keep pressing down with one hand as you turn the glass upside down with your other hand. Press the paper for a minute more. Finally, take your hand away. The paper will seem to hold the water in the glass.

Exercise Making a Final Copy and Sharing

Proofread your final draft one more time for errors in grammar, capitalization, punctuation, and spelling. Think of a good title. Then, make a clean, final copy of your explanation. Finally, check this final copy for any errors. Turn to pages 114-115 and choose a method of sharing your writing with your classmates.

Speaking and Listening

Oral Explanations

In this chapter, you learned how to write an explanation that tells *how*. You can also give a talk that explains how to do something.

For example, you might demonstrate a simple science experiment or craft project. Begin by telling the class what you are demonstrating. Be sure the class can see the materials and tools you are using. Explain each step in the process in time order. Pause after each step. Use signal words to help your listeners follow your demonstration. At the end of your talk, answer any questions your classmates may have.

Here are some guidelines to help you prepare your demonstration talk.

1. Do the demonstration several times yourself. Practice until you feel sure of yourself.
2. Make notes as you practice. Do not write your notes on 3″ x 5″ cards. Instead, write the same information you would put on a card, a fact or two, on a sheet of paper. Write in large letters. You will be able to place your notes so that you can read them, but your hands will be free to do the demonstration.
3. Practice doing the demonstration and telling about it at the same time. Practice in front of family or friends. Ask them to suggest ways you can improve your demonstration.

Exercise Giving a Demonstration Talk

Give a demonstration of a science experiment. Choose a simple experiment from your science book, or ask your teacher to help you choose one. Use the guidelines above and on page 199 to help you practice. When you feel ready, present the experiment to your class.

Creative Writing

Have you ever heard of Rube Goldberg? Reuben Lucius Goldberg was an American cartoonist during the early and middle 1900's. He became famous for his comical drawings of incredibly complicated machines. Although his machines always looked complicated, it turned out that they usually performed some very simple or silly task. Here is one of Goldberg's drawings.

Pencil Sharpener

Professor Butts gets his think-tank working and evolves the simplified pencil sharpener.

Open window (**A**) and fly kite (**B**). String (**C**) lifts small door (**D**), allowing moths (**E**) to escape and eat red flannel shirt (**F**). As weight of shirt becomes less, shoe (**G**) steps on switch (**H**) which heats electric iron (**I**) and burns hole in pants (**J**). Smoke (**K**) enters hole in tree (**L**), smoking out opossum (**M**) which jumps into basket (**N**), pulling rope (**O**) and lifting cage (**P**), allowing woodpecker (**Q**) to chew wood from pencil (**R**), exposing lead. Emergency knife (**S**) is always handy in case opossum or the woodpecker gets sick and can't work.

Imagine you are Rube Goldberg. However, instead of just drawing inventions, you also write about them. Think of a wonderfully complicated invention that performs some simple or silly task. Draw a colorful picture of your machine. Under the picture, write a paragraph that explains what your invention does and how it works. Be sure to use time order to explain your invention. Think about what you have learned in this chapter as you plan and write your paragraph.

Using English in Science

The planet Earth is home to billions of people. Most of the time, Earth is a gentle home. The seas and the soil feed us. The rain provides nourishment for crops. Melting snow from the mountains keeps the rivers flowing. The winds blow the clouds away.

Sometimes, however, Earth is not so gentle. The seas rise up in tidal waves. The ground trembles and splits from earthquakes. Soft rains become hurricanes. Mountains explode in volcanic eruptions. Breezes turn into tornadoes.

What causes these natural catastrophes? Scientists are busy trying to discover the answers. They believe that the more we know about our planet, the better we will be able to predict when the gentle Earth is about to become destructive.

Exercise **Explaining the Natural World**

How much do you know about the not-so-gentle side of your planet? Do some research in the library about tidal waves, earthquakes, hurricanes, volcanoes, or tornadoes. You might also explore other natural occurrences like clouds, fog, waterspouts, or snow. Write a paragraph explaining *how* about your topic. Use what you have learned in this chapter to help you plan and write your explanation.

Chapter 17 Review

A. Organizing an Explanation Look at the following prewriting notes telling how to give a dog a bath. Copy the notes on your own paper. Number them in the order in which they would be presented. Add any details that might have been left out.

wet down with hose
equipment needed: hose, dog, water, brush, bucket, comb
put soap and water in bucket
scrub dog
rinse dog with hose
dip brush in soapy water
groom dog with comb
dry dog with towel

B. Finding Signal Words Read the following paragraph. Then answer the questions.

It's easy to start a new geranium plant from a cutting. First, you will need a geranium, a knife or pruning shears, a pot, a mixture of soil and sand, and water. Next, put the mixture of sand and soil in the pot. Then cut a leafy stem off the geranium. Cut just below a node, or bump. Now place the cutting in the pot of soil and sand. Finally, water your new plant.

1. How many steps are listed in this process?
2. Make a list of the signal words that are used in the paragraph.

Cumulative Review

Composition

A. Writing Descriptions Write a brief description of the school cafeteria at lunchtime or a restaurant at suppertime. Include good sensory images and a simile or a metaphor in your description.

B. Explaining *How* Write a brief explanation of how to do something or how something works. Choose subjects that are familiar to you. If you like taking pictures, you could explain how to put film in a camera or tell how a camera works.

Grammar

Adjectives and Adverbs Number your paper from 1 to 10. Choose the correct word from the parentheses. Write it on your paper.

1. The train was (a, an) hour and (a, an) half late.
2. (Those, Them) codes are difficult to solve.
3. The detective said that this was the (more, most) difficult of the three cases.
4. Alma's cold is (worse, worst) today than it was yesterday.
5. Do not move (quick, quickly) or the frightened fawn will run away.
6. Both of the performers were (real, really) good, but I thought that the magician was (better, best) than the clown.
7. A beehive was the (most interesting, more interesting) thing I saw on the nature trail.
8. Neal used (this, these) kinds of tools to make the designs on his belt.
9. Popcorn tastes (good, well) with salt and butter.
10. Which of the two tan horses in the field is (tamer, tamest, most tame)?

Related Skills

A. Improving Sentences Improve the following sentences. Follow any directions in parentheses. Leave out words in italics.

1. No one plays that piano anymore. *It is* old. *It is* broken.
2. Mr. Jackson took us fishing last week and I caught two striped bass and Jerry caught three large trout.
3. Guavas may be eaten raw. *Guavas may be* cooked to make jelly. (Join sentence parts with **and** or **or**.)
4. Our town had an art fair for the children and Kevin's model won a blue ribbon and Shirley's wire sculpture took second prize.
5. In the forest, rangers found raccoon tracks. They did not find any bear or deer tracks. (Join sentences with **, but**.)

B. Poetry Read the following poem, "Ways of Composing." On your paper, answer the questions that follow.

typewriter:
a mouthful of teeth chattering
afraid to be quiet

a pencil can lie down and dream
dark and silver silences

—EVE MERRIAM

1. Give an example of a sensory image that appeals to the sense of sound.
2. Give an example of alliteration in the poem.
3. How many stanzas does the poem contain?
4. Which does the poem contain, a simile or a metaphor? Write it. What two things are being compared?

UNIT 4

Horizons

In Unit 4 you will combine and expand the skills you have been learning in this book. You will use your knowledge to explore new horizons.

You will discover how to find information in a library. You will see how to organize the facts you gather to write a report or to explain an opinion. You will learn to think clearly about information you find.

You can use the skills you have learned in all areas of your life. The opinions you hold will be stronger. Your library skills will help you to find any information you need. Your writing skills can help you tell about how you feel in a letter to the editor. The skills you gain can help you break free from everyday things. What you learn will help you stretch your wings and soar to new worlds and ideas.

YOUR WORLD

Your world is as big as you make it.
I know, for I used to abide
In the narrowest nest in a corner,
My wings pressing close to my side.

But I sighted the distant horizon
Where the sky line encircled the sea
And I throbbed with a burning desire
To travel this immensity.

I battered the cordons around me
And cradled my wings on the breeze
Then soared to the uttermost reaches
With rapture, with power, with ease!

—GEORGIA DOUGLAS JOHNSON

31

Chapter 18

Using Prepositions

Tom and Ted are finalists in this year's bikeathon. Tom is trying to overtake Ted. Read each sentence below. Certain words show where Tom is riding in relation to Ted. Can you tell who won?

Tom is riding behind Ted.
Tom is riding around Ted.
Tom is riding beside Ted.
Tom is riding beyond Ted.

The words *behind, around, beside,* and *beyond* are prepositions. These prepositions help you see the location of both Tom and Ted. A preposition is a word that relates the noun or pronoun following it to another word in the sentence.

In this chapter, you will learn all about prepositions, objects of prepositions, and prepositional phrases. You will learn how prepositions differ from adverbs. You will find that you can add interest to your writing by using prepositional phrases.

1 What Are Prepositions?

Focus

A **preposition** is a word that relates the noun or pronoun that follows it to some other word in the sentence.

A **preposition** relates words to each other in a sentence. Read this sentence. Let it form a picture in your mind.

Jim sat beside his friend.

One word tells you where Jim should be in your picture in relation to his friend. The word *beside* is placed before *friend* to show the relationship between Jim and his friend. The word *beside* is a preposition.

Read these sentences. Two words show the change in the relationship between Jim and his friend.

Jim sat near his friend.
Jim sat behind his friend.

The words *near* and *behind* show different relationships between Jim and his friend. *Near* and *behind* are prepositions.

Here is a list of words often used as prepositions.

about	before	down	of	through
above	behind	during	off	to
across	below	for	on	under
after	beside	from	outside	until
around	between	in	over	up
at	by	near	past	with

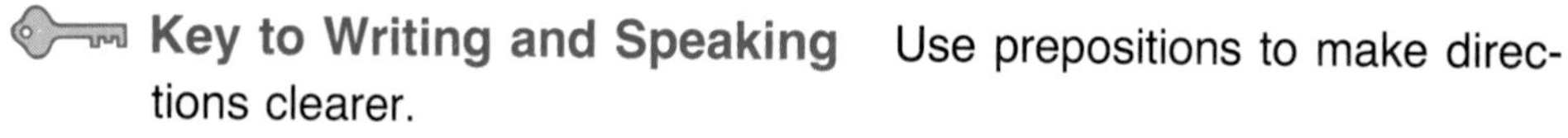

Key to Writing and Speaking Use prepositions to make directions clearer.

Example: Climb *over* the hill, walk *around* the lake, and go *by* the waterfall.

Exercises Finding Prepositions

A. Number your paper from 1 to 10. Find the preposition in each sentence and write it.

1. The train stopped at the station.
2. Please stand between Omar and Franklin.
3. Sara found the book under her bed.
4. The crowd cheered for their team.
5. Pam walked across the beach.
6. Ben fell off his skateboard.
7. The jet flew through the clouds.
8. Barbara threw a penny into the wishing well.
9. The letter is from my aunt.
10. Jung Lee skipped a stone on the water.

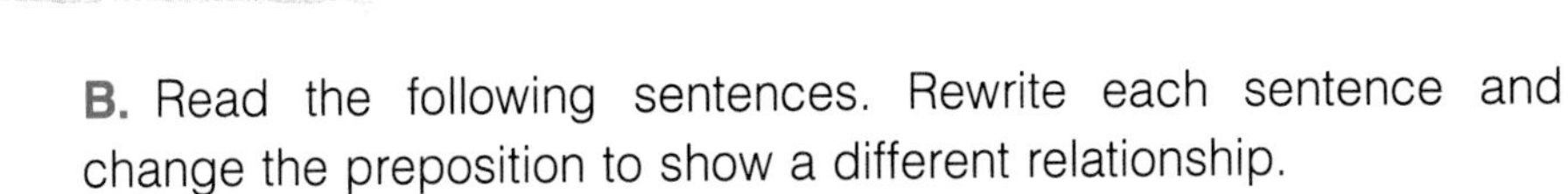

B. Read the following sentences. Rewrite each sentence and change the preposition to show a different relationship.

1. Larry found his shoes under the couch.
2. When we stood, Wendy was behind me.
3. Math class is before English.
4. Dad drove across the overpass.
5. Did you leave a postcard on the ledge?
6. Sadie went past the store every afternoon.
7. Jack was at the gym when the bell rang.
8. Two birds flew through the window.
9. John said, "Sit beside me."
10. A music box lay behind the dresser.

C. Writing Imagine that you are floating weightlessly in a spaceship. You may feel very strange as you tumble around. Write a brief paragraph describing how you feel and how you are moving. Use prepositions to help you describe your movements.

2 Prepositional Phrases

Focus

The noun or pronoun following a preposition is called the **object of the preposition.**

A **prepositional phrase** is a group of words that includes a preposition, its object, and the modifiers of the object.

Objects of Prepositions

Read these sentences.

I had a glass of *water*.
I had a glass of cold *milk*.
I had a glass of cold, refreshing *juice*.

Of is the preposition in each of the sentences. *Water, milk,* and *juice* are nouns following the preposition. They are objects of the preposition *of*. Look at these sentences.

Calvin wrote a story about *me*.
Mr. Marinas depends on *her* to finish the job.

Her and *me* are objects of prepositions. *Her* and *me* are **object pronouns**. Subject pronouns are never used as objects.

Prepositional Phrases

The group of words that includes a preposition and its object is called a **prepositional phrase**. The phrase also includes all words that modify the object. Here is an example.

The clown gave a balloon *to the happy little child.*

The prepositional phrase is *to the happy little child.*

A prepositional phrase can be found anywhere in a sentence. It may be at the beginning, in the middle, or at the end. Some sentences can have more than one prepositional phrase. Find the prepositional phrases in these examples.

> During the thunderstorm, my dog hid under my bed.
> The ball rolled to the bottom of the hill.

Key to Writing Add prepositional phrases to make your writing more descriptive.

Examples: The terrapin pulled his head *into his spotted shell.*
A bullfrog *with very large eyes* watched us.

Exercises **Recognizing Prepositional Phrases**

A. For each sentence, write the preposition and its object. Draw one line under the preposition and two lines under its object.

1. The sale will continue until Saturday.
2. Cindy brought an extra sandwich for her grandfather.
3. Kimberly hung her painting on the wall.
4. Pour the lemonade into the tall glasses.
5. Ann's seeing eye dog goes everywhere with her.
6. Gina searched everywhere and then found her glasses on the seat beside her.
7. Nicole rode her bike over the narrow bridge.
8. Tom was late, and the bus left without him.
9. Christopher lives near me.
10. The circus parade was led by the ringmaster.

B. For each sentence, write the prepositional phrase. Draw one line under the preposition and two lines under its object.

Example: Kim went out the door.
out the door

1. Ms. Strade drove carefully through the thick fog.
2. Beth took the money from her and wrote a receipt.
3. Near the river, Jackson found footprints.
4. Superman leaped over the tall building.
5. Rochelle tiptoed past the old, deserted house.
6. As we entered the movie theater, the usher took our tickets from us.
7. Sally saw her reflection in the still, quiet water.
8. Write your name on your own paper.
9. Sean saw the exit sign above the door.
10. Behind the shed, you will find the wheelbarrow.

C. Writing The children's song "Over the River and Through the Woods" describes how to get to grandmother's house. Draw an imaginary map from your house to grandmother's house. Then write a paragraph that describes the entire route. When you draw your map, make sure you include trees, lakes, bridges, hills, and other things to go over, around, into, or on.

3 Identifying Prepositions and Adverbs

Focus

Some words may be used in sentences as either **adverbs** or **prepositions**.

Look at these sentences.

Bob fell down.
Bob fell down the steps.

The word *down* appears in both sentences. In the first sentence, *down* is used as an adverb. In the second sentence, it is a preposition.

To tell if a word is used as a preposition or an adverb, examine the sentence. If the word is used alone, it is probably an adverb. Prepositions are never used alone. They are used in phrases. If the word has an object, it is a preposition. A preposition always has an object.

In the first sentence above, *down* is used alone. *Down* also answers the question *where,* one of the jobs of an adverb. Therefore, *down* is being used as an adverb. In the second sentence, *down* is used in a phrase. It has an object, *steps.* Therefore, it is being used as a preposition.

Read these sentences. How is *along* used in each one?

Janet rode along the trail.
Janet rode along.

In the first sentence, *along* is used in a phrase, *along the trail.* It has an object, *trail. Along* is a preposition in that sentence. In the second sentence, *along* is used alone. It is an adverb.

Exercises **Identifying Prepositions and Adverbs**

A. Number your paper from 1 to 10. After each number write *a* and *b*. After each letter, write if the word in italics is used as a preposition or an adverb.

1. a. Jackie looked *up*.
   b. Jackie looked *up* the elevator shaft.
2. a. Don't come *near*.
   b. Don't come *near* the broken glass.
3. a. The ferocious tiger walked *around* her cubs.
   b. The ferocious tiger walked *around*.
4. a. Merilee peeked *outside*.
   b. Merilee peeked *outside* the front door.
5. a. No one drove *past* us.
   b. No one drove *past*.

B. Rewrite the following sentences. Change the adverb to a preposition by adding an object and making a prepositional phrase.

1. Jump over.
2. Max followed behind.
3. Katie painted the letters on.
4. The cat climbed up.
5. Our band marched in.
6. The baby crawled around.
7. A train zoomed by.
8. Can you squeeze through?
9. Don't reach across.
10. Denise looked down.

C. Writing Write a paragraph describing an imaginary place. Since this place exists only in your mind, you must give an exact description. Include at least six of the following words.

above	below	near	over	under
around	between	of	through	with
behind	in	on	to	

Exercises for Mastery

Chapter 18

Using Prepositions

A. Finding Prepositions Write each preposition and the object of that preposition for each of the sentences below. Draw one line under the preposition and two lines under the object.

1. The subway train sped past him.
2. Will you be going to the store?
3. She will be finished in a minute.
4. How many of those do you have?
5. Two players from the Dodgers came to our banquet.

B. Finding Prepositional Phrases Write the prepositional phrase in each sentence below.

1. The ball fell between the two outfielders.
2. Tony's father planned a surprise party for him.
3. Alone in the house, I heard a strange noise.
4. Neil Armstrong was the first person on the moon.
5. After the storm, the streets were flooded.

C. Identifying Prepositions and Adverbs In each pair of sentences below, one word is used as both a preposition and an adverb. Write the word that is used two ways. Then write the letter of the sentence in which it is used as a preposition.

1. a. Doug sailed on.
   b. Doug sailed on the Ohio River.
2. a. The puppies jumped around the room.
   b. The puppies jumped around.
3. a. Renee leaned over the desk.
   b. Renee leaned over.
4. a. A light hung above.
   b. A light hung above the door.
5. a. The circus elephant walked slowly past.
   b. The circus elephant walked slowly past us.

Using Grammar in Writing

A. Pretend the newest student in your school is from Pluto. You and your classmates are writing a book explaining how Earth people do things. Your job is to write a paragraph explaining how to turn a somersault. Make sure your directions are exact. Underline all the prepositions with one line. Underline all the adverbs with two lines.

B. Write directions for finding buried treasure on a small deserted island. Use prepositions correctly.

C. **Using Prepositions in Health** Younger children often need help and instructions as they learn good daily grooming habits. Choose three of the items below. Write brief instructions to explain how these items should be used. Remember, you are telling someone much younger than you. Keep your directions simple and clear. Use prepositions correctly.

comb	dental floss	shampoo
toothpaste	soap	cotton swabs

Chapter 18 Review

A. Finding Prepositional Phrases Number your paper from 1 to 10. Find the prepositional phrases in the following sentences. Write them on your paper. Draw one line under the preposition and two lines under its object. Some sentences have more than one prepositional phrase.

1. Two of the girls at the fair won blue ribbons.
2. She sat across the aisle and behind us.
3. The bright sunshine beamed through the stained glass window.
4. His chances were one in a million.
5. The pride of lions moved slowly through the tall prairie grass.
6. The covers fell off the bed during the night.
7. If the ball rolls into the street, don't run after it.
8. We should wait until morning.
9. The firefighter climbed up the ladder with the hose.
10. Before this game, no one had ever scored that many points.

B. Finding Adverbs and Prepositional Phrases Divide your paper into two columns. Label one *Adverbs* and the other *Prepositional Phrases*. Find all the adverbs and prepositional phrases in the following paragraph and write each one in the correct column. You should find five adverbs and seven prepositional phrases.

Denny looked around. He checked outside, above the rafters, and under the loose floor boards. After that, he thought he heard a sound coming through the walls. What was happening? Nothing had knocked over the garbage can inside the shed before. Across the room, he saw the culprit behind the lawn mower. It was a baby raccoon that had turned the can over!

Chapter 19

Thinking Clearly

Suppose you read an ad that promises using a certain toothpaste will give you gorgeous teeth. Should you believe the ad?

Perhaps you hear someone say, "Everyone should know how to use a computer." Is this statement true? Should every person be comfortable at a keyboard?

You arrive home from school and find the door to your house locked. Can you figure out what to do?

Throughout your life, you will find yourself in situations that require you to think carefully and sensibly. Certain skills are necessary for clear thinking. These skills include telling fact from opinion, recognizing errors in thinking, drawing conclusions, and solving problems.

In this chapter, you will learn how to develop good thinking skills. These skills will be useful to you throughout your life.

1 Fact and Opinion

Focus

A **fact** is a statement that can be proved true. An **opinion** tells what someone believes or feels about something. Opinions cannot be proven.

Facts and opinions make up almost all of what you read, write, say, and hear. It is important to know the difference between the two.

Understanding Fact

A fact is a statement that can be proved true. For example, the sentence *George Washington was our first President* states a fact. You can prove that this information is true.

You can prove facts in different ways. Read the following:

1. My dad is chopping down the tree.
2. The sand dollar is a sea urchin.
3. A house can be built in four months.

You could use personal observation to prove some facts; for example, the first statement. If you can see your dad chopping down the tree, then the sentence states a fact.

You can also check a reliable source to prove a fact. Sometimes the source is a book. For example, you could look up *sand dollar* in the dictionary or encyclopedia to check the second statement.

Sometimes the reliable source is a person. An expert can be a good source of information. To prove that the third statement is true, you might talk to a carpenter or builder.

Recognizing Opinion

An opinion tells what someone believes. The sentence *Abraham Lincoln was our best President* states an opinion. The word *best* tells how someone feels about Abraham Lincoln. This opinion cannot be proved true.

You can recognize an opinion by looking for certain words called judgment words. **Judgment words** express feelings. Some examples are *best, worst, exciting, boring, should, believe,* or *feel.*

When you recognize an opinion, study it carefully. Decide whether you can accept or believe it. A good opinion will be supported by facts.

The sentence *Abraham Lincoln was our best President* states an opinion. Supporting facts should tell why someone might think he was our best President. Such facts might be these:

1. He worked to free the slaves.
2. He kept the country from being divided.
3. He was a self-made man.

Exercise Recognizing Fact and Opinion

On your paper, write whether each of the following statements is *Fact* or *Opinion.*

1. Products with well-known brand labels are better than generic products.
2. A liter bottle is larger than a quart bottle.
3. Nonfiction books are boring.
4. Vampire bats have sharp V-shaped teeth.
5. All states should pass a seat belt law.
6. Windsurfing is fun and exciting.
7. A pommel is located below the horn on a saddle.
8. Porcupine quills make the best fishing bobbers.
9. Ice-skating is harder to learn than roller-skating.
10. In bowling, the number five pin is the kingpin.

2 Errors in Thinking

Focus

Errors in thinking can occur when people use overgeneralization or slanted language. Knowing about errors in thinking can help you recognize weak opinions.

Overgeneralization

A **generalization** is a statement about a whole group. For example, suppose that the Wilson family has seven members. Five have blonde hair. You could say that most of the Wilsons have blond hair. You have made a generalization.

An overgeneralization is also a statement about a whole group. However, an **overgeneralization** is too broad to be true.

Everyone loves pizza. (absolutely everyone?)
No one travels by train these days. (not anyone?)

Overgeneralizations are usually unfair and often harmful. To correct overgeneralizations, replace words such as *all, every, never,* and *nobody*. Use limiting words such as *most, some,* or *usually* instead.

Most people like pizza.
Few people travel by train these days.

Slanted Language

Look at the following sentences.

He lives in a *cramped shack.* He lives in a *cozy cottage.*

When words are used to create a certain feeling, the speaker or writer is using **slanted language**. How do the italicized words change the sentences? Which sentence creates a positive, or good, feeling? Which one creates a negative, or bad, feeling?

Slanted language often appears in opinions. It can be used to sway the feelings of a listener or reader. The idea in the examples can be expressed without using slanted language. You could say:

He lives in a *small house.*

Think clearly about the words you hear and read. Do they make you feel a certain way? If so, study the facts again. As you write and speak, choose words carefully. Try to state a fact fairly. Be aware of the kind of feeling your words create.

Exercises Correcting Errors in Thinking

A. Rewrite the following examples of overgeneralization. Remove or limit the overstatement.

1. That weather forecaster is never right.
2. Jeremy gets a hit every time he goes to bat.
3. Athletes are always poor students.
4. All the colonists bravely resisted the British.
5. You never listen to anything I say.
6. No one would drive in this kind of weather.
7. I don't like Swiss cheese. Cheese doesn't taste good.
8. Gina was stung by a bee. All insects are harmful.
9. The three o'clock train is always late.
10. All sweets are junk food.

B. Identify the slanted words in the following sentences. Rewrite the sentences to create a different feeling.

1. Ticket agents give ridiculous excuses for late flights.
2. The house showed signs of flimsy construction.
3. Charm shampoo gives your hair glorious, golden highlights.
4. Dorothea is such a stingy person.
5. Uncle Eliot stubbornly refused to change his mind.

3 Drawing Conclusions

Focus

If you are given a series of related facts, you can **draw a conclusion.**

A **conclusion** is an opinion or decision you reach after you study the available facts. You are often asked to draw conclusions based on a set of facts. In geography, you may learn facts such as the average temperature and amount of rainfall in a country. These facts allow you to draw conclusions about the climate of that country. In math class, you may be given word problems to solve. From the facts given in the problem, you decide what arithmetic process you will use to find the answer. You are even drawing conclusions when you read a mystery and find the solution. Follow these steps.

1. **Look at the facts.** Read the following facts.

A woman lives in a house. One evening, she feels very tired. She decides to go to sleep. She turns off the light and goes to bed. In the morning, she reads the newspaper headline: "Ship Sinks, Search for Survivors." She is very upset and feels it is all her fault. ***Mystery***—Why is she upset? What did she have to do with the ship sinking?

2. **Think about how the facts fit together.** The woman felt she caused the ship to sink. This tells you to look for a cause-and-effect connection among the facts. What things did the woman do that might have caused the ship to sink?

3. **Compare the facts with what you already know.** You know that the woman turned off a light. Now think of any time that turning off a light could cause a ship to sink. What do you know about warning devices for ships?

4. Come to a conclusion. Decide what is true after looking at all the available information. Come to a conclusion. In step three, you probably thought about a lighthouse. The set of facts given could lead to the sinking of a ship only if the woman were a lighthouse keeper and had turned off the warning light.

Exercises Drawing Conclusions

A. Read the situation below. Study the facts that you find. Then write your conclusion.

In his will, an old prospector told the secret location of a stream rich in gold to two old friends. However, the friends had to sign a contract that stated, "The amount of gold that can be carried home in one trip shall be given to that individual."

The next day Seth and Jep arrived at the stream. They had only the clothes they were wearing, two pans, and Jep's mule. After five months, they had enough gold dust to make them rich. To prevent the gold dust from being blown away, they melted it into a gold brick. The brick was a foot long, six inches high, and six inches wide. After they returned, they argued about who rightfully owned the brick. They took their case to court. A judge peered at the brick and the contract. What was his decision? Who got the gold? ***Clue:*** What do you know about the weight of a gold brick?

B. When you answer a riddle, you are drawing a conclusion. Look at this riddle.

Twelve little figures
In a circle round
No legs but two hands
And a special sound
What am I?

Was *clock* your answer? Now write a riddle of your own. Make it rhyme if you wish. Exchange riddles and try to answer several.

4 Solving Problems

Focus

Use a five-step thinking process to help you solve problems more easily.

Every day you are faced with many kinds of problems. If you know how to approach a problem, you can solve it more easily. Follow these five steps.

1. Identify the Problem. Before you can solve a problem, you must have a clear idea of what the problem is. For example, Roger asks Chet to join some friends after school. They are going to play flag football. Chet would like to go. However, today his mom is picking him up right after school so they can shop for his dad's birthday gift. Also, Chet has a spelling test tomorrow he must study for. Chet wants to do all these things.

2. Think About the Choices. After you have identified the problem, think about all the possible solutions. Remember the sample situation. Chet can (a) go shopping with his mom, as planned, not play football, and study for spelling after dinner; (b) shop first, meet Roger and his friends later, and study spelling after dinner; (c) play flag football, not go shopping, and study spelling after dinner.

3. Find a Solution. After you have thought about all the choices, select the one that seems best. Chet decides to go shopping as planned and play flag football afterwards. He will study after dinner.

4. Try Out Your Solution. Once you have made a choice, try it out. Chet tells Roger about his decision. Roger reminds Chet that by the time Chet gets back from shopping it will be almost dark. They will have very little time for a game.

5. Think Again and Make Adjustments. If your first solution does not work, go over your choices again. Adjust your solution. Chet decides to call his mom to see if they can shop at any other time. His mom suggests shopping the next day. Chet will play football after school and study his spelling after supper. He used the problem-solving process to find a solution.

Exercise Solving Problems

Read the following problems. Choose one. Use the five-step problem-solving process to tell how you would solve your problem. Write your answer on your own paper.

1. You want to buy a special book on model building. The book costs $8.99. You have $6.00.
2. School closes early because of a snowstorm. When you get home, the door to your house is locked.
3. You are almost late for school. You notice your neighbor's frightened kitten high in a nearby tree. Your neighbor is not home.
4. You are invited to two parties at the same time on the same day. Both of the people having the parties are good friends of yours.

Using English in Science

You have learned that you can draw conclusions from facts. Scientists do this, too. When scientists want to find out why something happens, they use a process that is called the *scientific method.*

First, the scientists identify the problem. Then, they gather facts. They may experiment to gather facts. Next, the scientists carefully observe all the facts. Then they can draw conclusions about what is going on and why something happens. They may repeat the process to be sure the conclusion is correct.

Exercise **Drawing Conclusions from Experiments**

Watch your teacher do the following experiment or do it at home by yourself. Answer the questions that follow.

Making Raisins Dance

Materials needed:	Clear or light-colored soda Clear glass or cup About one-half dozen raisins
Procedure:	Fill the glass or cup one-half full with soda. Drop raisins into the liquid.

1. What happens to the raisins?
2. Does the same thing happen the second time you drop in the raisins?
3. Why do you think this happens?
4. Would the same thing happen if you dropped the raisins in water? Explain your answer.
5. What conclusion can you draw about why the raisins behave as they do?

Chapter 19 Review

A. Recognizing Fact and Opinion Write whether each of the five following statements is a *Fact* or an *Opinion*. Rewrite each opinion so that it is a fact. Be sure to take out any overgeneralizations or slanted language.

1. The Great Lakes were made during the last Ice Age.
2. All dinosaurs were terrifying creatures.
3. Bats are pests and should be destroyed.
4. Inchworms eventually become moths.
5. John Green is a shrewd horse-trader.

B. Drawing Conclusions Study the following sets of facts. Write the conclusions you draw.

1. Scientists have discovered cave paintings in the area of the Sahara desert. The paintings show men hunting animals on a grassy plain. Regular rainfall is necessary for a grassy plain to exist.
2. If you measure the angles inside a triangle, the total is always one hundred eighty degrees. Look at the triangle below. How many degrees does angle *C* contain?

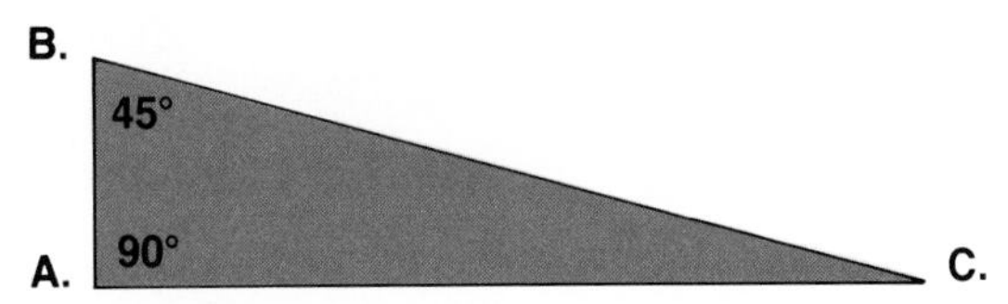

3. Chicken belongs to the protein food group. Protein should be cooked over low temperatures for a limited time. If it is cooked too long or the temperature is too high, it will be tough. Here are some oven temperatures: 200°–295° slow, 300°–375° moderate, 375°–425° hot, above 425°, very hot. Russell baked a chicken for three hours at 275° degrees. The chicken was tough and rubbery.

Chapter 20

The Process of Writing About Opinions

Have you ever read contest rules that began, "Explain in twenty-five words or less why . . ."? This type of contest asks you to do two things. First, you must state an opinion. Then, you must support that opinion with reasons.

You may never enter a contest like this. However, you will often be asked to state or write your opinion. An opinion is a strong belief about a subject or issue. You may write an opinion when you answer an essay question. You may also present and support an opinion when you speak with friends.

In this chapter, you will discover a writing process that will help you explain an opinion. You will learn how to state your opinion clearly. You will support your opinion with reasons and organize those reasons logically. You will see how the skills you learn can help you present your opinions more clearly when you speak to others.

1 Thinking About Opinions

Focus

An **opinion** is a feeling or belief about something.

You are often asked to explain an opinion. For example, imagine that you saw this advertisement on a grocery store bulletin board. You would like the job. How would you explain why you are the best person to take care of Rags?

Needed: Responsible young person to walk my dog, Rags.
Must be available early morning and late afternoon.
Must like animals.
Please write: Send a short letter to the address listed below.
Explain why you are qualified for this job.

Example 1

Read and Think. Gerry wrote this paragraph explaining why he would be a good dog-walker. Notice how he states his opinion. Then he supports it with good reasons.

> I would be the ideal person to walk Rags. First, I can walk Rags early in the morning before school, and again at 3:30 when I get home from school. Also, I have read many books about dogs, and know something about them. Most importantly, dogs always seem to wag their tails when they see me. That can mean only one thing—they know I'm a friend!

Think and Discuss. Read Gerry's paragraph again. Then discuss the following questions with your classmates.

1. Which sentence states Gerry's opinion?
2. What reasons did Gerry give to support that opinion?
3. Are his reasons based on facts or personal feelings?
4. Can you describe how Gerry organized his reasons?

Example 2

Read and Think. Read the paragraph below by Sam Levenson. The writer tells why he thinks students should wear school uniforms. As you read, look for his reasons. How do you feel about this issue?

> I should like to propose school uniforms for all children. On first thought, this sounds like the destruction of individuality. The fact is that in many countries students wear attractive uniforms embroidered with their school insignia [emblem]. They can be very colorful. The child is pleased to be recognized as a "student," an honor in itself. The wearing of a school uniform also influences personal behavior, since the child wishes to bring credit to his school whenever he appears in public.

Think and Discuss. Think about these questions. Share your ideas with your classmates.

1. What is Levenson's opinion? Where is it stated in this paragraph?
2. Explain the reasons that the writer gives to support this opinion.
3. What reason does the writer think is most important? How do you know?

Now It's Your Turn

You have now read two paragraphs that explain opinions. Each one states the opinion clearly. Each uses facts to support the author's opinions.

Now you will learn how to write an explanation of your own. As you explore your ideas in this chapter, keep these examples in mind. They will help you to think through opinions in your own writing. Remember to support all of your opinions with facts.

2 Prewriting: Discovering and Supporting Opinions

Focus

Explore your feelings to discover your opinions. Support an opinion with reasons.

Discovering Your Opinions

You may not realize it, but you have probably already formed many strong opinions. The simplest way to discover your opinions is to think about the world around you. Think about your school, your community, and your friends. For example, you might feel that there ought to be more crossing guards before and after school.

When you read, watch television, listen to records, or go to the movies, think about what you see and hear. Why is one TV program your favorite? Why do you dislike detective stories? Do you believe records should be rated as movies are? When you state a personal feeling, you state an opinion.

List your ideas and opinions in your journal. Your journal will become a valuable source of writing ideas.

Supporting Opinions

Opinions, by themselves, do not say much. Anyone can state an opinion. You also need strong reasons to help others understand and accept your opinion. For example, in part 1, Gerry wrote that he was ideal for the dog-walking job. He stated his opinion and gave three reasons to support it.

Gerry's opinions were facts. He did not use other opinions to support his opinion. He did not say, "I would be perfect for this job because I'm the best dog-walker in town."

Beginning a Writing Plan

Here is how one student, Julie, prepared an explanation of her opinion. She wrote an essay to convince the town council that an indoor pool was needed in her neighborhood.

First, Julie listed her opinion and all of her reasons.

Opinion: We need an indoor swimming pool.

There is no nearby place to swim.

We need supervised activities after school.

We could have a contest to name the pool.

Kids forget how to swim if they don't practice.

Swimming is my favorite sport.

Pool Closed for the Season

As Julie looked over her reasons, she noticed that *Swimming is my favorite sport* was a personal feeling, not a fact. She also noticed that *We could have a contest to name the pool* wasn't a reason at all. She crossed out both sentences. Later, Julie will arrange her reasons in a logical order.

Exercises Discovering Your Opinions and Finding Reasons

A. Finding Reasons Study the four opinions below. Choose one, and write four facts that support it. You may use reference books to find good reasons. Share your reasons with your classmates.

1. Mickey Mantle was a great baseball player.
2. Dolphins seem to be very intelligent creatures.
3. Natural gas is the safest source of fuel.
4. There are many advantages to owning a computer.

B. Choose a Topic Choose an opinion to use as the topic of a paragraph. Use ideas discussed in this chapter to discover a topic, or refer to the **Power Handbook.** Be sure to include your reasons.

3 Prewriting: Organizing Reasons

Focus

Organize reasons in the order of their importance.

You have listed three or four reasons that will support your opinion. Now decide in what order you will present those reasons.

Reasons are usually arranged in the order of their importance. State the least important reason first. Save the most important reason for the end. Then you leave the readers with the strongest and most convincing reason fresh in their minds.

When you organize reasons in the order of their importance, you must think about your audience. Which reasons would be most convincing to the people you are writing for?

Look at Gerry's paragraph on page 332. Gerry thought that Rags's owners were looking for someone who likes dogs, and who is liked by dogs in return. Gerry kept this in mind as he arranged his paragraph. He saved this reason for last.

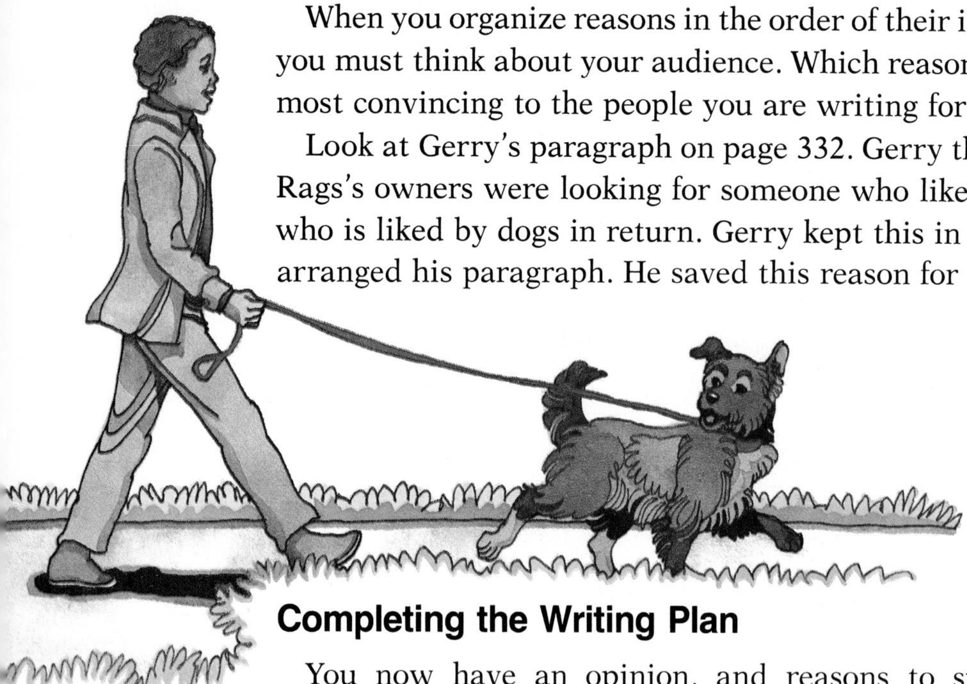

Completing the Writing Plan

You now have an opinion, and reasons to support the opinion. Next, you should organize the ideas in a writing plan.

Look again at Julie's writing plan. She has organized her reasons in the order of their importance. As she worked, Julie also made her reasons more specific. Look on the next page at her thoughts as she studied her plan.

Opinion: I think the Oak Leaf Park District needs an indoor swimming pool.

Reason 1: There is no nearby place to swim.

Reason 2: We need supervised activities all year round, not just in summer.

The town council will think this is the most important reason. I should save it for last.

Reason 3: Water safety and swimming skills are important. Kids forget many skills unless they can practice all year.

This reason should come earlier.

Exercises Putting Reasons in Order

A. Organizing Reasons Read the following list of reasons. They support the opinion, "Seat belt laws are necessary to save lives." Organize this list on your paper from the least important to the most important reason. Your audience is a state senator. Organize the reasons to convince the senator. Be ready to discuss why you organized the details in the way you did.

Statistics show that death and injuries in traffic accidents have gone down in states where seat belts must be worn.

Without the law, many people will not bother with seat belts.

Insurance costs have gone down in states where wearing seat belts is required.

B. Making a Writing Plan Look over the reasons that you have listed to support your topic. Then think about your audience. Decide which reason will be most important to your audience. Save it for last. Finally, make a writing plan. List your reasons in the order you will write them.

4 Drafting an Explanation

Focus

Follow your writing plan as you write your rough draft.

Once you have a clear writing plan, you are ready to begin drafting your explanation. When drafting a paragraph that explains an opinion, follow these steps.

1. Write a strong topic sentence. Begin your paragraph with a topic sentence that states your opinion. Never begin with the words "In my opinion" or "I think." Express your opinion in a more interesting way. Look at this topic sentence.

> I think reading mystery stories is fun.

This sentence states the writer's opinion. However, it should be more specific and not include the phrase "I think." The following sentence is more specific.

> Reading mystery stories is a great way to spend a rainy Saturday afternoon.

Avoid **overgeneralizations** in your topic sentence. A statement that uses words such as *everyone, nobody, always*, and *never* might be difficult to support. Instead, use words such as *most, few, usually*, and *seldom*. To learn more about overgeneralization, see Chapter 19, page 322.

2. Develop your paragraph. After you have written a strong topic sentence, follow your writing plan to develop the rest of your paragraph. State your reasons in the order of their importance. You might end your paragraph with your most important reason. You might also want to end with a sentence that summarizes all of your reasons. Your last sentence might ask that the reader take some action on your topic.

3. Use signal words. As you draft your explanation, check to see that each sentence flows smoothly into the next. Use signal words such as *first, next, then, finally,* and *most importantly* to show order in your paragraph. Use a comma to separate a signal word from the rest of the sentence.

A Sample Draft

Julie developed her writing plan into a draft. Notice her thoughts as she worked.

> ~~I think~~ our park district needs an indoor swiming pool. When our outdoor pool is closed, the children in my nieghborhood have no nearby place to swim. Children forget water safety and swimming skills unless they practice all year round. They should practice these skills all year round. Children need safe and supervised activities all year, not just in summer. ~~It sure would be great to have a gym for volleyball and basketball, too.~~

I shouldn't say "I think."

This is a new idea. I should stick to my topic.

Sometimes you have many details to support each reason. Then you should write about each reason and its supporting details in a separate paragraph.

Exercise Writing Your Rough Draft

Use your writing plan to draft your explanation. Start with a strong topic sentence. Remember to put your reasons in the order of their importance. Use signal words to show order in your paragraph.

5 Revising Your Explanation

Focus

Revise your explanation carefully. Make sure your reasons are presented clearly. Then proofread your work.

Explanations must be clear and well organized. As you revise your paragraph, ask yourself the questions below.

Guidelines for Revising an Explanation

1. Did I state my opinion clearly in my topic sentence?
2. Did I support my opinion well?
3. Are all my reasons facts?
4. Did I arrange my reasons from the least important to the most important?
5. Did I use signal words to make my order clear?

Ask one or two friends to read your draft. Ask them whether or not your reasons are clear. Find out whether or not they were persuaded by your paragraph. If they were not, ask why.

Julie studied her draft. She decided that she would make several changes. Notice Julie's thoughts as she worked.

Pool closed for the Season is a sign no one wants to see. Yet, our outdoor pool is closed from Labor day to Memorial day every year.

I'll add a short introduction to my topic.

Because of this, ~~O~~ur park district needs an indoor swiming pool. When our outdoor pool is closed, the children in my nieghborhood have no nearby place to swim. *This is bad because* ~~C~~hildren forget water safety and swimming skills unless they practice ~~all year round.~~ *often.* ~~They should practice these skills all year round.~~ Children need safe and supervised activities all year, not just in summer.

I don't want to repeat this phrase.

Julie studied her draft one more time. She found two more problems. She decided to make the following changes.

Problem: I should point out my most important reason.

Result: Julie added a signal phrase: *Most importantly, children need safe and supervised activities all year round.*

Problem: My paragraph just ends with my last reason.

Result: Julie added a good concluding sentence: *Let's put up a permanent sign that says Pool Open.*

Proofreading

When you write an opinion, your reasons must be stated clearly. Your facts and statistics must be accurate. Errors in capitalization, punctuation, and spelling can confuse your readers. Carefully proofread your paragraph and neatly correct any errors.

For more information, see the guides to capitalization, punctuation, and spelling in your **Power Handbook.**

Finally, read your paragraph out loud. You may hear mistakes that you might not otherwise notice. For example, you might notice that some words have been left out.

Look at the changes Julie made as she proofread.

> Pool Closed for the Season is a sign no one wants to see. Yet, our outdoor pool is closed from Labor day to Memorial day every year. Because of this, our park district needs an indoor swiming pool. When our outdoor pool is closed, the children in my nieghborhood have no nearby place to swim. This is bad because children forget water safety and swimming skills unless they practice often. Most importantly children need safe and supervised activities all year, not just in summer. Let's put up a permanent sign that says Pool Open.

Exercise **Revising Your Explanation**

Use the guidelines on page 340 to help you revise your explanation. After you finish your revision, ask a friend or classmate to read your paragraph. Ask him or her to point out any unclear sentences, or sentences that are out of order. Ask whether your topic sentence is interesting. Finally, proofread your work carefully. Make any necessary corrections.

6 Writing and Sharing a Final Copy

Focus

After you proofread your explanation, make a neat final copy.

Make your final copy as clean and neat as possible. Include all of the changes that you made during the revising and proofreading steps.

Add a title to your final copy, if needed. Be sure that the title includes the main idea. It should also catch the reader's attention.

Here is Julie's final copy. Notice how she has included all of the changes she made in the revising and proofreading steps.

Summer Fun All Year Round

"Pool Closed for the Season" is a sign no one wants to see. Yet, our outdoor pool is closed from Labor Day to Memorial Day every year. Because of this, our park district needs an indoor swimming pool. When our outdoor pool is closed, the children in my neighborhood have no nearby place to swim. This is bad because children forget water safety and swimming skills unless they practice often. Most importantly, children need safe and supervised activities all year, not just in summer. Let's put up a permanent sign that says "Pool Open."

Exercise **Writing and Sharing a Final Copy**

Write a good title for your explanation. Then make a final copy of your paragraph. Proofread one more time for errors in grammar, capitalization, punctuation, and spelling. Neatly correct any mistakes you find.

Speaking and Listening

Conducting a Survey

Have you ever seen the results of a survey printed in a newspaper or magazine? A reporter stops people on the street and asks them a question. Sometimes it is a serious question such as "Do you think city taxes should pay for a new domed stadium?" Other times it is a fun question such as "What do you think is the best way to celebrate July 4?"

The results of these surveys are then printed in a newspaper or magazine. The survey often states how many people had a particular opinion. In that way, readers know what most people think about the issue.

Exercise Surveying Your Friends

Now it is your turn to run a survey. First, write a fun question that you can ask classmates and friends. For example, you might ask classmates if they think your school should adopt a mascot.

Next, interview at least ten people. Ask your question. Then ask each person for at least two reasons to support his or her answer. Carefully record the answers in your notebook.

Now, report to the class on the results of your survey. State your question. Then tell how many people gave each answer. Also state some of the reasons that were given. The reasons that were given most often were probably the most important.

Finally, what conclusion, if any, can be made from the results of your survey? Give your classmates some examples to support your conclusion.

Creative Writing

A. Choose a character from a children's story. Decide what opinion that character might have had about what happened in the story. Write as if you are that character. Give reasons in your paragraph why you feel the way you do. Some suggestions for characters and opinions are listed below.

1. Jack—"I was right to climb the beanstalk."
2. Cinderella—"Everyone should have a fairy godmother."
3. The Tortoise—"I have learned that it pays to be patient."

B. Have you ever wondered whether animals have opinions? How would a gorilla feel about living in a zoo? How would a robin feel about the coming of spring? Pretend you are an animal. Write a paragraph that introduces yourself and states your opinion. Be sure to give several reasons to support your opinion in the order of their importance.

C. What one thing do you think would help make the world a better place? Write a paragraph in which you state your opinion and support it with reasons.

Using English in Social Studies

An editorial can be found in a newspaper or magazine. It gives the opinion of the editor or the publisher. Editorials are often about events that are currently in the news. They are about issues that affect many people.

A good editorial begins by stating an opinion. The opinion is followed by several supporting reasons. Finally, the writer often ends the editorial by adding a statement that refers back to his or her opinion.

Read this editorial.

> A hot line for runaways would provide a valuable service to children and their parents. Runaways often change their minds and want to return home, but they don't know how. They are often afraid, hurt, or out of money, and need help. They have nowhere to turn. A hot line could give runaways the help they need. Parents of a missing child could call the hot line for information or news about their child. Others who knew about a runaway could call the hot line with that information. The hot line would serve as an information center. It would help frightened runaways and worried parents. Most importantly, it might bring families back together again.

Exercise Reading and Writing About Editorials

Find two editorials in either newspapers or magazines. In each editorial, underline the opinion. Then put a number next to the beginning of each reason that supports the opinion. Finally, write a letter to the editor that tells whether you support or oppose the opinion in the editorial. Include good supporting reasons for your own opinion.

Chapter 20 Review

A. Supporting an Opinion with Facts Study the following opinion and possible reasons. Choose the reasons that can be used to support the opinion. Remember, you should not support one opinion with another opinion. Select only reasons that are facts.

Opinion:

Everyone should eat a nutritious breakfast.

Reasons:

1. Breakfast provides fuel for our bodies to make it through the morning.
2. Breakfast is my favorite meal.
3. Studies show that students who eat a good breakfast do better in school.
4. Students should learn about proper nutrition in their health classes.
5. Nothing beats a breakfast of a cheese omelet, wheat toast, and fresh orange juice.
6. A nutritious breakfast provides vitamins and minerals that are needed for good health.

B. Writing Topic Sentences Rewrite each of the following topic sentences. Make each one clearer and more specific.

1. I think summer is the best season of all.
2. In my opinion, ______ was a good movie.
3. I think that baby-sitting is a good job for sixth graders.
4. In my opinion, everyone should learn how to play a musical instrument.
5. I think that we should start a softball team.

Chapter 21

Sharpening Library and Research Skills

Did you ever wonder why the grass is green or what makes the sky look blue? As a child you asked questions to find out about the world around you. Now, as a student, you not only ask questions but you have to answer them as well.

People never stop looking for information. That is why knowing how and where to find information is such an important skill.

This chapter will help you to learn how and where to locate facts about a topic. You will learn how to use the library and how to do research. You can use these skills to gather information, answer questions, and satisfy your curiosity.

1 The Classification of Books

Focus

There are two kinds of books, **fiction** and **nonfiction**.

Materials in a library are divided into two categories: fiction and nonfiction. Each group is shelved in a different way.

Fiction

Fiction books are stories that are created by an author. Some parts of a fiction book may be based on real events, but most of the story comes from the author's imagination.

Fiction books are arranged alphabetically according to the author's last name. For example, books by Carol Ryrie Brink are placed before books by Scott O'Dell. Books by Scott O'Dell are placed before books by Donald Sobol.

All the books by one writer are shelved in one group. These books are then arranged alphabetically, according to the first word in the title. First words like *a*, *an*, and *the* are not considered. If a title begins with *a*, *an*, or *the*, the book is alphabetized according to its second word. For example, *The Children's War*, by Theodore Taylor, is alphabetized under *C* not *T*.

Nonfiction

Nonfiction books report facts or ideas. They tell about real people and events. There are nonfiction books written on every subject you can imagine. In the library, nonfiction books are arranged according to their subjects. These subjects are grouped together in large categories. Most libraries use the categories of the Dewey Decimal System. You will learn more about the Dewey Decimal System in part 2.

Exercises **Finding Books**

A. Number your paper from 1 to 10. Decide whether each book listed is fiction or nonfiction. Write *Fiction* or *Nonfiction* on your paper.

1. *The White House: A History of Presidents*
2. *The Mathematical Princess and Other Stories*
3. A book about the search for new energy sources.
4. *Bicycles: All About Them*
5. *Encyclopedia Brown Solves Ten Mysteries*
6. A book about a boy's adventures on Earth one hundred years in the future.
7. Biographies of four outstanding black women.
8. *The House That Sailed Away*
9. *The Amateur Magician's Handbook*
10. An adventure tale set in ancient China.

B. Number your paper from 1 to 10. Copy these authors' names in the order in which you would find their books on the shelves.

Eleanor Lattimore
Roald Dahl
Margaret E. Bell
Astrid Lindgren
Mary Norton
Hester Burton
Mary Rodgers
James L. Collier
Madeleine L'Engle
John Christopher

C. Number your paper from 1 to 5. List these books by Beverly Cleary in the order in which they would be arranged on the shelves.

Socks
Runaway Ralph
Mitch and Amy
Ribsy
Ramona the Brave

2 The Dewey Decimal System

Focus

The **Dewey Decimal System** classifies all nonfiction books into ten major categories. A specific identification number, a **call number**, is assigned to every nonfiction book.

Most libraries arrange books in the nonfiction section according to a system of numbers called the Dewey Decimal System. The Dewey Decimal System groups all nonfiction books into ten categories.

The Dewey Decimal System

000–099	**General Works**	encyclopedias, almanacs, handbooks
100–199	**Philosophy**	conduct, psychology
200–299	**Religion**	the Bible, mythology, theology
300–399	**Social Science**	law, education, government, folklore
400–499	**Language**	languages, grammar, dictionaries
500–599	**Science**	mathematics, chemistry, physics, astronomy
600–699	**Useful Arts**	gardening, cooking, sewing, television, cars, farming, inventions, nursing
700–799	**Fine Arts**	music, drawing, acting, games, sports
800–899	**Literature**	poetry, plays, essays
900–999	**History**	biography, travel, geography

Each category in the Dewey Decimal System is assigned a number counting by 100's. For example, the call numbers from 900 to 999 are assigned to History. This category includes books about real people, called biographies. It also includes books about historical events and other countries.

In the Dewey Decimal System, each book has an identification number. This number is the **call number**. The call number is printed on the spine of every nonfiction book. The book is shelved in numerical order according to its call number.

Exercises **Using the Dewey Decimal System**

A. Number your paper from 1 to 10. Assign the correct Dewey Decimal category to each of the following nonfiction books.

1. *Ginnie and Geneva Cookbook* by Catherine Woolley
2. *Mr. Nonsense: A Life of Edward Lear* by E. Kelen
3. *The Backyard Astronomer* by Alan E. Nourse
4. *Double Fun: 100 Outdoor and Indoor Games* by Alma Heaton
5. *Guinness Book of Young Recordbreakers* by Norris and Ross McWhirter
6. *British Isles* by Robert Clayton
7. *142 Ways To Make a Poem* by James W. Swanson
8. *Fun with Growing Things* by Joan Eckstein and Joyce Gleit
9. *The Story of Folk Music* by Melvin Berger
10. *The I Hate Mathematics! Book* by Marilyn Burns

B. Go to the library. In the nonfiction section, find a book on each of the following topics. On your paper, write the title, author, and Dewey Decimal number of each book.

1. A cookbook
2. A book on the Civil War
3. A collection of poems
4. A book of folk tales
5. A book about atomic energy

3 Finding a Book

Focus

Use the **card catalog** to find a book in the library.

A library may have hundreds or even thousands of books that you can use. You may want only one particular book. Finding one book among so many is not difficult when you use the card catalog. If the library has the book you want, it will be listed in the card catalog.

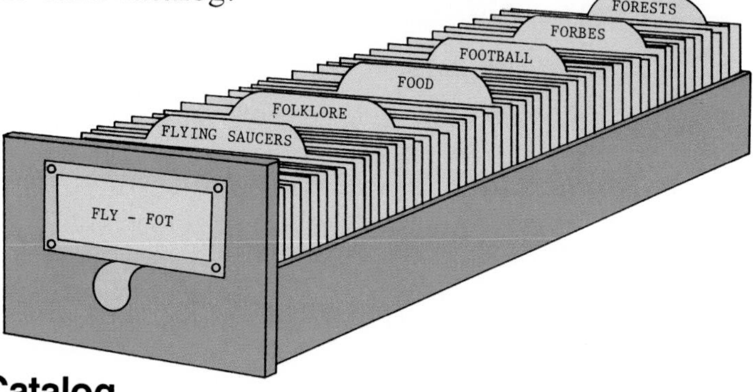

The Card Catalog

The card catalog is a cabinet of small drawers filled with cards. On the outside of each drawer there is a label that tells the letters of the alphabet for cards in that drawer. Each card is printed with information about a book in the library. The cards are arranged alphabetically according to the top line of each card. Cards for nonfiction books have the call number of the book in the upper left-hand corner. If no call number appears in the upper left corner of the card, the book is fiction.

There are usually three cards for the same book in the card catalog: the **author card**, the **title card**, and the **subject card**. All three cards give you the same information about the book, but in slightly different order. In this way, you can find a book no matter what information you have about it. You will learn more about these cards in part 4 of this chapter.

When you look for a book, be aware that some libraries now use a computer catalog. Computer screens display the information. The librarian can help you learn how to use this computer catalog.

To find a particular book, remember these steps.

1. Go to the card catalog. Use whatever information you have about a book to find its card in the card catalog.

2. Locate the book on the shelves by using the author's name or the call number of a book.

Exercise Using the Card Catalog

Read the five words or phrases in each group below. Each word or phrase is the first line of a card in the card catalog. Copy the words or phrases in the order in which you would find them in the card catalog.

1. Haywood, Carolyn
   Hidden Heroines
   HELICOPTERS
   Hicks, Clifford
   HOCKEY

2. Charlie and the Chocolate Factory
   Calhoun, Mary
   CAMPING
   Champions of the Little League
   CITIES AND TOWNS

3. Sharp, Margery
   Sachs, Marilyn
   Science Fiction Trilogy One
   SKIING
   The Secret of the Seven Crows

4 Types of Catalog Cards

Focus

Each book in the library has three catalog cards: an **author card**, a **title card**, and a **subject card**.

In part 3 you learned that the card catalog has an author card, a title card, and a subject card for every book. Each card has the same information about a book. Only the order of the information is different. An author card has the name of the author of the book on the top line. A title card has the title of the book on the top line. A subject card has the general subject or topic of the book on the top line.

Look carefully at the following examples of catalog cards.

The Author Card

When you know the author of a book you want to read, use the card catalog to look up the author's name. There will be an author card for each book in the library written by that author. All the cards for one author will be together, filed alphabetically under the author's last name.

J921 **Clark, Electa**
Ro

Cherokee chief; the life of John Ross. Illustrated by John Wagner. New York, Crowell-Collier Press 1970

118 p. Illus.
Bibliog. pp. 115–116

A biography of the Cherokee chief who struggled to maintain his tribe's independence and rights to its homeland.

1. Cherokee Indians 2. Trail of Tears

The Title Card

You might know the title of a book, but not its author. Then look for the title card of the book in the card catalog. Title cards are filed alphabetically by the first word in the title.

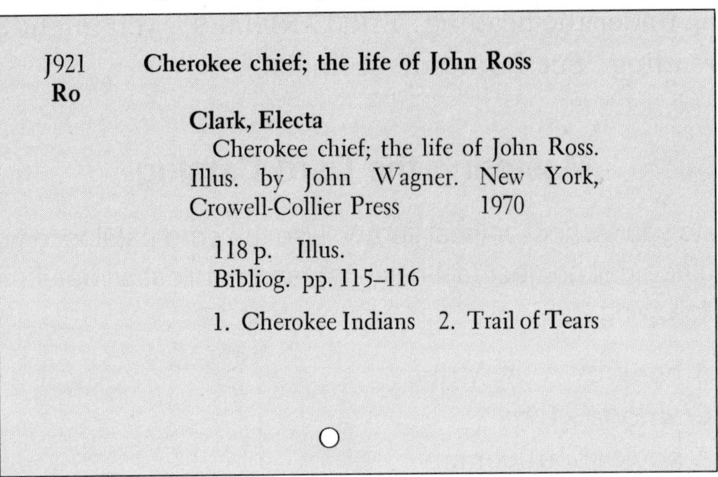

J921 Ro — **Cherokee chief; the life of John Ross**

Clark, Electa
Cherokee chief; the life of John Ross. Illus. by John Wagner. New York, Crowell-Collier Press 1970

118 p. Illus.
Bibliog. pp. 115–116

1. Cherokee Indians 2. Trail of Tears

The Subject Card

If you were writing a report on Cherokee Indians, you probably would want to find several books on this subject. The best way to do this would be to look in the card catalog under the subject heading CHEROKEE INDIANS. The subject is often printed completely in capital letters. This helps you tell the difference between it and an author or title card.

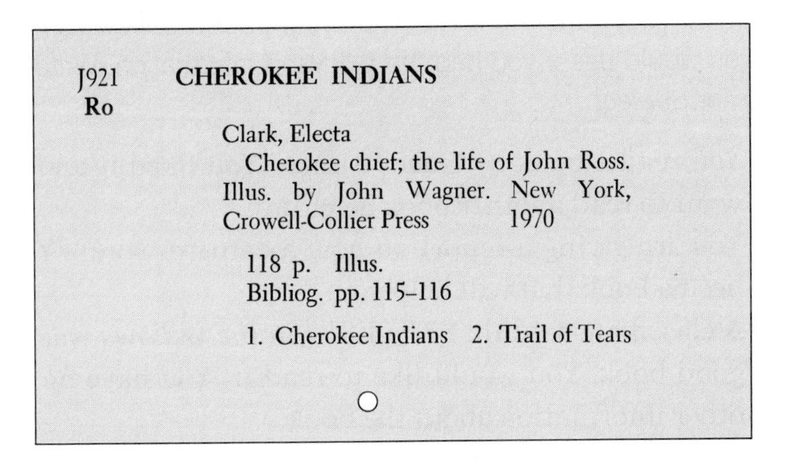

J921 Ro — **CHEROKEE INDIANS**

Clark, Electa
Cherokee chief; the life of John Ross. Illus. by John Wagner. New York, Crowell-Collier Press 1970

118 p. Illus.
Bibliog. pp. 115–116

1. Cherokee Indians 2. Trail of Tears

Cross-Reference Cards

Sometimes when you look up a subject you will find a card that reads "See" or "See also." The "See" card refers you to another subject heading in the card catalog. For example, looking under the heading "FARM ANIMALS," you might find a card reading "See Domestic Animals."

Exercises Mastering the Card Catalog

A. Go to your school or local library. Use the card catalog to find the title, author, call number (if it has one), and publication date for each of the following.

1. A book by A. A. Milne
2. *Charlotte's Web*
3. A book about comets
4. A book of short stories

B. Number your paper from 1 to 3. On your paper, write what kind of card you would use if you had the following information. Write *Title*, *Author*, or *Subject.*

1. You read a book by Isaac Asimov. You liked it and want to read another book he wrote.
2. You are giving a report on how a camera works. You need a book that will help you.
3. A classmate said that *The Wind in the Willows* was a good book. You would like to read it. You have no other information about the book.

5 Using Other Resources

Focus

Most libraries have a **reference section**. This area has special books and materials that offer you facts and information on every topic you can think of.

Where do you look to find facts and answer questions about a topic? Most libraries have a reference collection. This collection contains many valuable sources of information.

Here are some common reference works found in a library.

Dictionary

You have already learned about the dictionary and thesaurus in Chapter 8. Most libraries have an unabridged dictionary. An **unabridged dictionary** is the most complete collection of English words available. *Webster's Third New International Dictionary,* for example, contains 450,000 words on 2,662 pages. Shorter **abridged** dictionaries are available, too.

Encyclopedia

An **encyclopedia** is a collection of articles on many topics. General encyclopedias have many volumes arranged alphabetically. The spine of each volume is labeled with the letters of the subjects contained in that volume. This helps you find the volume you need. For example, suppose you were doing a report on the stages in the life of a bee. *Bee* is the most important word in your topic, and it starts with the letter "B." Therefore, you would look in the "B" volume of the encyclopedia. Like a dictionary, encyclopedias use guide words to help you find the article you want.

Atlas

An **atlas** is a book of maps. To use an atlas, refer to the index in the back of the book. Here you will find the page numbers of the maps. The index gives the exact location of cities or towns. The index may also give population figures.

Magazines and Newspapers

In most libraries, you can find current issues of popular magazines. Local newspapers and often papers from other cities are also available. Libraries also save back issues of magazines to be used for research. To locate an article on a specific topic, use the *Readers' Guide to Periodical Literature*. Ask the librarian to help you use this guide.

Almanac and Yearbook

Almanacs and **yearbooks** are collections of current facts and statistics. For example, you can find the current prime minister of Canada or last year's Super Bowl winner in an almanac. To find information, use the index. Two popular almanacs are *The World Almanac* and *Information Please Almanac*.

Exercises Using Reference Works

A. Number your paper from 1 to 10. Read the report topics listed below. Write the key word in each topic that tells you where to find the answer in an encyclopedia.

1. Countries where diamonds are found
2. The life of Wild Bill Hickok
3. The people of Denmark
4. The exports of Japan
5. The history of soccer
6. Where the puffin lives
7. Harry Houdini's magic
8. The inventions of Thomas Edison
9. Earth's weather cycle
10. The art of Marc Chagall

B. Number your paper from 1 to 8. Then write two reference sources you could use to answer the following questions. Try to use some reference sources in addition to an encyclopedia.

1. What is the population of Tucson, Arizona?
2. Where in the U.S. is rice grown?
3. What river forms part of the western border of the state of Idaho?
4. Who won the women's singles tennis competition at Wimbledon in 1986?
5. What language is spoken in Tanzania?
6. Draw and color a picture of the national flags of Poland and Monaco.
7. Who are the current United States senators from West Virginia?
8. In what ocean are the Canary Islands?

6 Taking Notes

Focus

Sometimes you read to gather information. Take complete and accurate notes as you read. Notes help you remember important facts and ideas.

Often you will be in the library to gather information for a report or composition. As you read, you will want to take notes. Notes will help you remember the facts and ideas you may want to include in your paper.

Many writers take notes on 3″ × 5″ note cards. They write each fact or idea on a separate card. This makes the notes easier to organize. The following note card shows information on the topic "Hawaii." It was taken from an encyclopedia. The note card gives the name and date of the encyclopedia and the volume and page number of the article.

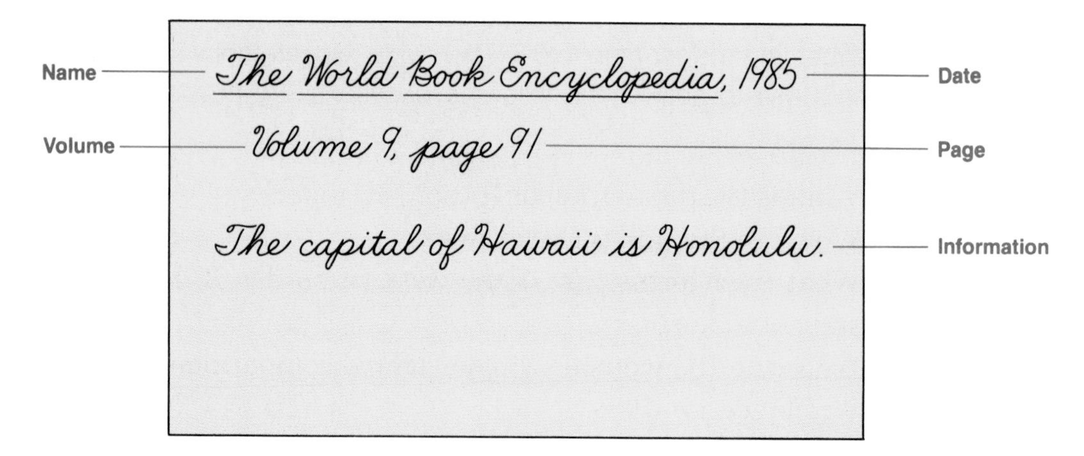

Note cards for books should include the title of the book, the author, and the page number where you found the information. For magazines, include the name and date of the magazine, the title and page numbers of the article, and the author's name, if it is given.

Do not try to write down everything you read. Include only key ideas. Your notes will help you remember what you read.

When you take notes, you should not copy the author's words exactly. You should **paraphrase**. That is, you should write the information in your own words. **If you do copy an author's words exactly, you must enclose them in quotation marks.**

Exercise Taking Notes

Read the following paragraphs. They were taken from the article "Undersea Odd Couples" published in the October, 1985, issue of *National Geographic World* on pages 6–10. Make two note cards for this article. Remember to put only one fact on each card. Write the information in your own words.

> Sea anemones come in flower-like colors and shapes. Although anemones may look somewhat like plants, they are really animals. They range in size from less than an inch to three feet across.
>
> Most land animals use their feet to move around. The anemone uses its single foot to stay in one place. It fastens the foot to the seafloor, and waits for food to come along. Poison in the anemone's tentacles can paralyze or kill smaller animals.

7 The Interview

Focus

An **interview** with an expert is a way to gather information.

Sometimes, the best source of information on a topic is an expert. For example, you might want to find out how weather forecasters know about the weather ahead of time. You could interview a meteorologist, or weather forecaster.

There are two parts, or stages, to every interview. First you get ready for the interview. Then you actually interview the person. Here are some guidelines for completing an interview.

Guidelines for Interviewing

Before the Interview

1. Call or write the person you want to interview. Arrange a time and date. This way the person can be prepared.
2. Know something about the subject. If you have done some research, you can ask better questions.
3. Try to find out about the person you will be interviewing. For example, learn about the person's hobbies or experiences.
4. Write a list of questions you will ask. Try to write questions that cannot be answered with a *yes* or *no*.

At the Interview

1. Be on time. Be sure that you have paper and pencil.
2. Listen carefully and take good notes.
3. If you do not understand an answer, ask the person to explain more clearly.
4. Check over your notes. Fill in anything that is incomplete while the interview is fresh in your mind.
5. Thank the person when you have finished. Send a thank-you note in a day or so.

Exercises Interviewing

A. Number your paper from 1 to 10. Name an expert that you could interview for each of the following topics.

1. How to start a savings account
2. How to become a police officer
3. Caring for a puppy
4. Life in ________ (another country)
5. What to look for when buying a bicycle
6. Duties of a lifeguard
7. What is necessary to become a teacher
8. Your own family's history
9. Equipment necessary for hiking
10. How to cut and style hair

B. Choose one of the experts from Exercise A. Make a list of questions you would use for an interview.

8 Getting Information from Graphic Aids

Focus

Graphic aids present information clearly and quickly. **Graphic aids** include photographs, illustrations, diagrams, maps, graphs, and charts.

We get most of the facts we learn by reading. However, sometimes a graphic aid can present information more clearly than words can.

Photographs and illustrations can often show ideas better than words can. Always read captions that appear with pictures.

Maps are drawings of areas of land and water.

Diagrams help you identify the parts of an object. They may also show how each part is related to other parts.

Tables and charts present groups of facts. They are often arranged in columns.

A **graph** is a special kind of chart. It shows how one fact is related to another. First, read the title and the key to any symbols used in the graph. Then, read what is printed inside and next to the graph.

Here are some sample graphic aids.

Table ▼

VITAMINS AND THEIR SOURCES	
Vitamin A	green/yellow vegetables, yellow fruits, liver, eggs, milk
B Vitamins	lean meats, liver, milk, eggs, peas, beans, whole grains, fish, green vegetables, corn
Vitamin C	oranges, grapefruit, tomatoes, strawberries, broccoli, turnip and mustard greens, potatoes

Map ▼

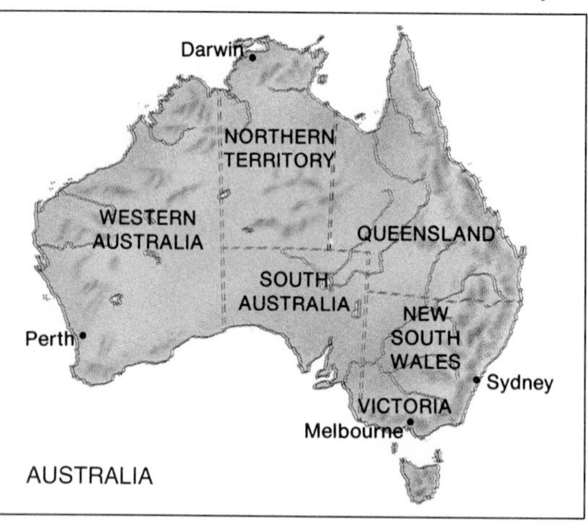

Diagram ▶

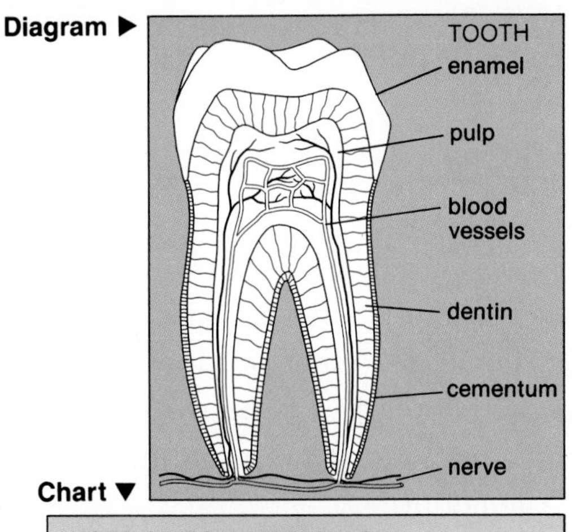

Chart ▼

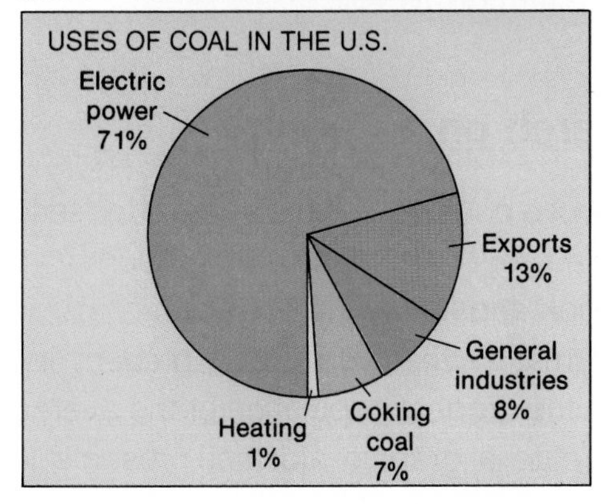

Illustration ▲

Exercise Using Graphic Aids

Use the graphic aids in the lesson to answer these questions.

1. What vitamin does grapefruit provide?
2. What is just inside the enamel of a tooth?
3. Do you find the city of Melbourne, Australia, north or south of Sydney?
4. What is shown in the illustration on the right above?
5. For what purpose is most coal used in the U.S.?
6. Into how many areas is Australia divided?
7. Which vitamins can you get from eggs?
8. What percent of coal is exported from the U.S.?
9. What part of the tooth contains the blood vessels?
10. Would a macaw seem more closely related to a robin or a parrot?

Using English in Geography

When you study any country, there is always a great deal to learn. What does the country look like? What products does it export? Where and how do the people live? The resources in the library help you find this information. For example, an atlas will contain a map of the country.

Exercise Doing Research on a Country

Choose a country or an area of a country that interests you. Use the card catalog to find five sources your library has on the country you chose. List the title of each book and its call number.

Look in the books for information that you could present in a graphic aid: the five cities with the biggest population or the average rainfall for certain months. Create a graphic aid that presents the information you have found. Label your graphic aid carefully. Make it colorful and interesting. The map below is an example of a kind of graphic aid you can make.

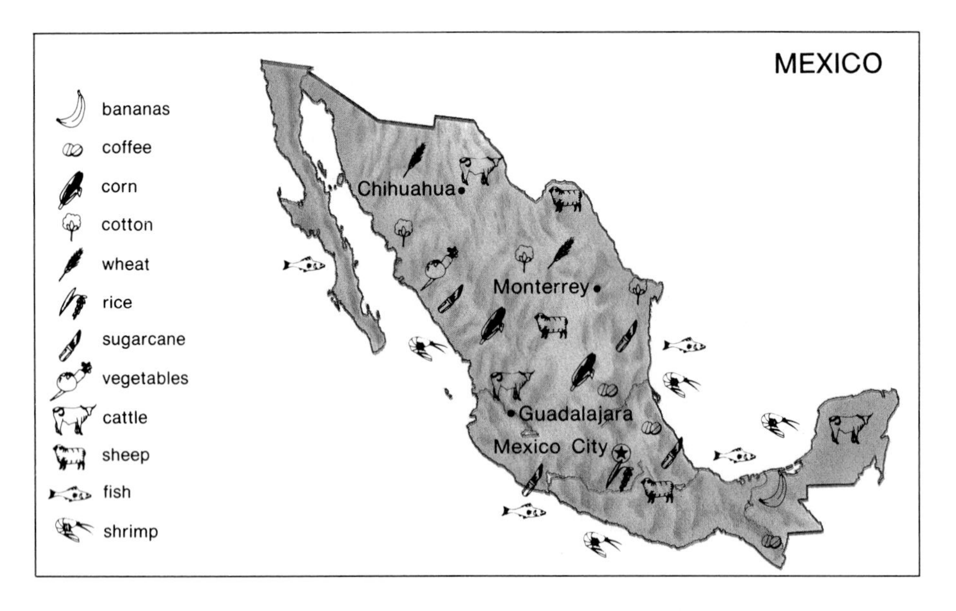

Chapter 21 Review

A. Mastering the Dewey Decimal System Refer to the Dewey Decimal list on page 352. Number your paper from 1 to 5. Write the correct number grouping for each of these nonfiction books.

1. *Solids, Liquids, and Gases* by Jeanne Bendick
2. *Geronimo: The Fighting Apache* by R. Syme
3. *Buying the Wind: Regional Folklore in the United States* by Richard M. Dorson
4. *Dance Is a Contact Sport* by Joseph Mazo
5. *The World Almanac and Book of Facts, 1987*

B. Writing Note Cards Read the following paragraph from "Little Known Mammals," published on page 78 of the book *Best in Children's Books*. Write two note cards from the article.

> Many strange creatures live in the vast jungles of tropical South America. Douroucoulis, or "night monkeys," are among the oddest of them all. These red-eyed monkeys spend the day sleeping in tree cavities or other dark places. At night they wake up and go climbing through the treetops looking for food. That is when you hear their amazing calls.

C. Understanding Graphic Aids Study the diagram below. Write answers to the questions on your paper.

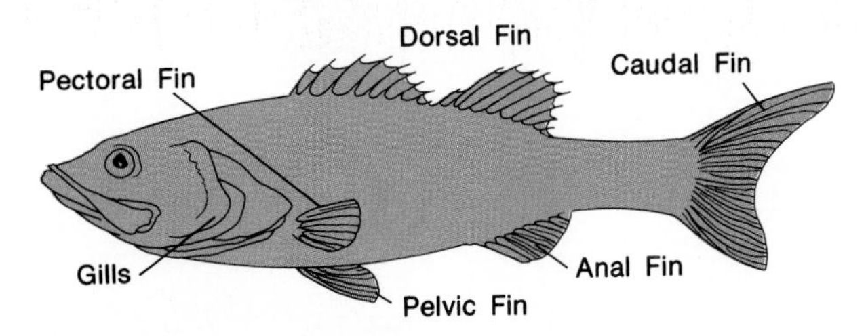

1. The fish's tail is actually a fin. Which fin is it?
2. Which fin is located just behind the gills?
3. Name a fin located on the belly of the fish.
4. Which fin is along the spine?
5. How many fins are named in the diagram?

Chapter 22

The Process of Writing a Report

Did you ever wonder why Saturn has rings? Do you know why lightning bugs light up on a summer night, or how the Grand Canyon was formed?

You can learn about these and other subjects when you write a report. A report is a composition that uses information from books, magazines, newspapers, and other sources.

At school you will often be asked to write reports. Your social studies teacher may assign you to write a report on life in a medieval castle. Your science teacher may ask you to write a report on the space shuttle. Writing a report can help you to discover new worlds of knowledge.

In this chapter, you will learn the process of writing a report. You will select an interesting subject. Then you will look for information about your subject in the library. Finally, you will present your subject in a written report.

1 Prewriting: Finding and Limiting a Topic

Focus

Find a subject you are interested in. Narrow it to a topic that can be written about in a short report.

How To Find a Subject

Many times you will be assigned a subject for a report. Sometimes, however, you must find a subject on your own.

Explore Your Interests. Think about subjects that interest you. If you take music lessons, you might write about the instrument you play. If you enjoy sports, you could write about a famous athlete you admire. Brainstorm with a friend to find other subjects that might be interesting.

Find Subjects in the Library. Another way to find a subject is to look through books on subjects you are interested in. Next, check the reference books. Encyclopedias, almanacs, and dictionaries on special topics may suggest interesting subjects. A third place to check is the magazine shelf. Look through magazines that interest you. Keep a list of all the topics and ideas you discover.

How To Narrow Your Subject

Now choose the subject that you think would be the most interesting to report on. Then narrow your subject. That means that you find the particular part of your subject you wish to write about. For example, imagine you wanted to report on the piano. Would you write about the history of the piano? Would you explain how a piano makes sounds? Would you tell how pianos are made? Each of these topics is a narrower version of the subject, *piano*.

Using the Table of Contents and Index The table of contents and the index of a book can help you to narrow a subject. One writer, Kenji, wanted to learn more about extinct animals. He looked under *extinct animals* in the index of an encyclopedia.

INDEX

Kenji decided that he wanted to learn more about *extinct birds*. He read about his topic in the encyclopedia. Finally, he decided to write about one extinct bird, the dodo bird.

Exercises Finding and Narrowing a Subject

A. Using a Table of Contents Look at the following table of contents. Use it to develop at least three topics for a brief report.

THE MAGIC OF DRAWING CARTOONS

B. Finding Your Own Topic Make a list of possible subjects for a report. When you finish your list, select the subject you want to write about. Narrow it down to a topic you can write about in a brief report.

2 Prewriting: Gathering Information

Focus

Once you have a topic for a report, gather information about it.

Finding Sources

The best place to find specific information about a topic is the library. Check the card catalog for books on your topic. Look through the indexes of the general encyclopedias. Ask the librarian to help you find magazine articles on your topic by using the *Readers' Guide to Periodical Literature*. Make a list of all the sources you find with information about your topic. You will include this list at the end of your report.

You may need to review how to use the library. If so, see Chapter 21, "Sharpening Library and Research Skills," which begins on page 349.

Taking Notes

As you read through the sources you have found, take notes on what you learn. Write each fact that you learn about your topic on a separate 3″ × 5″ note card. This will help you to organize your information more easily. Be sure to write the fact in your own words. Never copy it exactly from the source you are using. At the top of each card, write the name of the book or magazine that the fact came from. Also write the name of the author, if there is one. Put in page numbers.

One student, Tanya, chose spider webs as her topic. One of her note cards is shown at the top of the next page. She got her information from a book.

For more information about taking notes, see Chapter 21, pages 362–363.

Animals and Plants That Trap — Title of Book

by Philip Goldstein — Author

pages 55–56 — Pages

Spiders produce several kinds of silk. Some silk forms sticky threads or droplets. Other silk forms dry threads. — Information

Exercises Gathering Information

A. Taking Notes Read the following information carefully. It comes from *The World Book Encyclopedia*. There is no author. Make two note cards on what you read. Remember to write the notes in your own words.

> **MARS** was the god of war in Roman mythology. The ancient Romans gave Mars special importance because they considered him the father of Romulus and Remus, the legendary founders of Rome.
>
> Originally, Mars was a god of farmland and fertility. The month of March, the beginning of the Roman growing season, was named for him. Since ancient times, the area enclosed by a bend in the Tiber River in Rome has been called the Field of Mars. The early Romans dedicated this section of land to Mars because of its fertility.

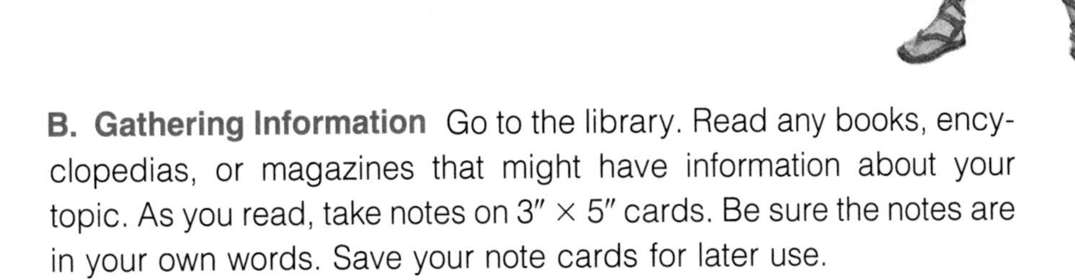

B. Gathering Information Go to the library. Read any books, encyclopedias, or magazines that might have information about your topic. As you read, take notes on 3″ × 5″ cards. Be sure the notes are in your own words. Save your note cards for later use.

3 Prewriting: Organizing Notes

Focus

Once you have written your information on note cards, organize the notes in a logical order.

When you write a report, you share a great deal of information with your readers. This information must be well organized. If it is not, your report may confuse your readers instead of adding to their knowledge.

Organizing Notes into Idea Groups

When you begin to organize your information, carefully read through the facts on your note cards. Put all of the cards that tell about the same main idea together. For example, if you were writing a report on life in the Rocky Mountains, you might put all of the cards that tell about animal life in one pile. Cards that tell about plant life could go in another pile, and so on. If you were writing a report about a famous baseball player, you might organize your cards into several piles. One pile might tell about the player's early life. Another pile might tell about how the player broke into baseball. A third pile might list all of the player's accomplishments.

When you sort your cards, you will probably have some that do not seem to fit with any others. Set these cards aside. You may not be able to use them for your report.

Tanya had five groups of cards.

1. Cards with facts about where spiders build webs
2. Cards about different types of webs
3. Cards about how spiders build webs
4. Cards about spiders' silk
5. Cards about how spiders use webs

After Tanya grouped her cards around main ideas, she decided to write a sentence that stated the main idea of each group of cards. First she read through the cards in each group. Then she wrote the following sentences.

1. Spider webs are found everywhere, indoors and out.
2. Each kind of spider builds it own type of web.
3. A spider builds a web thread by thread.
4. All spider webs are made from silk.
5. Spiders use their webs in many ways.

When Tanya begins drafting her report, she will probably talk about each of these main ideas in a separate paragraph. She can use each of the sentences she wrote as the topic sentence of a paragraph.

Exercises Organizing Information

A. Organizing Notes into Main Idea Groups Look at the following notes for a report on our solar system. Imagine each note is on a separate note card. Group these notes around these three main ideas.

Facts about planets
Facts about satellites
Facts about comets

1. The moon is Earth's only satellite.
2. The largest of all planets is Jupiter.
3. Halley's comet is seen from the Earth every 76 years.
4. Mercury is the closest planet to the sun.
5. Mars's satellites are named Phobos and Deimos.
6. Pluto was the last planet to be discovered.
7. Comets are made up of a nucleus, a head, and a tail.
8. Human beings could not survive on any other planet.

B. Organizing Your Notes Study the notes you have made for your report. Group your note cards around main ideas. For each group of cards, write a sentence that states the main idea of those cards.

4 Prewriting: Making an Outline

Focus

Make an outline to arrange your ideas.

Now that you have grouped your note cards around main ideas, you are ready to make an outline for your report. An **outline** is a writing plan. It shows the order in which ideas will be presented in a report.

Arranging Main Ideas

Arrange the main ideas on your list in a logical order. This will be the order you will follow when you write your report. These main ideas will become the main topics of your outline.

Remember the following when writing your main topics.

1. Each topic is numbered with a Roman numeral followed by a period.
2. The first letter of each main topic is capitalized.
3. The main topics are lined up under each other.

Arranging Facts

The facts on your 3″ × 5″ note cards will become subtopics on your outline. Subtopics are listed under each main topic.

Here are some guidelines to follow when writing subtopics.

1. Do not use just one subtopic under a main topic. If the main topic cannot be broken into at least two ideas, it should not be broken at all.
2. Subtopics are labeled with capital letters followed by periods.
3. The first letter in each subtopic is capitalized.
4. Subtopics are indented. They begin under the first letter of the main topic.
5. Subtopics are lined up under each other.

Topics and subtopics can be written as sentences, phrases, or words. However, once you decide on a form, you should write all your topics and subtopics in that same form.

Here are the first two parts of Tanya's outline.

Spider Webs

I. Webs found everywhere
   A. On mountains
   B. In tropical forests
   C. Underground
   D. Underwater
   E. Inside folded leaves
   F. Inside houses
II. Webs made from silk
   A. Made in special glands
   B. Carried by tubes to spinnerets
   C. Both sticky and dry

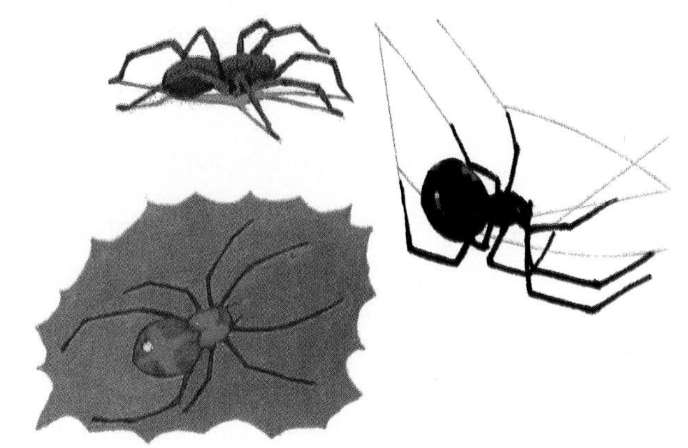

Exercises Writing an Outline

A. Completing an Outline Copy the outline on the left. Fill in the missing title, main topic, and subtopics. They are listed on the right.

__________ (Title)	Flying machines
	Jet fighters
I. Air-powered	Blimps
A. __________	Helicopters
B. __________	Engine-powered
II. __________	Hot-air balloons
A. Space shuttles	
B. __________	
C. __________	

B. Writing Your Own Outline List the main ideas for your report in logical order. Then make an outline. Use the main ideas as the main topics of your outline. Use the facts from your 3″ × 5″ note cards as the subtopics. Use the sample outline in this lesson as a guide.

5 Drafting the Introduction

Focus

There are three parts to a written report. The first part is the **introduction.**

A written report has three parts.

1. It has an introductory paragraph. This paragraph gives the main idea of the report. It should also capture the interest of the reader.
2. It has body paragraphs. These paragraphs explain the main idea of the report.
3. It has an ending paragraph. The ending pulls together all the ideas in the report.

When you are writing the three parts of a report, be sure to follow your outline. The outline includes all the ideas you want to cover. The ideas are arranged in logical order.

It is also important to refer to your note cards once in a while. In that way, you will not forget details that are not on the outline.

Writing the Introduction

Just as in any other piece of writing, the introduction is an important part of a report. The **introduction** gives the main idea of the report and captures the reader's attention.

You can begin your introduction by stating your main idea right away. You might use a quotation that relates to your topic. You might give an example or some interesting piece of information.

However you choose to begin, be sure that your introduction catches your readers' interest. It should make them want to read more.

When Tanya began drafting her report, she wrote the following introduction:

> Spider webs are pretty. They are found everywhere. They are interesting to study.

Although this paragraph gives the main idea of Tanya's report, it does not do so in a very interesting way. It does not give any facts about spider webs or make the reader want to read more. Tanya rewrote her introduction this way.

> Spider webs are wonders of nature. They are found everywhere, indoors and out. They can be high on a mountain slope or deep in a tropical forest. They can be underground or underwater. They can be inside a folded leaf or in a corner of your living room.

Tanya's new introduction lets you know the main topic of her report. It also gives you some specific information.

Exercises Writing an Introduction

A. Improving a Draft Read the following introductory paragraph. Think about how you could make it more interesting. Rewrite the paragraph on a separate sheet of paper.

> Sports are fun. There are many kinds of sports. Everyone can find at least one sport they can enjoy. I think the most interesting sport is ski jumping.

B. Writing Your Own Introduction Draft the introductory paragraph of your report. Be sure to give the main idea of your report, and to catch the reader's interest.

6 Drafting the Body

Focus

The **body** of a report gives most of the information about the topic.

The middle paragraphs are called the **body** of the report. These paragraphs give many facts about the topic. Each paragraph begins with a topic sentence. This sentence is usually a main topic from the outline. The rest of the sentences explain the idea of the topic sentence. They cover the subtopics on the outline. In other words, each paragraph in a report covers a main topic and its subtopics.

Here are the four body paragraphs of Tanya's report. Notice how she begins each paragraph with a topic sentence taken from her outline. The rest of each paragraph gives many facts about the topic sentence. The paragraphs work together to tell about the topic of the report.

> All spider webs are made from silk. Silk comes from special glands. They are inside a spider's body. Tubes connect the glands to openings on a spider's underside. The openings are called spinnerets. Some spinnerets have silk that stays sticky. Others have silk that hardens into dry threads.
>
> A spider builds a web thread by thread. It first draws a thread of dry silk out of a spinneret. It attaches the thread to a starting point with a drop of sticky silk. As it builds its web, the spider bites off extra threads. It discards them. It joins certain threads and weaves others in and out. Little by little the spider forms an intricate pattern.
>
> Each kind of spider builds it own type of web. A spider is born knowing how to build its special web. Some webs are as small as a postage stamp. Others measure two feet across. Some webs look like jumbles of tangled threads. Others form perfect circles or triangles. Webs can be shaped like bowls, domes, tents, platforms, or funnels. Some webs are complicated mazes.

Spiders use their webs in many ways. They use them as homes and as places to lay their eggs. They do not have to worry about getting caught in their own sticky threads. Their bodies are coated with an oil that prevents sticking. Other creatures are not as lucky. When they walk or fly into a spider web, they are caught by the sticky threads. The spider bites each captive and paralyzes it. Then it wraps the victim in silk and saves it.

Using Signal Words

When writing paragraphs that give facts, you can use signal words and phrases such as *first, next,* or *finally* to link your facts together. Other signal words, like *in addition* or *also,* can let a reader know that a new fact is coming up. You can also use signal words to make paragraphs flow smoothly and work well together.

For more about signal words, see Chapter 17, page 293.

Exercises Drafting Body Paragraphs

A. Paragraphing Study the following draft about hobbies. Decide where each new paragraph should begin. Write the first three words of each new paragraph.

Knitting is a hobby many people enjoy. It is fun to make your own sweaters, scarves, or gloves. It is also less expensive than buying these items in a store. Other people like vegetable gardening. They like raising their own vegetables. Most people say that their own vegetables are tastier than the ones they buy in the grocery store. Stamp collecting is a third popular hobby. Some people collect stamps because they are so pretty. Others collect stamps for their monetary value.

B. Drafting the Body of Your Report Draft the body paragraphs of your report. Follow your outline as you write. Be sure each paragraph has a topic sentence. Check your note cards to make sure you do not leave out any details.

7 Drafting the Ending and Giving Credit

Focus

Write a strong ending for your report. Give credit to the sources you used for your information.

Writing a Good Ending

A good ending paragraph should let your readers know that your report is finished. It should not introduce any new topics.

You may want to end your report by summarizing all of your main ideas. Or you may want to end your report by including your personal opinion on the topic.

An ending does not have to be long. However, it must be clear. You must let your readers know that you have said everything you are going to say about the subject.

Here is the first ending Tanya wrote for her report.

> Spiders need their webs to live. Other insects need safe living places also. Bees need hives and ants need ant hills.

This is a weak ending paragraph. It does not bring the report to a satisfactory close. Instead, it introduces a new topic—where other insects live.

Tanya then wrote a much stronger ending to her report. She included a personal opinion in her ending.

> Web-building spiders cannot live without their webs. Think about that the next time you are tempted to brush away a web. You may decide not to destroy it after all.

Giving Credit

You write a report in your own words. However, you get the information you use from outside sources. It is important to give credit to these sources. You do this at the end of your report. There, you list the books and magazines from which you got information.

Tanya used these sources. She listed them at the end of her report like this.

I got my information from the following sources.

1. Animals and Plants That Trap by Philip Goldstein
2. The World Book Encyclopedia, 1985, Volume 18, page 615
3. The Spider's World by Jim Dune
4. Insect World, November, 1984, "The Busy Spider," pages 10–12

Notice that Tanya underlined the titles of the books and magazines that she used. She put the title of the magazine article in quotation marks. Follow this same form when you list the sources for your report. To learn more about capitalizing and punctuating titles, see the **Power Handbook** at the back of this book.

Exercises Writing an Ending

A. Improving an Ending Rewrite the following ending paragraph. Make it clear that the report is over. The topic of the report is how computers help students learn at school. You may want to include your personal opinion when you rewrite the paragraph.

> Computers can help you learn. They can also help your parents organize their records at home. And, computers help businesses in many ways.

B. Ending Your Report Write the final paragraph for your report. Credit your sources. Use the examples in this lesson to guide you.

8 Revising, Proofreading, and Sharing

Focus

Revise and proofread your report carefully.

It is important to revise your report so that it will be clear and interesting. As you revise, ask yourself these questions.

Guidelines for Revising

1. Does my introduction state the topic of the report? Will the introduction capture the readers' attention?
2. Is the body of my report informative?
3. Are my ideas presented in a logical order?
4. Does my ending clearly let the reader know that my report is finished?
5. Did I begin a new paragraph for each main topic? Did I include all of the right subtopics in each paragraph?

A Sample Revision

Here is a paragraph from one writer's report. Luis wrote about the famous Mayan ruins in Mexico. Notice Luis's thoughts as he revised his paragraph.

I should tell what it is.

The ~~biggest thing~~ tallest building at Chichén Itzá is a temple called El Castillo. It is 75 feet tall. It has ~~lots of~~ 364 stairs. There are two snakes carved ~~on it~~ along the stairs. At times, when the light is right, the snakes actually seem to move~~ sometimes. I told some of my friends this, but they didn't believe me.~~

I should use a more exact word.

This last sentence shouldn't be here. It's not about my main idea.

Proofreading

Proofread a report carefully. Check the correctness of all the facts you used. Pay special attention to the correct spelling of names and special words. Check the correctness of dates, too. Be sure that your grammar, capitalization, and punctuation are also correct.

Making a Final Copy

When you have finished revising your report, make a clean, final copy. Write neatly. Be sure to give your report a good title. When your final copy is done, proofread it one last time. Neatly correct any mistakes you find.

Exercises Revising and Sharing a Report

A. Revising Your Report Revise your report, using the guidelines in this lesson. Then proofread your report carefully. When you are satisfied that your report is the best it can be, make a neat, final copy. Remember to give your report a good title.

B. Sharing Your Report Brainstorm with your classmates for ways to share your reports. One suggestion might be to have each student create a colorful cover for his or her report. The cover should include the name of the report, the name of the student who wrote it, and some type of design or illustration. When the covers are completed, display the reports where others can see and read them—in the school library, perhaps.

Speaking and Listening

Oral Reports

Not all reports are written. Some are given orally. Oral reports are like written reports in many ways. They are developed by following many of the same steps.

Preparing To Give Your Report

Writing Notes Oral reports are not written out word for word. However, most people use notes when they give an oral report. Notes help them to remember main ideas.

Notes can be written in several ways. One way is in outline form. A speaker would record each main topic of the outline and its subtopics on a separate 3″ × 5″ inch card. Cards are easy to hold and can be easily set aside.

Using Pictures Pictures can make an oral report more interesting. You can show slides during a report. You can pass pictures around after a report. You may also be able to display pictures on the chalkboard in the classroom.

Practicing Your Report

Practice your report in front of a mirror or present it to members of your family. You could also record your report on tape and play it back for yourself.

Exercise Giving an Oral Report

Prepare to give an oral version of the report you wrote for this chapter. Follow the guidelines given in this lesson.

Creative Writing

Imagine that you are an explorer. You have just come upon a fabulous discovery. Your discovery is one of the following.

a pirate ship that has been underwater for hundreds of years

a new species of animal

a mysterious cave in which you find treasures from an ancient civilization

a rocket ship from another planet, with no one in it

Write a report on what you have found. Make it as creative and as interesting as you can. First, make notes on your imaginary discovery. Then, organize your notes and make an outline. Finally, use your outline to write your report.

Using English in Reading

One way to share what you read is by writing a book report. When you write this type of report, you share with others the knowledge you have gained from reading.

Reporting on a Book A book report may be a two- or three-paragraph composition about a book you have read. You can write a book report on a fiction book or a nonfiction book. In either case, a book report should answer these five questions.

1. What is the title of the book?
2. Who is the author of the book?
3. What is the book about?
4. What is special about the book?
5. Why do you like or dislike the book?

When you report on a fiction book, tell who the book is about and one problem that character faces. You needn't tell the whole story. Let the ending be a surprise to the reader.

When you report on a nonfiction book, share the most interesting parts with your audience. Again, explain your feelings about the book.

Your teacher may ask you to read your book report to the class. Before you present your report, choose a part of the book that you want the class to hear. Then read it at the end of your report. Reading a part of the book lets your listeners know how the book is written.

Exercise Writing Your Own Book Report

Choose and read a fiction or nonfiction book. Write a book report that includes answers to the five questions listed above. Select a part of the book to read to the class.

Chapter 22 Review

A. Paragraphing Rewrite the following draft, separating it into paragraphs.

Savannas are grasslands with widely scattered trees and shrubs. In Africa, savannas cover two-fifths of the land and contain a large variety of animals. Grazing animals are one group that lives on the savanna. Grazing animals live by feeding on the grasses and trees. These animals include the giraffe, elephant, and zebra. Another kind of animal found on the savanna is the predator. Predators eat other animals. The best known predator is the lion. The leopard, cheetah, and hyena are also predators.

B. Organizing Notes Here are some notes about the islands of Hawaii. Organize them into the following idea groups.

Hawaii's climate
Hawaii's economy
Hawaii's natural beauty

1. The temperature is warm all year long.
2. Lush flowers are always in bloom.
3. Some beaches are covered with beautiful black sand.
4. Many tourists go to Hawaii.
5. Hawaii's main crops are pineapples and sugar cane.
6. There are strong winds in Hawaii.
7. Hawaii is surrounded by clear, blue waters.
8. There can be severe tropical storms in Hawaii.

C. Making an Outline Here are a title, main topics, and subtopics. Put them into outline form.

String instruments	Cello
Percussion instruments	Guitar
Musical instruments	Violin
Drums	Cymbals

Chapter 23

Communicating Through Letters

Everyone loves getting mail. You might get a letter from a friend, an invitation to a party, or birthday wishes from a favorite aunt. Letters like these can really make your day. Letters are special because the writer puts a part of himself or herself on paper.

Letter writing is probably one of the first kinds of writing you learned. This chapter will help you to improve your letter-writing skills. You will learn how to write friendly letters and social notes. You will also learn how to write business letters to get information or to order a product. Finally, you will learn another important skill—how to address envelopes for all your letters.

1 Writing a Friendly Letter

Focus

A **friendly letter** is a conversation on paper.

Write a friendly letter to say "hello" to someone you know well. Make the letter sound natural, as if you were talking to your friend.

Read the following letter. Look carefully at each part.

A Friendly Letter

Heading
7500 South State Street
Midvale, Utah 84047
May 12, 1987

Greeting
Dear Michelle,

Body
I just got your letter. When are you moving back to Midvale? Do you know your new address yet? I hope it's near me!

My brother and I are learning kite-making at the Y. When you come, I can teach you, too.

Write back soon. Tell me all about your move.

Closing
Your friend,

Signature
Danielle

The Parts of a Friendly Letter

A friendly letter has five parts. Each part has its own purpose. Follow these rules for writing each part of a friendly letter.

1. Heading The heading tells where you are and when you are writing. It is written in the upper right-hand corner. The heading has three lines in the following order.

house address and name of street
city, state, and ZIP code
month, day, and year

Follow these punctuation and capitalization rules for writing the heading.

1. Capitalize all proper names.
2. Place a comma between the city and the state.
3. Put the ZIP code after the state. No comma is needed to separate the state and the ZIP code.
4. Place a comma between the day and the year.
5. Avoid abbreviations.

2. Greeting The greeting is the way you say "hello" to your friend. Here are examples of some common greetings.

Dear Ted, *Hi Frank,*

Write the greeting on the line below the heading and begin at the left margin. Do not indent the greeting. Capitalize the first word and all proper nouns. Place a comma after the greeting.

3. Body In the body of the letter, you talk to your friend. Begin the body on the line below the greeting. Always arrange your information in paragraphs. Indent the first line of each paragraph. Use your best handwriting.

4. Closing In the closing you say "goodbye" to your friend. Capitalize only the first word. Place a comma at the end. Here are some suggestions for closings.

Love, *Your friend,* *Sincerely,*
Always, *Missing you,* *Yours truly,*

The closing lines up with the heading.

5. Signature Your signature should be written clearly. If you do not know the person very well, include your first and last names. Write your signature below the closing.

Exercises Writing Friendly Letters

A. Copy the following words and phrases. Capitalize and punctuate them as if they were in a letter.

1. 4802 page street
2. yankton south dakota 57078
3. january 18 1987
4. dear uncle dave
5. your nephew
6. mike larsen

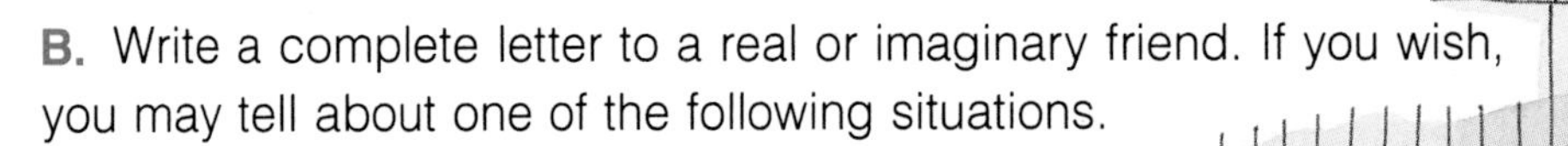

B. Write a complete letter to a real or imaginary friend. If you wish, you may tell about one of the following situations.

1. a class field trip
2. what your pet has been up to
3. a sports event you attended
4. a new hobby you started
5. a movie you saw
6. a picnic

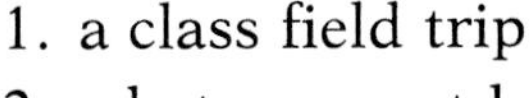

2 Writing Social Notes

Focus

A **social note** is a polite way to thank someone, to invite someone to an event, or to reply to an invitation.

Writing a Thank-You Note

Write a thank-you note when you have received a gift, when someone has done you a special favor, or when you have stayed overnight at someone's house.

Write a thank-you note soon after receiving a gift or favor. Promptness shows your appreciation.

Here is an example of a thank-you note. Notice that only the date is needed in the heading.

A Thank-You Note

February 24, 1987

Dear Mr. Owen,

Thank you for letting me have that old tricycle. I plan to fix it up and paint it for my younger brother. He will really be surprised.

You certainly are a good neighbor. I hope I can do a favor for you sometime.

Sincerely,
Doug Martin

Writing an Invitation

Use an invitation to ask someone to a party or an event. Use a complete heading on your invitation. Also include the following information.

1. What the activity is
2. Why the activity is being held
3. Where the activity will take place
4. When the activity will be held: day, date, and time
5. Any special instructions

Answering an Invitation

When you receive an invitation, you should reply as soon as possible. Reply with either a note of acceptance or a note of regret. In both notes, thank the person for the invitation. Use the same form you use for a thank-you note.

Exercises Writing Social Notes

A. Write a thank-you note for one of the following situations. Check your punctuation and use your best handwriting.

1. Thank a friend or a relative for a birthday gift.
2. Thank a friend of your parents for the information he or she gave you for a report.
3. Thank a relative for a Christmas or Hanukkah gift.
4. Thank your friend's parents for letting you spend the weekend.

B. Write an invitation for a party you would like to give. Exchange invitations with a classmate and reply to your classmate's invitation.

3 Writing Business Letters

Focus

A **business letter** may be written to get information or order a product.

A business letter can be used to request information or order materials. A business letter is more formal than a friendly letter. It should be clear and to the point.

Parts of a Business Letter

1. Heading Write your street address on the first line in the upper right-hand corner. Write your city, state, and ZIP code on the second line. Write the date on the third line. Remember to follow rules for capitalization and punctuation.

2. Inside Address The inside address tells the name and address of the person or company you are writing to. This is the same address you will use on the envelope. Write the inside address below the heading but at the left margin.

3. Greeting The greeting of a business letter is more formal than that of a friendly letter. If you are writing to a specific person, use *Dear* and then the person's name.

Dear Ms. Courtney: *Dear Mr. Dylan:*

You will often write directly to a company rather than to a person in the company. In this case, use a general greeting such as *Dear Sir or Madam,* or *Ladies and Gentlemen.* The greeting begins two lines below the inside address and ends with a colon (:).

4. Body The body of a business letter should be short and polite. It should clearly state your subject.

A Letter of Request

Heading

9204 Palm Drive
Tampa, Florida 33603
October 4, 1987

Inside Address

Science and Health Reports
Division of Research Resources
National Institutes of Health
Bethesda, Maryland 20014

Greeting

Dear Sir or Madam:

Body

In our fifth-grade science class we have four white mice and two guinea pigs. I am writing a report about how these animals are used in research. Do you have any brochures or information on this topic? I would appreciate any information you have available.

I need this information by November 1 for my report. Thank you for your help.

Closing

Respectfully,

Signature

Jacob Corley
Jacob Corley

A **letter of request** should include these three points: *what* specific information you need, *why* you need that information, and *when* you need it.

An **order letter** should include: the name of the product and how many you want, where the product was advertised, and the catalog number, size, and color. Also include the price plus postage and handling fees, and what you are enclosing, such as a check, money order, or coupon.

5. Closing Write the closing on the second line below the body. Line it up with the heading. The most common closings for a business letter are these.

Sincerely, *Yours truly,* *Respectfully,*

6. Signature Print your name four spaces below the closing. Then write your signature in the space between. In this way the reader will have no trouble reading your name so that he or she can reply to you.

Exercise Writing Business Letters

Write a business letter to order or request one of the following.

1. Order the book *Canoeing*. This book teaches the proper way to paddle a canoe. It costs $5.40. Write to the American Red Cross, 617 North Main Street, Mount Prospect, Illinois 60056.
2. Request information about wildlife refuges and bird migration. Write to the Assistant Director—Public Affairs, United States Fish and Wildlife Service, Department of the Interior, Washington, D.C. 20240
3. Ask for a list of films on farming in the United States. Write to Broadcasting and Film, Office of Governmental and Public Affairs, Department of Agriculture, Washington, D.C. 20250.

4 Addressing an Envelope

Focus

An envelope must be addressed correctly so that it arrives at the destination quickly.

Use the following guidelines for preparing an envelope.

Guidelines for Addressing Envelopes

1. Make sure the envelope is the right size for the paper. You should not fold the paper more than three times.
2. Make sure the envelope is right-side up.
3. Write the address almost half-way down the envelope and about two-thirds of the way from the left edge.
4. Put your own name and address, called the return address, in the upper left-hand corner.
5. Check the accuracy of street numbers and ZIP codes.
6. Use the two-letter postal abbreviations for states.

Study this example of a correctly addressed envelope.

Miss Nancy Shafer
92 Laurel Trail
Wheeling, IL 60090

Ms. Naomi Martinez
423 St. Catherine Avenue
Phoenix, AZ 85040

Envelopes for social notes are often smaller in size than business envelopes. In this case, the return address may be put on the back of the envelope, as in the following example.

Exercises **Addressing Envelopes**

A. Look at the organizations listed in the exercise on page 401. Then draw three envelopes on your paper and correctly address them to these organizations. Use your own home or school address as the return address.

B. Using your local telephone directory, look up the names and addresses of three of the following businesses. Draw three envelopes on your paper and address them correctly. Use your own home or school address as the return address.

1. a sporting goods store
2. an arts and crafts store
3. a pet store
4. a record store
5. a pharmacy
6. a dentist
7. a music store
8. a bicycle repair shop

C. Draw two envelopes on your paper. Address one envelope for each social note you wrote in Exercises A and B on page 398. Use your own address as the return address.

Using English in Health

If you know how to write letters of request, you can discover a whole world of information. For example, everyone should be familiar with basic first aid facts. You never know when you will be called upon to treat a minor injury or to help someone who has had a serious accident. You can use your letter-writing skills to learn proper first aid.

Exercise Writing for First Aid Information

Here are some sources for information on first aid. Choose one. Write a letter of request or an order letter asking for the book or pamphlet. Review what should be included in a letter of request and an order letter on page 401. After you have written the letter, address an envelope for it.

1. *Standard First Aid and Personal Safety*. This book costs $2.50 and is available through your local chapter of the American Red Cross. Check your telephone book for the proper address.
2. "First Aid Fact Chart." This free chart is distributed by the Consumer Service Department, Johnson & Johnson, New Brunswick, New Jersey 08903.
3. *Standard First Aid Training Course*. This book is published by the Department of Defense. It costs $3.75, and its order number is (S/N 088–047–00260–2). Write to the Superintendent of Documents, Government Printing Office, Washington, D.C. 20402.
4. *First Aid*. This pocket guide to first aid costs $1.70. It is available through the Consumer Information Center, Pueblo, Colorado 81009.

Chapter 23 Review

Writing Letters and Addressing Envelopes Find the errors in the following business letter and envelope. Copy the letter and envelope on your paper. Make the necessary corrections.

2362 Jackson St.
Green Bay Wis. 54302
Feb. 4, 1987

Mr. Basil Connors
Home Robots Company
1205 Seventh Ave.
Morton; Minn. 51622

Dear Mr. Connors,

I would like a brochure explaining the uses of your household helper robots. Also, please send a price list.

Sincerely:
Sybil Abrahams
Sybil Abrahams

Sybil Abrahams
2362 jackson street
Green Bay, wi 54302

Mr. Basil connors
home robots company
1205 Seventh ave.
Morton, minn. 51622

Cumulative Review

Unit 4

Composition

A. Writing Opinions Explain why everyone should learn to cook. If you prefer, explain why everyone should or should not exercise regularly. Remember to include facts to support your opinions.

B. Writing Reports The five following statements are incorrect. Rewrite the statements correctly.

1. When you write a fact on a note card, copy it exactly from the source.
2. A report should be written mainly from your own knowledge or experience.
3. Each group of notes should become a subtopic on your outline.
4. The introduction contains most of the important information in your report.
5. List all of your sources at the end of your report to make it longer.

C. Letter Writing Write a letter to a friend or relative. Tell about your plans for summer vacation. Prepare a correctly addressed envelope to go with your letter.

Grammar

Prepositions Number your paper from 1 to 10. Write the prepositional phrases from the following sentences. Draw one line under the preposition and two lines under the object of the preposition in each phrase.

1. Hundreds of cars drive through the tunnel daily.
2. Potatoes cook quickly in the microwave.
3. The ambulance sped across town to the hospital.
4. Debbie's report is about a famous inventor.

5. A jackrabbit scampered across the desert and hid behind a cactus.
6. The racers sped around the track.
7. The boys pulled their sleds up the steep, icy hill.
8. Mom parked the car near the corner.
9. Pull the shades on the window before the show.
10. I put my hands over my eyes during the scary part of the monster movie.

Related Skills

A. Thinking Clearly Number your paper from 1 to 10. Tell if each statement below is *Fact* or *Opinion*.

1. Computers can store information.
2. Broiled hamburgers taste better than fried ones.
3. Jupiter is the largest planet in our solar system.
4. Expensive shampoo will always make your hair softer and fuller.
5. Television is the best source for news.

B. Library and Research Copy the following sentences on your paper. Fill in the blanks with the word or words needed to make a correct sentence.

1. The ______ System classifies all books into categories and gives each a ______ number.
2. Each book in the library has three catalog cards: an ______ card, a ______ card, and a ______ card.
3. Dictionaries and encyclopedias can be found in the ______ section of the library.
4. Books are classified as ______ and ______ according to whether they are stories or fact.
5. The starting place for finding a book in the library is the ______ .

POWER HANDBOOK

Guidelines for the Process of Writing

Prewriting

1. Select a topic and narrow it. Write your topic as a main idea. Decide whether you are writing a **narrative**, a **description**, or an **explanation**.
2. Identify your purpose and your audience.
3. Make a list of details that you could use to develop your main idea.
4. Put your details into a logical order. Choose an order that suits the type of writing you are doing. Some common orders are **time order**, **order of importance**, and **natural order**.
5. As you organize your details, see if you can cover your main idea in one paragraph. If not, organize your details into several paragraphs.
6. Use your organized details to make a **writing plan**.

Drafting

1. Choose a method of drafting that works best for you. (See page 108.)
2. With your topic in mind at all times, begin to write. Follow your writing plan. However, do not hesitate to change your writing plan if necessary.

Revising

1. Read your draft. Keep questions such as these in mind:
   a. Do you like what you have written? Will others want to read it?
   b. Does your writing make sense? Have you achieved your purpose?
   c. Is your writing organized well? Is each paragraph well written? Does each have a strong topic sentence?
   d. Do all of the sentences in each paragraph tell about the main idea? Are they arranged correctly? Should any sentence be moved?
   e. Should any details be left out? Should any be added?
   f. Does every sentence express a complete thought?
   g. Is there variety in the sentence patterns? Do the sentences flow smoothly from one idea to the next?
   h. Is every word the best possible word? Have you chosen language that suits your audience?
2. Mark changes on your paper as you think of them. Keep making changes until you are satisfied with what you have written.

Proofreading

Proofread your revised draft. Consider questions such as those that follow. Refer to the pages indicated for specific help.

Grammar and Usage

a. Is every word group a complete sentence? (20–21)
b. When you use a pronoun, is it clear about whom you are writing? (158–160)
c. Is the form of each adjective correct? (216–226)
d. Is the form of each adverb correct? (234–240)

Capitalization

a. Did you capitalize the first word in each sentence? (424–425)
b. Did you capitalize all proper nouns and adjectives? (416–421)
c. Did you capitalize titles correctly? (428–429)

Punctuation

a. Does each sentence have the correct end mark? (432–438)
b. Did you use these punctuation marks correctly: commas, apostrophes, quotation marks, hyphens, colons, question marks, underlining? (439–451)

Spelling

a. Did you check unfamiliar words in a dictionary? (142–146)
b. Did you spell plural and possessive forms correctly? (46–51)

Sharing the Final Copy

1. Make a clean copy of your writing. Make all changes and correct all mistakes. Then check your work, asking the following questions:
   a. Is your handwriting easy to read?
   b. Is your paper neat?
   c. Did you leave wide margins?
   d. Is every paragraph indented?
2. Proofread your final copy, reading aloud. Correct any mistakes by erasing neatly and writing in the changes.
3. Choose a method of sharing your writing. Use the suggestions on pages 114–115.

Topics for Writing

Journal Starters

You may also use Creative Writing ideas as journal starters.

I wish I could trade places with:
- my older brother or sister
- someone in the year 2000
- an animal
- a famous person

I certainly hope that by this time next year . . .

I talked to a wonderful person today.

My worst nightmare was . . .

I don't like people who . . .

The best thing that happened to me this week was . . .

My favorite color is ____________ because . . .

When I'm feeling down, I . . .

_______ always puts me in a good mood.

I heard the best news on the radio today.

I would like to wake up one day and find myself . . .

I felt so lonely when . . .

My favorite time of year is . . .

Narratives

Tell a story about:

a person who should be in the *Guinness Book of World Records*

a mystery

a plant that answers when you ask it a question

a time when you failed, but tried again

the day all color left the earth

how you helped your team win the big game

a time that you were glad something was over or finished

a broken promise

a new invention—the anti-gravity machine

a time that you were embarrassed

a situation that wasn't fair

an odd-looking creature that came to town

a memorable birthday

a big storm

a hero

your first day at school

your life as a great dinosaur hunter

Descriptions

Describe each of the following:

a view from a hot-air balloon

an extinct animal

a constellation

a leprechaun

what your favorite book character looks like
the sound of a musical instrument
your favorite place outdoors
early morning sounds
sounds and smells in a neighborhood grocery store
most cherished childhood toy
sights and sounds of an amusement park
your bedroom
a sunrise
the treasure at the end of a rainbow
how it feels to float on a cloud
how a sunburn feels
swimming underwater
a ghost
the sound of thunder
Rip Van Winkle

Explaining *How*

Explain how to:
live with new eyeglasses
write a secret code
stop hiccups
play a new game
skateboard
hit a home run
make tacos
build a bird house
paddle a canoe
make a sling

Explain how:
a jet engine works
radio waves are transmitted
aluminum is recycled
a battery works
a glacier is formed
a spider catches its prey
a windmill works
cheese is made

Explaining *Why*

Give reasons for or against each of the following:
school buses should be equipped with seat belts
a new fad should be dropped
amusement park rides are dangerous and should be closed
your school should have support groups for students
there should be a national holiday to honor ________
your school should have a pool
dirt bikes are dangerous

Give reasons why:
a student should adopt a "grandparent" from a home for the elderly
________ is your favorite music
you participate in a sport
________ is the best vacation spot
friends always stand by you
your cafeteria should add ________ to the menu
________ is your favorite food

Reports

Write a report about:

an inventor (Eli Whitney, Gabriel Fahrenheit)

a famous woman (Clara Barton, Gloria Steinem)

an explorer (Sir Francis Drake, Neil Armstrong)

the formation of volcanoes

the life cycle of a seahorse

the Milky Way

sunspots

early model sports cars

the history of basketball

your state symbols: flag, flower, bird, motto

the early television shows

dinosaurs

hang gliders

panda bears

Peking Man

the pyramids—their design and how they were built

how hurricanes develop

how diamonds are formed

how money is minted

how a newspaper is printed

a breed of dog

the building of a bridge

Creative Writing

an announcement you might make over your school public address system

an advertisement for a brand new product

an introduction to a new TV show

a tall tale about a real person

What if? . . .
giraffes had short necks
a day had thirty-five hours
you could read minds
you were a famous explorer
people never made mistakes

Write about . . .
purple
sweet
prickly
fear

What happens to? . . .
yesterday's newspapers
a half-used notebook
old gym shoes
worn-out batteries

Write a conversation between . . .
a ball and a bat
a mouse and a trap
a foot and a shoe
a cactus and the sun

Guides to Capitalization, Punctuation, and Spelling

Capitalization

Punctuation

Spelling

Guide to Capitalization

1 Proper Nouns and Proper Adjectives

A **common noun** is a general name of a person, place, thing, or idea. Common nouns are not capitalized.

hero country planet peace

Capitalize proper nouns. A **proper noun** is the name of one particular person, place, or thing.

Hercules Switzerland Mars

If a proper noun is made up of more than one word, both words begin with capital letters.

Valentine's Day New Zealand Adirondack Mountains
Exton Mall Amazon River Mary Shelley

Capitalize proper adjectives. A **proper adjective** is an adjective made from a proper noun.

Herculean strength (made from Hercules)
Swiss cheese (made from Switzerland)

Proper adjectives are usually used with common nouns. Do not capitalize the common noun.

Proper Adjective	Common Noun	Adjective and Noun
American	flag	American flag
French	poodle	French poodle

Practice

A Number your paper from 1 to 10. Copy the sentences below, using capital letters where they are needed.

1. The olsens live in sweden.
2. Tomatoes and green peppers are two ingredients in spanish rice.
3. On columbus day, we do not have school.
4. Wisconsin, michigan, and minnesota border lake superior.
5. I hope that our family will vacation in maine this year.
6. Some of my new friends are margie, bobby, and bobby's sister, judy.
7. The school she goes to is noble elementary school.
8. My english teacher is miss conlin.
9. The alaskan husky is a good sled dog.
10. During the christmas holidays, we are going to see the lincoln memorial.

B Complete this story by filling in the blanks below with proper nouns or proper adjectives.

Today was so exciting! I finally received a letter from my new pen pal. His name is ______, and he lives in ______. He wrote all about his family. They include his father and mother, two brothers named ______ and ______, and a dog called ______. His family lives on ______ outside the city of ______. In his country, the musical group ______ is very popular. He enjoys many things that I do. We even have the same favorite TV shows, ______ and ______. Writing to each other will be fun.

C **Writing**

Pretend that you are giving a Halloween party. Everyone must dress like a famous person in history. List the characters who come to your party. Include the countries they come from. Use this list to write a paragraph about your Halloween party. Capitalize all proper nouns and proper adjectives.

2 Other Kinds of Proper Nouns

Capitalize the names of people and pets.

Michael Snoopy Maria Tallchief James Earl Jones

Capitalize the pronoun *I*.

Most pronouns are treated like common nouns, and are not capitalized. The pronoun *I*, however, is capitalized.

Capitalize an initial and follow it with a period.

C. G. Rossetti Mary B. Martin O. J. Simpson

Capitalize words for family relations when they are used as names of specific people.

Father Mother Aunt Em Grandpa Smith

Capitalize titles used before names.

Often you use words called **titles** before a person's name. Titles are always capitalized when used before names.

Doctor Brown Judge Clark President Collins

Capitalize abbreviations of titles.

Many titles have short forms. A shortened form of a word is an **abbreviation**. Abbreviations for titles are always capitalized and followed by a period.

Mister = Mr. Mistress = Mrs. Reverend = Rev.

The title *Ms.* has no long form. It is always capitalized and marked with a period. The title *Miss* has no short form. Do not place a period after the word *Miss*.

Practice

A Number your paper from 1 to 10. Copy the following sentences. Change small letters to capital letters wherever necessary.

1. Last week professor nancy l. huse spoke at our school.
2. Mr. rodrigo wrote a letter to superintendent t. j. newman.
3. Were you there when senator cary dedicated the building?
4. Each year we see dr. hankel for a checkup.
5. President and mrs. reagan attended the ceremony.
6. The writer charles dodgson used the pen name lewis carroll.
7. Perhaps i'll name my new puppies pepper and salt.
8. The best players on rhonda's team are rhonda and i.
9. Some famous indian leaders are chief joseph and sitting bull.
10. At the state capitol, clara and i met governor ridge.

B Number your paper from 1 to 10. Copy the following sentences. Some nouns and adjectives are correctly capitalized. Some are not correctly capitalized. Rewrite the incorrect words correctly.

1. A Dog named benji adopted us.
2. Yes, aunt Aretha and I met doctor Cooley.
3. My neighbor, mrs. avellini, repairs cars.
4. Kathy Moran's Cousin produces a television show.
5. My favorite foods are Italian Spaghetti and swiss cheese.
6. One american champion golfer is judy rankin.
7. The Bill was introduced by senator edward m. kennedy.
8. "Stamp out forest fires," smokey tells us.
9. Yesterday, grandma and Jeremy made popcorn.
10. Pianist eubie blake was still performing in his nineties.

3 More About Proper Nouns

Capitalize the names of months, days, and holidays.

Do not capitalize names of seasons, such as *spring* and *summer*.

We observe Lincoln's Birthday on February 12.
Next Friday is the first day of summer.

Capitalize the names of cities, states, and countries.

Did you live in Kansas City, Kansas, or Kansas City, Missouri?
The United States shares borders with Mexico and Canada.

Capitalize both letters of the two-letter postal abbreviations for states.

California = CA   Maine = ME   Wisconsin = WI

Capitalize the names of streets, bridges, parks, and buildings such as schools.

Chambers Elementary School is on Shaw Avenue.
The Oakland Bay Bridge was being repainted.
Estes Park is in Colorado.

Capitalize all geographic names.

Also capitalize such words as *north*, *south*, *east*, and *west* when they refer to a section of the country. Do not capitalize them when they are used as directions.

The air in the Southwest is often hot and dry.

Père Jacques Marquette began his explorations at Lake Michigan. His party traveled south along the Mississippi River toward the Gulf of Mexico.

Practice

A Number your paper from 1 to 10. Copy these sentences. Change small letters to capital letters wherever necessary.

1. The midwest is known for its corn and soybean crops.
2. The postal abbreviation for massachusetts is ma.
3. The danube river flows into the black sea.
4. Americans celebrate thanksgiving day on the fourth thursday of each november.
5. On may 5, harper school will hold a carnival.
6. A good time for picnics is independence day, july 4.
7. Go east on main street until you see grant park.
8. The first monday in september is labor day.
9. The golden gate bridge spans a channel at the entrance to san francisco bay.
10. The aleutian islands are southwest of alaska.

B Copy the following sentences. Correct the errors in capitalization. If a sentence is correct, write *Correct* on your paper.

1. In december, january, and february, skiers travel to resorts near boulder, Colorado.
2. My friend daranee Yang is from bangkok, thailand.
3. Martin luther King, Jr.'s, birthday is now a National Holiday.
4. Whenever I have a chance, I visit Grandma Martin.
5. Mr. swaim teaches sixth grade at Middlebury School.
6. There is a city named paris in the state of Texas.
7. On March 17, many people celebrate St. Patrick's Day.
8. The thames river flows through london, england.
9. The capital of Montana is helena.
10. The northeast was the first U.S. industrial center.

4 Special Groups

Capitalize the names of religions, nationalities, and languages.

Three of the major faiths are Christianity, Judaism, and Islam.
My grandpa is Danish and my grandma is French Canadian.
Many Belgians speak Flemish and French.
Catholicism is the religion of many Spaniards and Portuguese.

Capitalize the names of clubs, organizations, and businesses.

Mary Ann belongs to the Junior Photographers Club.
The Boy Scouts of America was founded in 1910.
The Four Star Amusement Park opens on Memorial Day.
The Camp Fire Girls took a tour of O'Grady's Peanut Farm.

Practice

A **Number your paper from 1 to 15. Copy the following sentences. Change small letters to capital letters wherever necessary.**

1. The sierra club holds nature outings each summer.
2. The civic center hosted a russian dance company.
3. The national geographic society has a good magazine.
4. One indian craft is bead design.
5. Many chinese practice buddhism.
6. The journalism club and photography club at my school belong to the young journalists' association.
7. We held my birthday party at wheel roller rink.
8. Many operas are sung in italian.

9. My father flies a small plane for pegasus airlines.
10. Hanukkah is a jewish holiday.
11. The Masai of tanzania, africa, speak swahili.
12. The main religion of india is hinduism.
13. The spanish spoken by mexicans is different from the spanish spoken by peruvians.
14. My favorite restaurant is taco barn.
15. People all over the united states are helped by the red cross.

B Copy the following paragraph. Use capital letters where they are necessary.

When we were studying important women in history, I decided to learn about sally k. ride. She was the first american female astronaut to enter space. Sally ride was born on may 26, 1951. She received a Ph.D. in physics from stanford university in 1977. She was selected to be an astronaut in 1978. The historic dates of her first space flight on the space shuttle *discovery* were june 18–24, 1983.

C Writing

Imagine that you are living in the year 1902. You have decided to leave your country and emigrate to the United States. Write a short paragraph about the life you are leaving in your native country. What nationality are you? What language do you speak? What is your religion? Include the clubs and organizations you belong to and the business you work for. Complete your paragraph by telling why you are emigrating. Capitalize proper nouns.

5 First Words

Begin every sentence with a capital letter.

Capital letters are important sentence signals. They tell when a new sentence begins.

My brother likes mushrooms on his pizza.
Does February have twenty-nine days this year?
Look out!

Capitalize the beginning of every direct quotation.

When you write the exact words somebody else said, you are **quoting** that person. The words are a **direct quotation**.

"Today we can expect two inches of snow," said the forecaster.

Usually, when you write what a person said, you add some words before or after the direct quotation to tell who said it. If these explaining words come at the beginning of your sentence, use a capital letter there. Use another capital letter at the beginning of the direct quotation. If the explanatory words come after the quotation, you do not begin them with a capital letter unless the first word is a proper noun.

"Let's go fishing before breakfast," Kerry suggested.
(Direct quotation at beginning of sentence)
Ezra asked, "Will I play forward or guard?"
(Direct quotation after explanatory words)

Practice

A Number your paper from 1 to 10. Copy the sentences below. Change small letters to capital letters where needed.

1. giant reptiles lived long ago.
2. "a robot has no brain," mr. rodriguez said.
3. maria asked, "may i use the microscope?"
4. "would you like to take a bike trip?" roosevelt asked.
5. wildflowers grow in the forest.
6. i explained, "a spaceship has gone to mars."
7. a kayak is similar to a canoe.
8. mother reminded me, "your fish must be fed."
9. mona asked, "did you find any animal tracks?"
10. "admiral byrd was the first to fly over the south pole," the teacher said.

B Capitalize the following lines from "The Legend of King Arthur."

when Arthur returned to the shore, Merlin told him, "your sword is called Excalibur. keep it close to you."

as they rode back to court, Merlin asked Arthur, "which do you like better, the sword or the sheath?"

arthur answered, "the sword, of course."

"the sheath is far more valuable than the sword," said Merlin. "while you wear it, you will lose no blood, even if you are badly wounded. always keep it nearby."

from that day on, Arthur felt more capable of fighting against his enemies.

C **Writing**

Imagine that your best friend asks, "Do you want to hear a secret?" Write the conversation that follows. Be sure to capitalize the beginning of every quotation.

6 More First Words

Capitalize the first word in most lines of poetry.

An emerald is as green as grass;
  A ruby red as blood;
A sapphire shines as blue as heaven;
  A flint lies in the mud.
A diamond is a brilliant stone,
  To catch the world's desires;
An opal holds a fiery spark;
  But a flint holds fire.

—CHRISTINA GEORGINA ROSSETTI, "Precious Stones"

Capitalize the first word of each line of an outline.

The major ideas of an outline are marked with Roman numerals (I, II, III). The secondary ideas are marked with capital letters (A, B, C).

Systems of Measurement

I. The English system
  A. Inch, foot, yard, mile
  B. Ounce, pound, ton
  C. Cup, pint, quart, gallon
II. The metric system
  A. Meter
  B. Gram
  C. Liter

Capitalize the greeting and the first word of the closing of a letter.

Dear Sir:
  Sincerely,

Dear Lucy,
  Your friend,

Practice

A Copy the following poem. Capitalize it correctly.

the steam digger
is much bigger
than the biggest beast i know.
he snorts and roars
like the dinosaurs
that lived long years ago.
—ROWENA BENNETT, "The Steam Shovel"

B Copy the following outline. Capitalize it correctly.

The Lewis and Clark Expedition

I. why it was needed
  a. the Louisiana Purchase of 1803
  b. lack of good maps

II. why Lewis and Clark were chosen
  a. achievements of Meriwether Lewis
  b. achievements of William Clark

C **Writing**

You are a TV station manager. Your job is choosing programs to show. Complete the following outline of your Monday night programs. Do not name shows already on TV. You are trying to capture the TV audience with all new shows. Be creative!

I. Game shows
  A.
  B.
II. Sports events
  A.
  B.
III. Movies
  A.
  B.

7 Capitalizing Titles

Capitalize the first word, the last word, and any other important words in a title.

Do not capitalize an article (*the, a, an*) or a short preposition (*in, for, from, by*) unless it comes first or last.

Life on the Mississippi (book)
From the Mixed-Up Files of Mrs. Basil E. Frankweiler (book)
"The Legend of Sleepy Hollow" (story)
"The Song by the Way" (poem)

Titles are also enclosed in quotation marks or underlined. Rules for using these marks are given on page 447. In general, use quotation marks around the titles of short works, such as stories, poems, newspaper or magazine articles, and reports. Underline the titles of longer works, such as books, movies, television series, magazines, and newspapers. In printed works, these titles are in italic type instead of underlined.

Practice

A Copy the following titles. Capitalize them correctly.

1. *where the sidewalk ends* (book)
2. "the seeing stick" (story)
3. *the best christmas pageant ever* (book)
4. *knight rider* (television series)
5. "the pied piper of hamelin" (poem)
6. *a christmas carol* (book and movie)
7. "the top ten on television" (newspaper article)
8. *newsweek* (magazine)
9. "the horses of the sea" (poem)

10. *fantasia* (movie)
11. *people* (magazine)
12. "the mountain and the squirrel" (poem)
13. "the story of keesh" (story)
14. "casey at the bat" (poem)
15. "peace talks begin in geneva" (magazine article)

B Copy the following titles. Add capital letters where necessary. Use underlining and quotation marks correctly.

1. the lion, the witch, and the wardrobe (book)
2. the desert is theirs (poem)
3. 3-2-1 Contact (magazine)
4. the mystery of the rolltop desk (story)
5. the giving tree (book)
6. aftershock of disaster (newspaper article)
7. ghosts i have been (book)
8. the return of the jedi (movie)
9. three rolls and a pretzel (story)
10. the black stallion (movie)
11. the times of london (newspaper)
12. st. elsewhere (television program)
13. the rare tigers of india (magazine article)
14. like ghosts of eagles (story)
15. maple leafs take stanley cup (newspaper article)

C Writing

Pretend that your class is creating a time capsule. List what you will include. Write a paragraph describing the time capsule. The capsule should have a book, a short story, a poem, a magazine, and a movie. What else will you put in the time capsule? Capitalize and punctuate correctly.

Additional Practice

A Capitalizing Proper Nouns and Proper Adjectives

Correctly capitalize the following sentences.

1. Terry graduated from piedmont middle school.
2. Is it true that french toast did not originate in france?
3. At thanksgiving, aunt judy came from phoenix.
4. The advance insurance company is managed by president jerome rupert.
5. The spanish club meets at baker school.
6. The letter was addressed to dr. eugene m. yeazle.
7. In highland park, many people of the jewish faith attend beth israel synagogue.
8. On april 6, 1909, admiral r. e. peary reached the north pole.
9. Michelle is the editor of the panther press club.
10. Amelia earhart was a well known american flyer.

B Capitalizing Proper Nouns and First Words in Sentences and Quotations

Use correct capitalization in the following sentences.

1. *the new york times* is read all over the united states.
2. byrd baylor wrote *when clay sings*.
3. the little girl asked, "can you open this umbrella?"
4. on tuesday, i must give my book report on *sounder*.
5. janine said, "my sister susan has the measles."
6. "our team won the relay!" exclaimed dominic.
7. The fifth graders at edgemont school recited "the steadfast tin soldier" at the parent-teacher association meeting.

8. "sassafras is used in root beer," reported jeremy.
9. "There are eighty-eight keys on a piano," said mrs. roth.
10. i just read *the adventures of robin hood*.

C Capitalizing First Words, Outlines, and Letters

Correctly capitalize the following poem, outline, and letter.

1. listen, my children, and you shall hear
   of the midnight ride of Paul Revere,
   on the eighteenth of April, in seventy-five;
   hardly a man is now alive
   who remembers that famous day and year.

   —HENRY WADSWORTH LONGFELLOW

2. Hawaii

   I. major crops
      a. sugar cane
      b. pineapple

   II. flowers
      a. orchids
      b. jasmine
      c. carnations

3. april 19, 1987

   dear officer bolden:

   thank you for talking to the students in room 148 about careers in police work. everything you said was interesting. the best part was when you answered my question. i asked, "what was the most exciting thing that ever happened to you?"

   i think i'd like to be a police officer someday, too.

   your friend,
   lillian mays

Guide to Punctuation

1 Using the Period

Use a period at the end of a sentence.

A period signals the end of a sentence. All declarative and most imperative sentences end with a period.

Declarative Navaho Indians built homes called hogans.
Imperative Describe a hogan.

Use a period after an initial.

An initial is the first letter of a name. It is always followed by a period. Initials are always capitalized.

John Fitzgerald Kennedy   John F. Kennedy

Use a period after each number or letter in an outline.

An outline is used to organize information. Every outline has main topics and subtopics. Use a period after each number or letter that shows a main topic or subtopic of an outline.

How the Months Got Their Names

I. Months named for real people
   A. July
   B. August
II. Months named for gods
   A. January
   B. March
   C. May

Practice

A Copy these sentences. Use periods correctly.

1. Make yourself comfortable
2. J Fred Muggs is a chimpanzee
3. Be sure to bring warm mittens
4. Actor George C Scott once played General George S Patton
5. Author P L Travers wrote about Mary Poppins
6. Lyndon B Johnson was born near Stonewall, Texas
7. Please call back tomorrow
8. Orethal James Simpson is better known as O J Simpson
9. Alfred B Nobel invented dynamite
10. Look at the frogs in our aquarium

B Copy this outline. Use periods correctly.

Coral

I How coral is formed
II Kinds of coral
  A Hard coral
  B Soft coral
III Where coral is found
IV Types of coral reefs
  A Barrier reefs
  B Fringing reefs
  C Atolls

C **Writing**

You have just made a strange discovery. The initials in the names of several famous people do not mean what the public thinks they mean. In a paragraph, explain the real meaning of the initials in four of these famous names.

E. T.
R. E. O. Speedwagon
Dr. J.
Mr. T.
O. J. Simpson
A. J. Foyt
e. e. cummings
Z. Z. Top
P. T. Barnum

2 The Period After an Abbreviation

There are times when you do not need to write an entire word. You can use an abbreviation. **An abbreviation is the short form of a word.** For example, days of the week and months of the year are often abbreviated.

Sun. Mon. Tues. Jan. Feb. Mar.

Here are some common abbreviations and the words they stand for.

Common Abbreviations

Rev.	Reverend	doz.	dozen
Mr.	Mister	Rd.	Road
Mrs.	Mistress	Ave.	Avenue
Jr.	Junior	Blvd.	Boulevard
Sr.	Senior	St.	Street
P.O.	Post Office	apt.	apartment
cont.	continued	in.	inch(es)
E.	East	yd.	yard(s)
W.	West	mi.	mile(s)
N.	North	A.M.	before noon (ante meridiem)
S.	South	P.M.	after noon (post meridiem)
oz.	ounce	B.C.	before Christ
lb.	pound	A.D.	Anno Domini (year of the Lord)

Abbreviations are often used in certain types of writing, such as lists, addresses, or arithmetic problems. Do not use most abbreviations in sentences. The only exceptions are titles with names (Dr. Johnson), A.M. and P.M., and B.C. and A.D.

An abbreviation is usually followed by a period. When an abbreviation stands for more than one word, it has more than one period.

Washington, D.C. New York, N.Y.

Not all abbreviations use periods. Here are some examples.

Metric Measure			
meter	m	gram	g
centimeter	cm	milligram	mg
decimeter	dm	liter	l
kilometer	km	milliliter	ml

Key to Writing

When addressing an envelope, use abbreviations for states. Notice that these abbreviations do not need periods.

MN CA NY IA

Practice

A Copy these sentences. Use periods correctly.

1. Sue M Schneider refereed the game
2. Ask Dr Dale Casey for an appointment
3. The Capitol is in Washington, D C
4. Our troop leader is Mrs Jean Carmody
5. Sammy Davis, Jr, recorded that song
6. According to legend, the city of Rome was founded by Romulus in 753 B C
7. Mr Scott raises rabbits on his farm
8. In 1500 A D, the Portuguese naval commander Pedro Àlvares Cabral discovered Brazil
9. Mrs Schmidt is Becky's violin teacher
10. Mr and Mrs Harvey celebrated their fiftieth anniversary

B Copy the following chart. Abbreviate the words in italics. Add periods where necessary.

Doctor James Michael Cooper's Patients

name	height	weight
John *Earl* Meyer 44 *South* Ridge *Road*	4 *feet*,5 *inches*	70 *pounds*
Mario *Louis* Perez 317 *North* Adams *Street*	5 *feet*,1 *inch*	97 *pounds*

C **Writing**

Flight 005 is a space shuttle to the Orion galaxy. Write the ticket agent's announcement for this flight. Give the names of the flight crew, the dates and times of arrival and departure, and the destination. Correctly use at least five abbreviations in the flight announcement that you write.

3 Question Marks and Exclamation Points

Using the Question Mark

A **question mark (?)** is used at the end of every interrogative sentence. It is a signal that a question has been asked. When you are reading aloud, the question mark generally tells you to raise the pitch of your voice.

Are you ready to go?
What did you say?

Using the Exclamation Point

An **exclamation point (!)** tells the reader that the sentence or words should be read with strong feeling. An exclamation signals surprise, joy, fear, excitement, or shock. To signal these emotions to your readers when you write, use an exclamation point at the end of every exclamatory sentence. Remember that an imperative sentence that shows strong feeling also ends with an exclamation point.

Don't touch the hot stove!
I lost my watch!
Hey! I won first prize!
Fire! Good grief!

Key to Writing

Use an exclamation point only when you want to show strong emotion. Avoid using too many exclamation points. Exclamation points lose their power when overused.

Practice

A Copy these sentences. Use either a period or a question mark at the end of each sentence.

1. I built a sandcastle shaped like a turtle
2. Does Jason collect stamps
3. Fill out this application form
4. What is batik
5. Can you grow a plant from orange seeds
6. How does this camera work
7. Mom made the costumes
8. Go directly home after school
9. Have you ever made banana bread
10. Hand me the scissors, please

B Copy these sentences. Use periods, question marks, and exclamation points correctly.

1. Will you have braces put on your teeth
2. Hooray We won
3. Oh, no The bus has gone
4. Let's sing some songs
5. Where is your prize from the Science Fair
6. We went to the monkey house at the zoo
7. Get help fast
8. May I use the shovel
9. Start with a simple project
10. Halt

C **Writing**

"Scoop" Smith is a magazine reporter. "Scoop" is interviewing an Olympic gold medal winner. He wants to know how it feels to be the best in the world. Record "Scoop's" interview on your paper. Correctly use both question marks and exclamation points.

4 Using the Comma

There are eight uses of the comma that you should know.

1. Use a comma to separate the day of the month from the year.

The Civil War began on April 12, 1861.

If the date appears in the middle of a sentence, also place a comma after the year.

On April 2, 1805, Hans Christian Andersen was born.

2. Use a comma to separate the name of a city from the name of the state or country in which it is located.

Tokyo, Japan   Los Angeles, California

If the name of the city and state or country appears in the middle of a sentence, place a comma after the state or country.

Our neighbors will move to Philadelphia, Pennsylvania, next month.

3. Use a comma to set off the name of a person spoken to.

Blanca, are you going to the football game?
I think, David, that you won an award.
May I go to the park, Mom?

4. Use a comma after introductory words such as *yes*.

Yes, the store is open late tonight.
No, you do not have homework.
Well, maybe I'll go another day.

5. Use a comma to set apart the words in a series.

Two words are not a series. There are always at least three words in a series.

The farmer planted corn and beets. (not a series)
The farmer planted corn, beets, and soybeans. (series)

6. Use a comma before or after a direct quotation.

"I like the Museum of Science and Industry," my brother said.
Ellen asked, "Have you seen my new bike?"

7. Use a comma after the greeting of a friendly letter and the closing of any letter.

Dear Jeff, Sincerely yours,

8. Use a comma at the end of the first complete thought in a sentence with two complete thoughts.

Casey struck out, and the game was over.
The hamburgers burned, but we ate them anyway.

Key to Writing

Use commas correctly when joining sentences. A comma is always placed before the conjunction that joins two sentences.

It stormed on Saturday, but we still went to the family reunion.

Practice

A Copy the following sentences. Add commas where they are needed.

1. On April 3 1860 the Pony Express started.
2. Julie answer this riddle.
3. Are you coming with us Aaron?
4. Amelia Earhart was born in Atchison Kansas.
5. No I have never been to Paris France.
6. We saw bulls calves and horses at the rodeo.
7. Our plane landed in Raleigh North Carolina on its way to Miami Florida.
8. Mount St. Helens erupted on May 18 1980.
9. The birdcage fell and my parakeet screeched.
10. Courtney said "Pick some flowers."

B Copy this letter on your paper. Add commas where needed.

January 3 1987

Dear Terry

Sydney Australia is great! I have seen kangaroos koalas kiwis and kumquats. We are especially lucky that it is summer down here. In the morning we go swimming in the hotel pool. My mother just came in the room and said "Craig tell Terry hello from me." I can't wait to see you.

Your friend
Craig

C **Writing**

Think about some special events that you have attended. Have you been to ball games, concerts, picnics, or fireworks? Write a paragraph about some of these events. Tell when and where the events took place. Include people you saw and things that you did. Be sure to use commas correctly.

5 Using the Apostrophe

The Apostrophe To Show Possession

A **possessive** is a word that shows ownership.

To form the possessive of a singular noun, add an apostrophe and *s*.

The captain's ship passed through the Panama Canal.

To form the possessive of a plural noun that does not end in *s*, add an apostrophe and an *s*.

Newbury's is having a sale on all children's clothes.

To form the possessive of a plural noun that ends in *s*, add only an apostrophe.

The actresses' costumes are covered with sequins.

The Apostrophe in Contractions

A **contraction** is a word formed by combining words. When the two words are combined, letters are often left out. An apostrophe is used to show where a letter or letters have been left out.

could + have = could've

Here are some contractions that are used often.

hasn't	has not	haven't	have not
isn't	is not	it's	it is, it has
doesn't	does not	I'll	I will
don't	do not	I'm	I am
can't	cannot	they're	they are
won't	will not	we're	we are

Practice

A Copy the following groups of words. Make the single words in italics possessive. Combine the word pairs in italics to make contractions.

1. *is not* clear
2. a *princess* crown
3. *would have* driven
4. my *sisters* books
5. *I will* ski
6. *it is* finished
7. the *captain* orders
8. the *woman* office
9. *have not* forgotten
10. the *watchmen* keys

B Copy the sentences below. Add apostrophes where they are needed to show possession or to identify contractions.

1. Isnt that racket yours?
2. Whos building the fire?
3. I cant play tennis.
4. Doesnt your town have a childrens museum?
5. Youll enjoy Barrys records.
6. Vics room is full of pets.
7. Its a picture of a lions den.
8. The kittens are Mandys and hers.
9. Theyre in Mr. Baxters guitar class.
10. Both boys bikes were rusted by the rain.

C **Writing**

What kind of person will you be when you are old? Think about what you will look like and what you will do or will not do. List these details. Write five sentences to describe yourself. Write five sentences that tell what you will do or will not do. Correctly use contractions in all sentences.

6 Using Quotation Marks

If you repeat someone's exact words when you write, you are writing a **direct quotation**. To tell your reader that you are quoting someone's exact words, use **quotation marks (" ")**.

Use quotation marks before the first word and after the last word of every direct quotation.

Dad said, "Your favorite show starts in ten minutes."
Kenneth yelled, "There's a fire in the kitchen!"
Della asked, "Did anybody find a red glove?"

There is a direct quotation in every sentence above. Only the speaker's exact words are placed inside the quotation marks. Notice these other details in the sentences.

1. There is a comma before every direct quotation.
2. The first word of the quotation is capitalized.
3. The punctuation at the end of each sentence is placed before the end quotation mark.

A quotation can also be placed at the beginning of a sentence.

"This plant needs water," Mr. Crockett said.

In the sentence above, the comma ending the quotation is placed inside the quotation marks. If a punctuation mark other than a comma is needed, it is also placed inside the quotation marks.

"There's a fire in the kitchen!" yelled Kenneth.
"Did anybody find a red glove?" Della asked.

Divided Quotation

Sometimes a quotation is divided. Words that tell who is talking, like *she said* or *she asked,* come in the middle of the sentence.

"After three helpings," Vic admitted, "dessert will be too much."

Divided quotations follow the same rules of capitalization and punctuation you have already learned. In addition, remember these rules.

1. Two sets of quotation marks are used.
2. The words that tell who is talking are followed by a comma or a period. Use a comma if the second part of the quotation does not begin a new sentence. Use a period if the second part of the quotation is a new sentence.

   "Did you know," Katherine asked, "that mammoths once lived here?"

   "Turn off the TV," Larry suggested. "Nothing good comes on now."
3. The second part of the quotation begins with a capital letter if it is the start of a new sentence, as in the second example above. Otherwise, the second part begins with a small letter.

Key to Writing

Stories in which characters talk to one another are more exciting than stories that just tell what happened. Make your stories more interesting by including conversation between characters.

Practice

A Copy these sentences. Add correct punctuation.

1. Make up your mind Dennis urged.
2. I finished the puzzle he announced.
3. JoAnn asked Is that a robin?
4. The zookeeper warned Don't disturb the panda.
5. Where is the North Star she asked.
6. Lauren asked What causes a storm?
7. Mom raises bees said Jeff.
8. A chameleon changes color Terri explained.
9. Dad asked Where are your gloves?
10. Mr. Owens said Sing that verse again.

B Copy these sentences. Add punctuation and capital letters where they are needed.

1. Some people Josh noted don't laugh much.
2. I'm tired Suzanne said let's rest.
3. Will you write to me Jeff asked after you move?
4. During the summer Amy said we make ice cream.
5. What's cooking I asked it smells good.
6. We're late Mom said and the show has started.
7. When does camp start Sonia asked I'm ready.
8. I have a plan Bill said for a model railroad.
9. I made sculptures Tom said out of soap.
10. We've looked at stars Linn said we used a telescope.

C **Writing**

Many people believe that dogs and cats are natural enemies. Write a conversation between a cat and a dog that shows they are only pretending to be enemies. Use proper punctuation.

7 Punctuating Titles

Titles are always given special attention in writing. Sometimes they are put in quotation marks. Sometimes they are underlined.

Put quotation marks around the titles of stories, poems, reports, articles, and chapters of a book.

"The Elephant's Child" (story)
"Sea Fever" (poem)
"The Koala Bear" (student report)
"Fog Causes Traffic Jam" (newspaper article)

Underline the title of a book, magazine, newspaper, television series, play, or motion picture.

When these titles are set in print, they are in italics.

Charlotte's Web by E. B. White (book title in writing)
Charlotte's Web by E. B. White (book title in print)

Practice

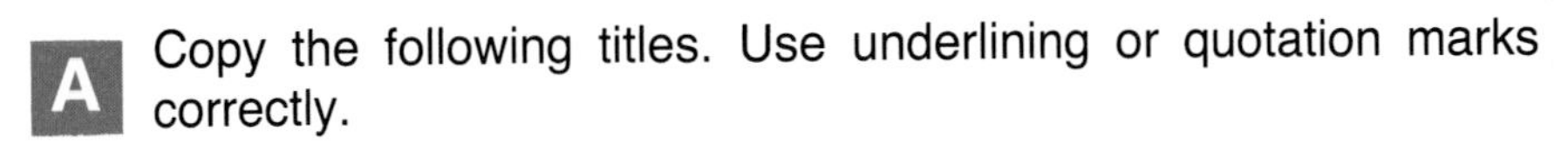

A Copy the following titles. Use underlining or quotation marks correctly.

1. To a Nightingale (poem)
2. Frankenstein (movie)
3. Time (magazine)
4. Eskimo Life (student report)
5. The First Women in America (chapter)

6. Star Trek (TV series)
7. Cheaper by the Dozen (book)
8. To Build a Fire (story)
9. Homer Price (book)
10. Owens Runs for Office (newspaper article)

B Copy the following titles. Use quotation marks or underlining as needed.

1. Two Escape from Jail (newspaper article)
2. Cricket (magazine)
3. Sounder (movie)
4. The Emperor's New Clothes (story)
5. The Ice Ages (chapter)
6. The Reason for Seasons (book)
7. The Legend of Bigfoot (student report)
8. Caddie Woodlawn (book)
9. Foul Shot (poem)
10. Ranger Rick's Nature Magazine (magazine)

C **Writing**

Year: 2050; You: Last librarian on Earth; Your Mission: To preserve samples of printed works and video art. Most of civilization has left Earth to colonize other planets. You remain behind to complete your task. What will you save? In a paragraph, list the titles of a story, poem, book, TV series, movie, newspaper article, and magazine that you would save.

8 Using the Colon

Use a colon (:) after the greeting of a business letter.

Dear Ms. Stratton: Gentlemen:

Use a colon between hours and minutes.

10:15 A.M.   7:30 P.M.

Remember to capitalize both letters of the abbreviations *A.M.* and *P.M.*, and to use a period after each letter.

Practice

A Copy the following business letter. Use colons and commas correctly.

May 12 1987

Dear Mr. Jenson

This letter is to tell you about the details for your magic show at our assembly on May 18 1987. Our class president will meet you at the office at 1245 P.M. The assembly will begin at 130 P.M., and your act will be announced at approximately 145. The assembly ends at 250.

We are looking forward to your show.

Sincerely
Camille Eberhard

B **Writing**

What did you do last Saturday? List your Saturday activities and the time you did each one. Then use the list to write a paragraph about your day.

9 Using the Hyphen

Sometimes when you are writing, you run out of space at the end of a line. You cannot fit in all of the next word on the same line. When this happens, you write part of the word, followed by a **hyphen (-)**, on that line. You write the rest of the word at the beginning of the next line.

Only words of two or more syllables can be divided at the end of a line. Never divide words of one syllable, such as *pound*, or *might.* If you are in doubt about dividing a word, look it up in a dictionary.

A single letter must not be left at the end of a line. For example, this division would be wrong: *a-part.* A single letter must not appear at the beginning of a line either. It would be wrong to divide *dictionary* like this: *dictionar-y.*

Divided Numbers

Numbers are usually spelled out in writing: ten, seventeen, thirty-five. Use a hyphen between all numbers of two words from twenty-one through ninety-nine.

My paint set has forty-four colors.
My dad just celebrated his thirty-seventh birthday.

Key to Writing

Hyphens can change the meaning of what you write.

Patricia saved thirty-five dollar bills. ($35)
Patricia saved thirty five-dollar bills. ($150)

A hyphen tells your reader that two words should be read as one.

Guide to Punctuation

Practice

A Divide each word as you would at the end of a line of writing. Add the necessary hyphen. Some words can be divided in more than one way. If the word cannot be divided, just copy it. Use a dictionary to help you.

Example: arithmetic
arith- or arithme-
metic tic

1. honest
2. adventure
3. sail
4. music
5. owl
6. copper
7. groceries
8. marbles
9. live
10. burrow
11. collection
12. together

B Divide the numbers below between their two parts. Write each number on your paper. Use hyphens correctly.

1. sixtythree
2. thirtyone
3. seventysix
4. fiftyseven
5. sixtythird
6. fortyfour
7. twentytwo
8. ninetyfive
9. fiftyfive
10. eightynine

C **Writing**

Pretend that you are the supervisor at a widget factory. You are in charge of taking inventory of all widgets, wheels, whistles, wiggles, and whydahs. Sales are up. You have less than ninety-nine of each item. Write a report to the company president listing these items and how many of each are in stock. Use hyphens correctly when you write numbers in your report.

Additional Practice

A Using End Marks, Quotation Marks, and Underlining

Copy these sentences. Add the needed punctuation.

1. What did Ben Franklin invent
2. I've never seen such a huge spider
3. Be careful Dad yelled There's broken glass
4. Help I can't swim
5. For her book report, Darda read A Wrinkle in Time
6. Cary asked Where is Zaire
7. Dominic spread hay over the newly seeded lawn
8. May I borrow your copy of Child Life (magazine)
9. Where do pineapples grow Chuck asked
10. The Cowardly Lion is my favorite character in The Wizard of Oz (movie)

B Using Commas, Apostrophes, Hyphens, and Colons

Copy these sentences. Add the correct punctuation.

1. Your flight arrives in Houston at 607 PM
2. Todd makes candles jewelry and pottery.
3. Youll like Ogden Nashs poems.
4. A meter is a little over thirtynine inches long.
5. On January 24 1848 gold was discovered in California.
6. No Ive never seen a wombat.
7. Whos been to the childrens zoo?
8. Amber sold thirtysix boxes of cookies before 10 00 A M
9. The tournament is in Shaker Heights Ohio.
10. Sean asked "Where is my backpack?"

Guide to Punctuation

C Punctuating a Letter

Correctly punctuate the following letter.

417 Laboratory Avenue
Seattle Washington 98188
July 1 9416

Dear Professor Mudd

This is incredible news On June 25 9416 I was fossil hunting near old Lake Michigan I dug in an area thirty five miles north of what was once called Lakeview Wisconsin Suddenly, I unearthed the partial remains of an unknown object It appears I have discovered something used by ancient Americans in A D 1987

I took my fossil to Dr I M Bright at the Ninety Fifth Century Co Dr Bright has written a book titled Famous Twenty Fifth Century Fossils but he could not identify my find Send your information to Professor Mudd in Newtown California he said He is the expert on the twentieth century I am sending you all the details Can you help me solve this mystery

The object I found is black smooth and plastic It is rectangular and measures 15 cm by 25 cm It weighs 2 kg Attached to it are dials buttons and an antenna. Numbers ranging from fifty four to eighty nine are written along with small marks. I also noticed the word *stereo* on one side.

I am working on a magazine article titled Digging Through Wisconsin It will be printed in the January 24 9417 issue of Archaeology Illustrated I certainly hope you can help me.

Please contact my office between 1000 AM and 400 PM I m eager to hear from you

Sincerely yours
Mr Rock E Boulder

Guide to Punctuation

Guide to Spelling

How To Become a Better Speller

Make a habit of looking at words carefully.

When you come to a new word, be sure you know its meaning. If you are not certain, look up the word in a dictionary.

Practice seeing every letter. Many people see a word again and again but don't really look at it. When you see a new word or a tricky word, like *government*, look at all the letters. To help you remember them, write the word several times.

When you speak, pronounce words carefully.

Sometimes people misspell words because they say them wrong. Be sure that you are not blending syllables together. For example, you may write *probly* for *probably* if you are mispronouncing it.

Find out your own spelling enemies and attack them.

Look over your papers and make a list of the misspelled words. Also keep a list of new words that are difficult for you. Study these words until you can spell them correctly and easily.

Find memory devices to help with problem spellings.

Some words are difficult to remember. In these cases, a memory device may help you. A memory device is a trick, or a catchy sentence, that you can remember easily. The device tells you how to spell the word. Here are two examples:

friend I will be your fri*end* to the *end*.
separate There is *a rat* in sep*arat*e.

Proofread what you write.

To make sure that you have spelled all words correctly, reread your work. Examine it carefully, word for word. Don't let your eyes race over the page and miss incorrectly spelled words.

Use a dictionary.

You don't have to know how to spell every word. No one spells everything correctly all the time. A good dictionary can help you to be a better speller. Use a dictionary whenever you need help with your spelling.

Mastering Specific Words

When you notice that you are having trouble with a certain word, take a few minutes to study it carefully. Give it all your attention. If you spend the time and energy to learn it correctly once, you will save yourself all the trouble of correcting it many times.
Follow these steps to master a specific word.

Steps for Mastering Specific Words

1. Look at the word and say it to yourself.

Pronounce it carefully. If it has two or more syllables, say it again, one syllable at a time. Look at each syllable as you say it.

2. Look at the letters. Spell the word aloud.

If the word has two or more syllables, pause between syllables as you say the letters.

3. Without looking at the word, write it.

Be sure to form each letter properly. Take your time.

4. Now look at your book or list to see if you have spelled the word correctly.

If you have, write it once more. Compare it with the correct spelling again. For best results, repeat the process once more.

5. If you have misspelled the word, notice where the error was.

Then repeat steps 3 and 4 until you have spelled the word correctly three times in a row.

Rules for Spelling

Adding Prefixes and Suffixes

Prefixes

A prefix is a word part added to the beginning of a word to change its meaning. When a prefix is added to a base word, the spelling of the base word stays the same.

Prefix		Base Word		New Word
re- (again)	+	write	=	rewrite (write again)
dis- (not)	+	approve	=	disapprove (not approve)
un- (not)	+	able	=	unable (not able)
in- (not)	+	formal	=	informal (not formal)
im- (not)	+	possible	=	impossible (not possible)
counter- (against)	+	act	=	counteract (act against)
pre- (before)	+	view	=	preview (see before)
mis- (incorrectly)	+	spell	=	misspell (spell incorrectly)
non- (not)	+	sense	=	nonsense (not sensible)

The Suffixes *-ly* and *-ness*

A suffix is a word part added to the end of a word to change its meaning. When the suffix *-ly* is added to a base word ending with *l*, both *l*'s are kept. When *-ness* is added to a base word ending in *n*, both *n*'s are kept.

Base Word		Suffix		New Word
total	+	**-ly**	=	totally
real	+	**-ly**	=	really
open	+	**-ness**	=	openness
mean	+	**-ness**	=	meanness

The Final Silent e

When a suffix beginning with a vowel is added to a base word ending with a silent *e,* the *e* is usually dropped.

hope + ing = hoping
refuse + al = refusal
expense + ive = expensive
fame + ous = famous
pale + er = paler
like + able = likable

When a suffix beginning with a consonant is added to a word ending with a silent *e,* the *e* is usually kept.

care + ful = careful
lone + ly = lonely
score + less = scoreless
move + ment = movement
same + ness = sameness
bore + dom = boredom

The following words are exceptions to these two rules:

truly argument ninth wholly

Words Ending in *y*

When a suffix is added to a word that ends with *y* after a consonant, the *y* is usually changed to *i.*

baby + es = babies
empty + er = emptier
happy + ly = happily
lazy + ness = laziness
carry + ed = carried
story + es = stories

Note this exception: When *-ing* is added, the *y* remains.

empty + ing = emptying
fly + ing = flying
carry + ing = carrying
apply + ing = applying

When a suffix is added to a word that ends with *y* following a vowel, the *y* usually is not changed.

boy + s = boys
buy + er = buyer
play + ed = played
stay + ing = staying

The following words are exceptions: paid, said

Words with *ie* or *ei*

When the sound is long *e* (ē), the word is spelled *ie* except after *c*.

The following rhyme provides some rules which will help you.

I before *e*
Except after *c*,
Or when sounded like *a*
As in ne*i*ghbor or we*i*gh.

I* before *E

belief	relieve	yield	fierce	achieve
niece	brief	field	chief	shield

Except after *C*

receive	ceiling	perceive	deceit
conceive	conceited	receipt	

Or when sounded like *A*

weight eight
neigh

These words are exceptions:

either	weird	species
neither	seize	leisure

Doubling the Final Consonant

Words of one syllable, ending with one consonant following one vowel, double the final consonant before adding *-ing*, *-ed*, or *-er*.

spin + ing = spinning fat + er = fatter
hot + est = hottest scrub + ed = scrubbed

The final consonant is **not** doubled when it follows two vowels.

trail + er = trailer shout + ed = shouted
steam + ing = steaming float + er = floater
peel + ed = peeled shoot + ing = shooting

Words with the "Seed" Sound

Only one English word ends in *sede: supersede.*
Three words end in *ceed: exceed*, *proceed*, *succeed*.
All other words ending in the sound of "seed" are spelled *cede.*

concede precede recede secede

Words Often Confused

Sometimes your problems in spelling are caused by the language itself. In English, there are many words that are easily confused. These words sound the same, or nearly the same, but are spelled differently and have different meanings. Words of this type are called **homophones**. Here are some examples of homophones.

horse—hoarse pare—pear—pair tail—tale do—dew—due

When you have problems with homophones, general spelling rules won't help you. The only solution is to memorize which spelling goes with which meaning.

Here is a list of homophones and other words frequently used and frequently confused in writing. Study the sets of words, and try to connect each word with its correct meaning. Refer to the list if you have further difficulties with these words.

accept means "to agree to something or to receive something willingly."
except means "to keep out or leave out."

▶ Ms. Daley will not *accept* excuses.
▶ Everyone *except* Carl won a prize.

capital means "chief, important, or excellent." It also means "the city or town that is the official seat of government of a state or nation."
capitol is the building where a state legislature meets.
the Capitol is the building in Washington, D.C., in which the United States Congress meets.

▶ Lincoln is the *capital* of Nebraska.
▶ The *capitol* in Lincoln is a new building.
▶ The nation's lawmakers meet at *the Capitol*.

hear means "to listen to."
here means "in this place."

▶ I *hear* a drumbeat.
▶ Drop your fishing line *here*.

it's is the contraction for *it is* or *it has*.
its shows ownership or possession.

▶ We visited Calico. *It's* a ghost town.
▶ We enjoy Mexico and *its* people.

lead (lĕd) is a heavy, gray metal.
lead (lēd) means "to go first, to guide."
led (lĕd) is the past tense of *lead* (lēd).

▶ The pipes were made of *lead*.
▶ The general will *lead* his army.
▶ Pioneers *led* the way west.

loose means "free or not tight."
lose means "to mislay or suffer the loss of something."

▶ My sister replaced the *loose* nail.
▶ If you leave, you will *lose* your place in line.

peace is calm or stillness or the absence of disagreement.
piece means "a portion or part."

▶ The rival tribes enjoyed a time of *peace*.
▶ Liz molded the *piece* of clay.

principal means "first or most important." It also refers to the head of a school.
principle is a rule, truth, or belief.

▶ The *principal* purpose of TV is to entertain.
▶ Our school *principal* spoke to the parents.
▶ Superman's *principle* is justice for all.

quiet means "free from noise or disturbance."
quite means "truly or almost completely."

- Our rabbit is a *quiet* pet.
- Those acrobats are *quite* daring.

their means "belonging to them."
there means "at that place."
they're is the contraction for *they are*.

- The children took *their* rafts to the beach.
- Plant the tomato seeds *there*.
- *They're* taking the train to Cleveland.

to means "in the direction of."
too means "also or very."
two is the whole number between one and three.

- Snowflakes drifted *to* the ground.
- My sister wants to come, *too*.
- The moose had *two* huge antlers.

weather is the state of the atmosphere referring to wind, moisture, temperature, etc.
whether indicates a choice or alternative.

- Tornadoes usually occur during warm *weather*.
- John asked *whether* wood sinks or floats.

who's is the contraction for *who is* or *who has*.
whose is the possessive form of *who*.

- *Who's* throwing those snowballs?
- *Whose* house is closest to school?

your is the possessive form of *you*.
you're is the contraction for *you are*.

- Did *your* wish come true?
- *You're* going to need a warmer coat.

Thesaurus

How To Use This Thesaurus

What Is a Thesaurus?

A strong vocabulary adds power to your speaking and writing. It allows you to express your ideas clearly. This thesaurus can help you to develop a strong vocabulary.

A thesaurus is a tool writers use to improve their writing. In a thesaurus, words with similar meanings—synonyms—are listed in groups. These groups of synonyms can help you find the best word to express an idea. They can also help you add variety to your speaking and writing.

Using This Thesaurus

To find synonyms for a word, first find the word in the index on pages 475–476. The index lists, in alphabetical order, every synonym that appears in the thesaurus. Look at the following portion of the index.

SMART	
smash *see* BREAK	468
snicker *see* LAUGH	470
spot *see* SEE	472
still *see* QUIET	471
STRANGE	
stride *see* WALK	474
strut *see* WALK	474
stunning *see* BEAUTIFUL	467
support *see* HELP	469

Some of the words in the index are printed in capital letters. These words are called **entry words.** *Strange* and *Quiet* are entry words. An entry word has a general meaning. It is the word under which one group of synonyms is organized.

The words in small letters in the index are synonyms for entry words. *Snicker* is a synonym for *laugh. Strut* is a synonym for *walk.*

Suppose you wanted to find a synonym for the word *weird.* First you would look up *weird* in the index. The index would tell you to look at the entry for *strange* on page 473. Here is what you would find.

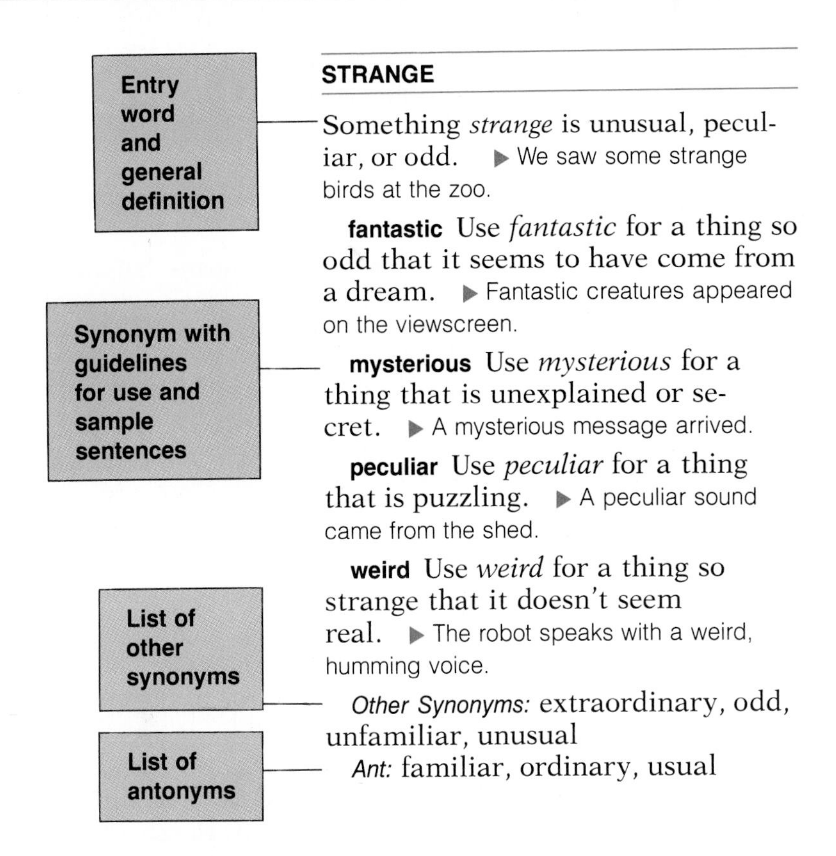

Understanding the Entries

The entry begins with the entry word, *strange.* This general word is then defined and used in an example sentence. Following the definition and example sentence are synonyms for *strange.* These synonyms include *weird,* the word you looked up in the first place. The group also includes *mysterious* and *peculiar.* Each synonym is followed by a sentence or two that tells how the word should be used. Then the word is used in an example sentence. Be sure to read all the synonyms before you decide which one best expresses your idea.

At the end of some entries, there is a list of other synonyms. These words are not defined and not used in example sentences. Be careful about using these words. Before you choose one, look it up in a dictionary. Study its meaning. Then decide whether it is really the right word for you to use.

AFRAID

Afraid means "feeling fear." The fear has lasted for a while and will probably last longer. ▶ Al is afraid of snakes.

alarmed Use *alarmed* for sudden fear caused by danger. ▶ We were alarmed by pictures of the monster.

frightened A person is frightened by something that has happened. ▶ The explosion frightened all of us.

scared A scared person is less afraid than a frightened one. ▶ Thunder scares me.

Other Synonyms: fearful, wary
Ant: unafraid, calm
see also **BRAVE**

ANGRY

Angry means "upset by something." ▶ Being cheated makes a person angry.

annoyed *Annoyed* means "a little angry." Something annoying usually lasts for a while. ▶ Mosquitos annoyed the campers.

enraged *Enraged* means "very angry." An enraged person may be shouting. ▶ The unfair law enraged him.

furious *Furious* means "very enraged." A furious person may be out of control. ▶ The attack on his castle made the king furious.

upset *Upset* is a mild word. Use it to show that a person feels troubled and angry. ▶ Jean's teasing upset me.

Ant: glad, happy, pleased

ANSWER

To *answer* is to react to a question or request by saying or doing something. ▶ Please answer this letter.

reply *Reply* is a more formal word than *answer*. ▶ Senator Jenks replied to our letter.

respond *Respond* suggests cooperation. ▶ Thousands responded to our appeal for help.

retort *Retort* means "answer in an angry or clever way." ▶ "I'm not through yet," Hank retorted.

Ant: see **ASK**

ASK

To *ask* is to request something. A person may ask for information. ▶ "Where do I send this form?" he asked.

inquire *Inquire* suggests a serious reason for asking. It is more formal than *ask*. ▶ "How many were hurt?" the reporter inquired.

request To request is to ask in a formal, polite way. ▶ Mrs. Banks requested an extra vacation day.

Ant: see **ANSWER**

BAD

Bad has two main meanings: "not satisfactory," and "evil." ▶ That was a bad movie. Avoid bad habits. **Caution:** do not use *bad* carelessly. Tell what was wrong with the movie or some habits. You may find that you don't need the word *bad*.

careless *Careless* means "not caring about doing a good job." ▶ Careless work is sloppy work.

evil *Evil* suggests doing wrong on purpose. An evil thing or person is all bad. ▶ Evil deeds can't be hidden forever.

poor A poor thing is worse than usual. ▶ I received a poor score on my spelling test.

vicious A vicious thing is cruel. It may be purposely cruel. ▶ He said vicious things to me.

see also **MEAN**
Ant: see **GOOD**

BEAUTIFUL

Beautiful and its synonyms mean "pleasing to look at." *Beautiful* suggests that a thing is perfect in some way. ▶ What a beautiful sunset!

attractive Use *attractive* for beauty that draws a person's attention. ▶ We set up an attractive display.

elegant Something elegant shows good taste, grace, and excellence. ▶ The hotel lobby is elegant.

gorgeous A gorgeous thing is dazzling. It may be gaudy. ▶ They have a gorgeous pink sofa.

lovely *Lovely* suggests cozy or comforting beauty. ▶ The fire gave off a lovely glow.

stunning A stunning thing is astonishing. Its beauty is striking. ▶ The view of earth from space is stunning.

Other Synonyms: fair, handsome, pretty
Ant: homely, hideous, ugly

BIG

Big and its synonyms mean "great in size or amount." ▶ Moths ate a big hole in my sweater.

colossal Something colossal seems "bigger than life." ▶ A colossal statue of a horse stands in the park.

enormous Something enormous is much bigger than usual. ▶ I can't ride that enormous horse!

immense An immense thing seems too big to measure. ▶ I was in a tiny boat on the immense sea.

mammoth A mammoth was a prehistoric elephant. *Mammoth* suggests great size and weight. ▶ At the dock was a mammoth oil tanker.

Other Synonyms: gigantic, great, huge, large, monumental
Ant: see **SMALL**

BRAVE

Brave and the other words in this group mean "facing up to danger or trouble." ▶ Six brave climbers reached the peak.

bold A bold person is quick to meet a challenge. *Bold* may suggest cockiness. ▶ A bold man faced the angry crowd.

courageous A courageous person welcomes the challenge that trouble brings. ▶ Courageous people traveled west in covered wagons.

daring *Daring* suggests a liking for risks and danger. A daring person may look for dangerous situations. ▶ Daring surfers were in the water right after the storm.

fearless *Fearless* means "without fear." A fearless person doesn't think about danger. ▶ A fearless woman grabbed the snarling dog.

Other Synonyms: plucky, valiant
Ant: see **AFRAID**

BREAK

Break and its synonyms mean "divide into pieces." ▶ The scissors broke when I dropped them.

shatter To shatter is to break with a sharp blow and make pieces scatter. ▶ The ball shattered the window.

smash *Smash* is a blend of *smack* and *crash*. To smash is to break into small pieces, making noise. ▶ He smashed the mirror on the ground.

wreck *Wreck* means "destroy." Use *wreck* for large things that are broken beyond repair. ▶ In the storm, the ship was wrecked on the rocks.

Other Synonyms: crack, crumble, crush, snap

BRIGHT

A *bright* thing reflects light or shines with its own light. ▶ The car had bright taillights.

brilliant *Brilliant* suggests strong light that catches a person's attention. ▶ Brilliant fireworks lit the night.

gleaming *Gleaming* suggests light like the light from a firefly. ▶ I saw only the cat's gleaming eyes.

glistening *Glistening* suggests flashes of light reflected from something smooth. ▶ Glistening icicles hung from the roof.

glowing *Glowing* suggests warm light coming from the thing itself. ▶ The blacksmith took a glowing bar of metal from the fire.

Other Synonyms: blazing, glittering
Ant: dark, dim

END

End and its synonyms mean "stop." ▶ When will this rain end?

finish *Finish* shows that a thing was completed when it stopped. ▶ Rita finished before the deadline.

halt Use *halt* for a quick stop. *Halt* suggests that the end was not expected. ▶ Officials halted the race.

Other Synonyms: close, conclude, stop
Ant: continue, go on, keep up

EXPLAIN

Explain means "to make plain or clear." ▶ I can explain the problem.

clarify *Clarify* means "make clear." Use it to emphasize that something was "foggy" before it was explained. ▶ Inspector Clouseau clarified the criminal's motives.

demonstrate Use *demonstrate* when explaining includes showing. ▶ Mr. Wilson demonstrated his invention.

describe To describe is to give a picture in words. ▶ She described the many kinds of corn.

FUNNY

Funny describes a thing that makes a person smile or laugh. So do the other words in this group. ▶ We saw a funny show last night.

amusing *Amusing* suggests smiles or chuckles, not loud laughs. ▶ Andy told an amusing story about fishing.

comical *Comical* suggests funny action. ▶ The clowns were really comical.

hilarious Use *hilarious* for something lively, active, and noisy. ▶ The movie ended with a hilarious chase.

silly A silly thing is foolish or ridiculous. ▶ Young children like silly riddles.

Other Synonyms: humorous, laughable, witty

GET

The words in this group have the meaning of *get:* "come to have."
▶ We can get two shirts for the price of one.

earn To earn is to get something for something done, usually work.
▶ "I've earned this vacation," Ann said.

gain To gain is to get something worthwhile by working. ▶ I gained self-confidence by learning to swim.

obtain *Obtain* means "get what is wanted." ▶ We must obtain more help.

receive To receive is simply to get. A person may not even want the thing received. ▶ We received some bad news.

Other Synonyms: acquire, buy, collect, obtain, purchase, win

GOOD

Good may mean "okay; meeting standards." ▶ We had a good time.
Caution: do not use *good* carelessly. Instead, describe what you like.

satisfactory Something satisfactory meets a person's wishes or needs. It is just what a person expected—no more and no less. ▶ Carlton Movers did a satisfactory job for a low price.

worthwhile *Worthwhile* means "worth the time or effort spent." ▶ Esther has a worthwhile plan for the festival.

see also: **TERRIFIC**
Ant: see **BAD**

GROUP

A *group* is a gathering of people, animals, or things. ▶ We'll travel in a group.

band A band is a group that got together for a purpose. ▶ A band of pirates attacked the ship.

crew A crew is a group working together or brought together by work.
▶ Crews of city workers repaired the storm damage.

crowd A crowd is a large group. *Crowd* suggests disorder. ▶ I hope we won't be stuck in a crowd.

gang A gang can be a group of workers. ▶ A gang of painters is working in the building. It can also be a group of lawbreakers. ▶ A gang of thieves robbed two local banks.

mob A mob is disorderly. It may be lawless. It is not just a large crowd. ▶ An angry mob gathered.

ANIMAL GROUPS Specific words are used for animal groups; for example: brood of chicks, colony of ants, flight of birds, flock of sheep (or camels), gaggle of geese, herd of elephants, pack of dogs (or wolves), pride of lions, school of fish, swarm of bees (or eels), troop of kangaroos.

HELP

To *help* is to make things easier or better for others. ▶ Ellie helped me wrap the gifts.

aid *Aid* is more formal than *help*. Use *aid* for serious help. ▶ The singers held a concert to aid famine victims.

assist Use *assist* when the help is less important than what the other person does. ▶ Lisa planned the show, and I assisted her.

rescue *Rescue* means "save from danger." ▶ The Coast Guard rescued us.

support *Support* may mean "give approval or understanding." It may mean meeting a person's needs by giving money or what is needed.
▶ We support the mayor's parking plan.

Ant: interfere, hinder

IMPORTANT

Something *important* has great meaning or influence. ▶ Cal has an important job.

serious *Serious* contrasts something really important with things that are not very important. ▶ "I have a serious question," she said.

urgent Use *urgent* for something important that should get quick attention. ▶ Wake Sue up; I have an urgent message for her.

vital *Vital* means "absolutely necessary." Don't use *vital* just to mean "important." ▶ Iron is vital to a person's health.

Ant: unimportant, unnecessary

LAUGH

To *laugh* is to make the sounds that show happiness. ▶ Claire's jokes always make me laugh.

chuckle To chuckle is to laugh in low tones. A person may chuckle when something is mildly amusing. Being pleased with oneself may also make a person chuckle. ▶ Larry chuckled at his good luck.

giggle *Giggle* means "make a high-pitched laugh." Something embarrassing or silly may make a person giggle. ▶ We giggled at the sight of Oscar's purple sneakers.

roar To roar is to laugh loudly. ▶ Everyone roared at the clown act.

snicker To snicker is to laugh slyly, often at someone. ▶ Phil snickered when I said that I could pitch.

Other Synonyms: cackle, chortle, crow, guffaw, howl

LIKE

Like and its synonyms have the general meanings "to be pleased with, to enjoy." ▶ Everyone likes Dan because he's so nice.

admire To admire something is to look up to it because you are impressed with its qualities. ▶ I admire Angela's singing voice.

adore To adore something is to love and honor it. Don't use *adore* just to mean "like very much." ▶ She has always adored her grandmother and grandfather.

enjoy *Enjoy* means "get pleasure from something." ▶ I enjoy hiking and boating.

love To love is to feel a strong and tender affection. ▶ You can see how much that father loves his son. People sometimes use *love* to mean "enjoy." ▶ Donna loves roller skating. In writing, avoid that use of *love*.

MAKE

Make means "bring into being." ▶ Jean made this bookcase.

construct *Construct* suggests following a plan to put parts together. ▶ Workers construct the building's steel framework.

create To create is to bring into being what did not exist. ▶ Rick has created a new musical instrument.

manufacture Once, *manufacture* meant "make by hand." Today, *manufacture* is used for making something by machine. ▶ Mammoth Company manufactures power tools.

Ant: destroy, dismantle

MANY

Many means "a great number of." **Caution:** it is better to tell how many, instead of using *many* or a synonym. Therefore, the second of the following sentences is better. ▶ Many people arrived early. More than twenty people arrived early.

a lot In casual speech, *a lot* is used to mean "many" or "much." Avoid *a lot* in most writing and speaking.

a number of *A number of* is more formal than *a lot*. However, it is just as vague. Choose a better synonym.

countless *Countless* means "too many to count." ▶ Countless tiny fish swam past.

numerous *Numerous* is more formal than *many*. It suggests more than expected. ▶ Numerous people helped make the fair a success.

several *Several* means "a few." It does *not* mean "many." ▶ We saw several birds, but most have gone south.

MEAN

Mean can mean "bad-tempered" or "unkind." ▶ A mean dog snarled at us.

bad-tempered A bad-tempered person is cranky. ▶ A bad-tempered customer shouted at Mr. Lasch.

nasty A nasty person's meanness disgusts people. ▶ Teasing Ann was a nasty thing to do.

selfish A selfish person gives little thought to others. ▶ It was selfish of you not to help your brother.

unkind *Unkind* means "not kind." It is stronger than *bad-tempered*. An unkind person treats others harshly. ▶ Scrooge was an unkind man.

QUIET

The words in this group mean "without noise." *Quiet* also suggests calm. ▶ We spent a quiet evening alone.

hushed *Hushed* suggests that usual sounds are missing or softened. ▶ The city was hushed by the snow.

silent *Silent* means "without any sound." ▶ The theater was empty and silent.

still *Still* means "without sound or movement." ▶ Before the storm, the birds and animals were still.

RIGHT

Right may mean "correct" or "proper." ▶ This is the right address.

correct *Correct* may mean "without errors." ▶ Is that the correct time? It may mean "proper." ▶ What is the correct way to set the table?

proper *Proper* means "what good judgment says is right." ▶ It wouldn't be proper to end the meeting now.

Other Synonyms: accurate, exact, fit, fitting

Ant: see **WRONG**

RUN

The words in this group share the meaning of *run:* "to go faster than walking." ▶ Lisa ran home to tell her mother the good news.

dash Use *dash* for a quick run over a short distance. ▶ Ralph dashed around the corner.

race Use *race* to suggest moving extremely fast or too hastily. ▶ We raced from shop to shop.

scamper *Scamper* suggests small, quick movements, like those of a kitten. ▶ Children scampered around the nursery school.

trot Use *trot* for a speed between walking and running. ▶ We'll trot around the track to warm up before the race.

Other Synonyms: gallop, jog

SAY

The words in this group share the meaning of *say:* "to speak words." Most suggest *how* the words are said. *Say* is the general word. It does not indicate how the words are spoken. ▶ "I'll be a little late," said Tom.

announce *Announce* is more formal than *say*. ▶ "I have important news," she announced.

cry To cry is to speak loudly. ▶ "Wait! Wait for me!" he cried.

exclaim To exclaim is to speak with excitement, surprise, or anger. ▶ "I know who did it!" she exclaimed.

roar To roar is to speak in a loud, lively way. ▶ "I won!" Chris roared.

Other Synonyms: blurt, boast, comment, declare, growl, grumble, remark, shout, state, whisper

SEE

To *see* is to sense through the eyes. ▶ I saw a bright flash of light.

glimpse To glimpse is to see briefly. ▶ I glimpsed Ann in the crowd before the train pulled away.

inspect To inspect is to look carefully. ▶ Inspect the finish for scratches or nicks.

observe To *observe* is to watch closely. ▶ Scientists observed the eclipse.

sight *Sight* means "see something for which one has been looking." ▶ At noon we sighted our first whale.

spot To spot is to see something that is hard to find. ▶ I spotted a hawk drifting high above us.

watch To watch is to observe for a reason. ▶ Watch for a signal from Burns. However, it is also used for looking at something without close attention. ▶ We watched the clouds roll by.

SMALL

The words in this group mean "little in size or importance." *Small* suggests that a thing is less than things like it. ▶ The car has one small dent.

little Use *little* when being small is good or nice. ▶ They live in a cozy little cabin. You can also use it to mean "some, but not much." ▶ I have a little money with me.

miniature Use *miniature* for a very small copy of something. ▶ Around the toy track raced two miniature cars.

tiny Use *tiny* for something so small that it can hardly be noticed. ▶ Gnats are tiny insects.

Ant: see **BIG**

SMART

The words in this group mean "intelligent, alert, clever." *Smart* is an informal word. ▶ Waiting is the smart thing to do.

bright *Bright* is also informal. It suggests a quick mind. ▶ One bright girl solved the puzzle right away.

clever *Clever* suggests new or unusual ideas. ▶ Paul found a clever way to patch the leak.

gifted *Gifted* stresses an inner intelligence or talent rather than learning. ▶ As a child, she was a gifted artist.

intelligent *Intelligent* stresses being able to learn new things quickly. ▶ He has no experience, but he's intelligent and hard-working.

STRANGE

Something *strange* is unusual, peculiar, or odd. ▶ We saw some strange birds at the zoo.

fantastic Use *fantastic* for a thing so odd that it seems to have come from a dream. ▶ Fantastic creatures appeared on the viewscreen.

mysterious Use *mysterious* for a thing that is unexplained or secret. ▶ A mysterious message arrived.

peculiar Use *peculiar* for a thing that is puzzling. ▶ A peculiar sound came from the shed.

weird Use *weird* for a thing so strange that it doesn't seem real. ▶ The robot speaks with a weird, humming voice.

Other Synonyms: extraordinary, odd, unfamiliar, unusual
Ant: familiar, ordinary, usual

TEACH

To *teach* is to help someone learn or show someone how to do something. ▶ I can teach you to speak Japanese.

coach *Coach* has the meanings of *instruct* and *train*. Coaching uses step-by-step help. ▶ Don coached the dancers before the show.

instruct To instruct is to teach according to some system, usually in one subject. ▶ Dan instructed me in Scuba diving.

train To train is to develop one skill, or to teach a person to do one job or follow one career. ▶ Ms. Sims was trained as a programmer.

Other Synonyms: drill, educate

TERRIFIC

Some people use the words in this group to mean "very fine or enjoyable." This is not the best use for them. Each has a specific meaning. *Terrific* actually means "terrifying." ▶ A terrific explosion shook the house.

fabulous *Fabulous* means "astounding." It refers to things that might be in a fable. ▶ On the hilltop was a fabulous marble castle.

remarkable A remarkable thing is unusual enough to make people notice it. ▶ Tony has a remarkable voice.

sensational A sensational thing causes excitement or strong feelings. ▶ The festival ended with a sensational fireworks display.

wonderful Something wonderful causes amazement. ▶ I couldn't believe what a wonderful gymnast Nan is.

TRAVEL

The words in this group share the meaning of *travel:* "go from one place to another." ▶ Mr. Bolt traveled to Brazil.

journey *Journey* once meant "a day's trip." Now, it suggests a long, hard trip. ▶ They journeyed across the desert.

roam *Roam* suggests freedom and pleasure. ▶ We roamed through the cool, beautiful woods.

wander *Wander* stresses lack of purpose. ▶ Ed wandered along, glancing in the shop windows.

WALK

To *walk* is to go on foot, not running. ▶ If the rain stops, I'll walk home.

pace *Pace* means "walk back and forth." It can also mean "measure by walking." Pacing may suggest nervousness. ▶ Jack paced the room, waiting for the election news.

stride Use *stride* for vigorous or bold walking. ▶ Paula strode into the room with a smile on her face.

strut Use *strut* for proud or showy walking. ▶ Nick strutted past with the trophy in his hand.

trudge Use *trudge* for the way a tired or sad person would walk. ▶ At the end of the day, we trudged home.

Other Synonyms: hike, march, parade, saunter, step, stroll, tramp, tread

WRONG

Wrong and the words in this group mean "not correct." ▶ My answer was wrong.

inaccurate Something inaccurate is not exact or precise. ▶ That clock is inaccurate.

incorrect *Incorrect* means "not correct." It is more formal than *wrong*. Many people think it is more polite. ▶ Your answer is incorrect.

mistaken *Mistaken* may mean "wrong by accident." It may mean "wrong by carelessness." ▶ I was mistaken about how many books were left.

Ant: see **RIGHT**

Index

Index

Answer to Exercise, p. 270
Left: A salt crystal
Right: The eye of a black ant

Acknowledgments

Atheneum Publishers, Inc.: For "Sometimes Poems" by Judith Viorst, from *If I Were in Charge of the World and Other Worries;* copyright © 1981 by Judith Viorst. For "To Dark Eyes Dreaming," from *Today Is Saturday* by Zilpha Keatley Snyder; copyright © 1969 by Zilpha Keatley Snyder. Bell & Hyman, Publishers: For "Rainy Nights," from *Come Follow Me* by Irene Thompson. Children's Television Workshop: For an excerpt on "Braces," from *3-2-1 Contact,* June, 1984; copyright © 1984 by Children's Television Workshop. Thomas Y. Crowell Publishers: For an adapted excerpt from *Chains, Webs and Pyramids: The Flow of Energy in Nature* by Laurence Pringle; copyright © 1975 by Laurence Pringle. Delacorte Press/Seymour Lawrence: For "The Toaster," from *Laughing Time* by William Jay Smith; copyright © 1953, 1955, 1956, 1957, © 1959, 1968, 1974, 1977, 1980 by William Jay Smith. Dodd, Mead & Company, Inc.: For "Roses and Pearls" by Paul Laurence Dunbar, from *The Complete Poems of Paul Laurence Dunbar.* For "Called Away" ("I Meant to Do My Work Today") from *The Lonely Dancer and Other Poems* by Richard Le Gallienne; copyright 1913 by Dodd, Mead and Company, Inc. Copyright renewed 1941 by Richard Le Gallienne. Doubleday & Company, Inc.: For "The Bat" by Theodore Roethke, from *The Collected Poems of Theodore Roethke;* copyright 1938. Greenwillow Books (A Division of William Morrow & Co., Inc.): For "Do Oysters Sneeze?" from *The New Kid on the Block* by Jack Prelutsky; copyright © 1984 by Jack Prelutsky. Harcourt Brace Jovanovich, Inc.: For "Broken Sky" by Carl Sandburg, from *Wind Song;* copyright 1928, 1956 by Carl Sandburg. Henry Holt and Company, Inc.: For an excerpt from "Out, Out," from *The Poetry of Robert Frost* edited by Edward Connery Lathem; copyright 1916, © 1969 by Holt, Rinehart and Winston, copyright 1944 by Robert Frost. Houghton Mifflin Co.: For an excerpt from *I Met A Man* by John Ciardi; copyright © 1961 by John Ciardi. Henry Lincoln Johnson: For "Your World" by Georgia Douglas Johnson, from *American Negro Poetry* edited by Arna Bontemps. G.P. Putnam: For an entry from *The New Roget's Thesaurus in Dictionary Form* edited by Norman Lewis; copyright © 1961, 1966 by G.P. Putnam's Sons, Inc. Random House: For an excerpt from *Born Free* by Joy Adamson; copyright 1974. Marian Reiner: For "Ways of Composing," from *Rainbow Writing* by Eve Merriam; copyright 1976 by Atheneum. Simon & Schuster: For p. 601, from *Webster's New World Dictionary,* Student Edition; copyright © 1981 by Simon & Schuster, Inc. Mrs. James Thurber and Hamish Hamilton, Ltd, London: A brief excerpt from "The Figgerin' of Aunt Wilma," in *Thurber Country,* published by Simon and Schuster, originally printed in *The New Yorker;* copyright 1953 by James Thurber, copyright © 1963 by Mrs. Helen Thurber. Viking Penguin Inc.: For a brief excerpt from "J.P. Sousa," from *American Tall-Tales* by Adrien Stoutenburg; copyright 1968 by Adrien Stoutenburg. World Book, Inc.: For an entry on "Mars," from *The World Book Encyclopedia;* copyright © 1986 by World Book, Inc. World Book-Childcraft International: For an excerpt from *The World Book Encyclopedia;* copyright © 1979 by World Book-Childcraft International, Inc. Every effort has been made to trace the ownership of all copyrighted material found in this book and to make full acknowledgment for its use. Portions of the material in this book were previously published under the title *Building English Skills,* © McDougal, Littell & Company.

Editorial Credits

Executive Editor: Kathleen Laya
Managing Editor: Geraldine Macsai

Executive Editor for Language Arts: Bonnie L. Dobkin
Senior Editor: James M. LiSacchi
Editor: Julie A. Schumacher
Associate Editors: Christine Iversen, Susan Nisson, Virginia Swanton
Assistant Editor: Marcia Mann
Rights and Permissions: Irma Rosenberg, Betty Godvik
Editorial Assistant: Nanci Connors

Senior Designer: Mary MacDonald
Design and Art Supervision: Dale Bēda, Donna Cook, Laima T. Gecas, Luis Ramirez, Chestnut House
TE: Diane R. Johnson
Cover Design: Mary MacDonald, Laima T. Gecas

Continued from Student Letter page.

Gilbreth, Frank B., Jr., and Ernestine G. Carey, from *Cheaper by the Dozen.* ▸*Belles on Their Toes*
Greenfield, Eloise, "Aunt Roberta," *Honey I Love You and Other Poems.* ▸*Sister*
Huff, Barbara A., "The Library," *Favorite Poems Old and New.*
Johnson, Georgia D., "Your World," *American Negro Poetry.*
Koch, Kenneth, "Ordinary Things," *Thank You and Other Poems.* ▸*Talking to the Sun: An Illustrated Anthology of Poetry for Young People*
Krantz, Hazel, from *They Ride Like the Wind.* ▸*One Hundred Pounds of Popcorn*
LeGallienne, Richard, "Called Away," *The Lonely Dancer and Other Poems.*
McCann, Rebecca, "Swallows," *The Complete Cheerful Cherub.*
Merriam, Eve, "Ways of Composing," *Rainbow Writing.* ▸*There Is No Rhyme for Silver*
Prelutsky, Jack, "The New Kid on the Block," *The New Kid on the Block.* ▸*The Snopp on the Sidewalk & Other Poems*
Roethke, Theodore, "The Bat," *The Collected Poems of Theodore Roethke.* ▸*Poems for Children*
Rossetti, Christina, "The Frog and the Toad," *The Complete Poems of Christina Rossetti.* ▸*Doves and Pomegranates*
Sandburg, Carl, "Broken Sky," *Wind Song.* ▸*Rainbows Are Made*
Sharpe, R. L., "A Bag of Tools."
Silverstein, Shel, "Hector the Collector," "Memorizing Mo," "Never," *A Light in the Attic.* ▸*The Giving Tree*
Smith, Dodie, from *I Capture the Castle.* ▸*The Hundred and One Dalmations*
Smith, William J., "The Toaster," *Laughing Times.* ▸*The Golden Journey: Poems for Young People*
Snyder, Zilpha Keatley, "To Dark Eyes Dreaming," *Today is Saturday.* ▸*The Egypt Game*
Starbird, Kaye, "Housemates," "December Leaves," *Don't Ever Cross a Crocodile.* ▸*The Covered Bridge House and Other Poems*
Stoutenberg, Adrien, from "J. P. Sousa," from *American Tall Tales.*
Thompson, Irene, "Rainy Nights," *Come Follow Me.*
Untermeyer, Louis, from *The World's Great Stories.* ▸*Rainbow in the Sky: Golden Anniversary Edition*
Viorst, Judith, "Sometimes Poems," *If I Were In Charge of the World & Other Worries: Poems for Children and Their Parents.* ▸*Alexander and the Terrible, Horrible, No Good, Very Bad Day*
Zolotow, Charlotte, "Scene," *River Winding Poems.* ▸*The Summer Night*

▸An additional work by the author

Photographs

Cleo Freelance Photo: 174. Click/Chicago, Ltd.: Robert Estrall 193; Vince Streano 193; Claudio Ferrer 196; John Bertrand 232. Four By Five Inc.: 318. The Image Bank: Nancy Brown 4; John Kelly 56; R. Joe Decke 140; Zao-Grimberg 156; Gary Cralle 284. International Stock Photo: Ray Solowinski 40; Mark Bolster 244. Magnum Photo: Dennis Stock 98; Eve Arnold 258. Science Source, Photo Researchers: Dr. Jeremy Burgess 270. Taurus Photos: Menschenfreund 330. Wide World: *Walking Man,* sculpture by Alberto Giacometti 275. Jim Cronk: 90, 370. Tony Freeman: 348. Tom Meyers: 306. Paul Robert Perry: 272. Norman Prince: 214. Carl Purcell: 124, 392. Jim Whitmer: 18.

Illustrations

"The Pencil Sharpener" (page 299). From *The Best of Rube Goldberg,* by Charles Keller © 1979, by Rube Goldberg, published by Prentice Hall, Inc.

Karen Ackoff: 147, 273; Wayne Bonnett: 44; Bradley Clark: 135, 267; Gwenn Connelly: 21, 28, 48, 92, 95, 200, 218, 281, 290, 384, 389; David Cunningham: 3, 32, 47, 63, 78, 93, 148-149, 172, 187, 189, 201, 213, 230, 240, 288, 293, 300, 310, 311, 324, 363, 377, 379, 398; Ben Denison: 316; Len Ebert: 9, 123; Larry Frederick: 142, 143, 168, 216, 220, 248, 249, 309, 332, 361, 365; Lydia Halverson: 102, 115; Gregory Hergert: 238; Ken Izzi: 354; JAK Graphics: 119, 366, 367, 368, 369; Tani Johnson: 27, 42, 54, 64, 80, 81, 129, 167, 190, 224, 225, 239, 253, 254, 269, 294, 295, 320, 345, 358, 360, 381, 396; Susan Lexa: 105, 111, 116, 287, 296; Diana Magnuson: 16, 162, 336, 338; Bob Masheris: 33, 118; Diane McKnight: 305; Todd Reifers: 11, 177, 235, 260; Judy Sakaguchi: 6, 22, 29, 38, 45, 51, 71, 75, 77, 131, 152, 153, 161, 165, 179, 183, 185, 194, 202-203, 207, 222, 242, 277, 312, 321, 327, 340, 355, 375, 387; Krystyna Stasiak: 144, 276, 351; Robert Steele: 25, 58, 264; Arvis Stewart: 335, 343; James Teason: 250, 284.

We wish to express our appreciation to Dr. Barry Moore, curator of the International Collection of Children's Art, University Museums, Illinois State University, and to his staff for their consultation and research.